FRESH WIND, FRESH FIRE

What Happens When God's Spirit Invades the Hearts of His People

TWO BOOKS IN ONE

FRESH FAITH

What Happens When Real Faith Ignites God's People

Resources by Jim Cymbala

Fresh Wind, Fresh Fire
(book and audio)

Fresh Faith
(book and audio)

Fresh Power
(book and audio)

The Life God Blesses
(book and audio)

The Church God Blesses
(book and audio)

Breakthrough Prayer
(book and audio)

When God's People Pray
(curriculum)

JIM CYMBALA

WITH DEAN MERRILL

FRESH WIND, FRESH FIRE

What Happens When God's Spirit Invades the Hearts of His People

TWO BOOKS IN ONE

FRESH FAITH

What Happens When Real Faith Ignites God's People

ZONDERVAN®

ZONDERVAN.com/
AUTHORTRACKER
follow your favorite authors

Fresh Wind, Fresh Fire/Fresh Faith
Copyright © 2008 by Jim Cymbala

Fresh Wind, Fresh Fire
Copyright © 1997 by Jim Cymbala
Study Guide Copyright © 2003 by Jim Cymbala

Fresh Faith
Copyright © 1999 by Jim Cymbala
Study Guide Copyright © 2003 by Jim Cymbala

Requests for information should be addressed to:

Zondervan, *Grand Rapids, Michigan 49530*

ISBN-10: 0-310-61024-9
ISBN-13: 978-0-310-61024-3

Printed in the United States of America

07 08 09 10 11 12 13 • 22 21 20 19 18 17 16 15 14 13 12 11 10 9 8 7 6 5 4 3 2 1

CONTENTS

FRESH WIND, FRESH FIRE

FRESH FAITH

Fresh Wind, Fresh Fire

PART 1

Waking Up to a Powerful Promise

ONE

❦

The Amateurs

I WAS STRUGGLING TOWARD the climax of my none-too-polished sermon that Sunday night back in 1972 when disaster struck. It was both pathetic and laughable all at once.

The Brooklyn Tabernacle—this woeful church that my father-in-law had coaxed me into pastoring—consisted of a shabby two-story building in the middle of a downtown block on Atlantic Avenue. The sanctuary could hold fewer than two hundred people—not that we required anywhere near that much capacity. The ceiling was low, the walls needed paint, the windows were dingy, and the bare wood floor hadn't been sealed in years. But there was no money for such improvements, let alone a luxury such as air-conditioning.

Carol, my faithful wife, was doing her best at the organ to create a worshipful atmosphere as I moved into my invitation, calling the fifteen or so people before me to maybe, just possibly, respond to the point of my message. Someone shifted on a pew to my left, probably not out of conviction as much as weariness, wondering when this young preacher would finally let everybody go home.

C-r-r-a-a-ck!

The pew split and collapsed, dumping five people onto the floor. Gasps and a few groans filled the air. My infant daughter probably thought it was the most exciting moment of her church life so far. I stopped preaching to give the

11

people time to pick themselves up off the floor and replace their lost dignity. All I could think to do was to nervously suggest that they move to another pew that seemed more stable as I tried to finish the meeting.

In fact, this kind of mishap perfectly portrayed my early days in ministry. I didn't know what I was doing. I had not attended Bible college or seminary. I had grown up in Brooklyn in a Ukrainian-Polish family, going to church on Sundays with my parents but never dreaming of becoming a minister.

Basketball was my love, all through high school and then at the U.S. Naval Academy, where I broke the plebe scoring record my first year. Late that year I hurt my back and had to resign from the navy. I resumed college on a full athletic scholarship at the University of Rhode Island, where I was a starter on the basketball team for three years. In my senior year I was captain of the team; we won the Yankee Conference championship and played in the NCAA tournament.

My major was sociology. By then I had begun dating Carol Hutchins, daughter of the man who was my pastor back in junior high and high school. Carol was a gifted organist and pianist even though she had never been formally trained to read or write music. We were married in January 1969 and settled down in a Brooklyn apartment, both getting jobs in the hectic business world of Manhattan. Like many newlyweds, we didn't have a lot of long-term goals; we were just paying bills and enjoying the weekends.

However, Carol's father, the Reverend Clair Hutchins, had been giving me books that piqued my desire for spiritual things. He was more than a local pastor; he made frequent trips overseas to preach evangelistic crusades and teach other pastors. In the States he was the unofficial overseer of a few small, independent churches. By early 1971 he was seriously suggesting that perhaps God wanted us in full-time Christian service.

"There's a church in Newark that needs a pastor," he commented one day. "They're precious people. Why don't you think about quitting your job and stepping out in faith to see what God will do?"

"I'm not qualified," I protested. "Me, a minister? I have no idea how to be a pastor."

He said, "When God calls someone, that's all that really matters. Don't let yourself be afraid."

And before I knew it, there I was, in my late twenties, trying to lead a tiny, all-black church in one of the most difficult mission fields in urban America. Weekdays found me spending hours in the systematic study of God's Word while on Sundays I was "learning" how to convey that Word to people. Carol's musical ability made up for some of my mistakes, and the people were kind enough to pay us a modest salary.

My parents gave us a down payment for a home, and we moved to New Jersey. Somehow we made it through that first year.

DOUBLE DUTY

THEN ONE DAY my father-in-law called from Florida, where he lived, and asked a favor. Would I please go preach four Sunday nights over at the multiracial Brooklyn Tabernacle, another church he supervised? Things had hit an all-time low there, he said. I agreed, little suspecting that this step would forever change my life.

The minute I walked in, I could sense that this church had big problems. The young pastor was discouraged. The meeting began on a hesitant note with just a handful of people. Several more walked in late. The worship style bordered on chaotic; there was little sense of direction. The pastor noticed that a certain man was present—an occasional visitor to the church who sang and accompanied himself on the guitar—and asked him on the spot to come up and render a solo. The man sort of smiled and said no.

"Really, I'm serious," the pastor pleaded. "We'd love to have you sing for us." The man kept resisting. It was terribly awkward. Finally the pastor gave up and continued with congregational singing.

I also remember a woman in the small audience who took it upon herself to lead out with a praise chorus now and then, jumping into the middle of whatever the pastor was trying to lead.

It was certainly odd, but it wasn't my problem. After all, I was just there to help out temporarily. (The thought that I, at that stage of my development as a minister, could help anyone showed how desperate things had become.)

I preached, and then drove home.

After the second week's service, the pastor stunned me by saying, "I've decided to resign from this church and move out of state. Would you please notify your father-in-law?"

I nodded and said little. When I called that week with the news, the question quickly arose as to whether the church should even stay open.

Some years earlier, my mother-in-law had met with other women who were interceding for God to establish a congregation in downtown Brooklyn that would touch people for his glory. That was how this church had actually started—but now all seemed hopeless.

As we discussed what to do, I mentioned something that the pastor had told me. He was sure one of the ushers was helping himself to the offering plate, because the cash never quite seemed to match the amounts written on people's tithing envelopes. No wonder the church's checking account held less than ten dollars.

My father-in-law wasn't ready to give up. "I don't know—I'm not sure God is finished with that place quite yet," he said. "It's a needy part of the city. Let's not throw in the towel too quickly."

"Well, Clair, what are you going to do when the other pastor leaves?" asked his wife, who was listening on their other phone. "I mean, in two weeks . . ."

His voice suddenly brightened. "Jim, how about if you pastor both churches for the time being? Just give it a chance and see if it might turn around?" He wasn't kidding; he really meant it.

I didn't know what to say. One thing I was sure of: I didn't have any magic cure-all for what ailed the Brooklyn Tabernacle. Still, my father-in-law's concern was genuine, so I went along with the plan.

Now, instead of being an amateur in one congregation, I could double my pleasure. For the next year, this was my Sunday schedule:

9:00 a.m.	*Leave home in New Jersey and drive alone to Brooklyn.*
10:00 a.m.	*Conduct the morning service by myself.*
11:30 a.m.	*Race back across Manhattan and through the Holland Tunnel to the Newark church, where Carol and the others would have already begun the noon service. Preach the sermon.*
Late afternoon:	*Take Carol and the baby to McDonald's, then head back to Brooklyn for the evening service there.*
Late evening:	*Drive back home to New Jersey, exhausted and usually discouraged.*

Vagrants would wander in occasionally during the meetings in Brookyn. The attendance dropped to fewer than twenty people because a number of folks quickly decided I was "too regimented" and elected to go elsewhere.

Sunday mornings without Carol were especially difficult. The pianist had mastered only one chorus, "Oh, How I Love Jesus." We sang it every week, sometimes more than once. All other selections led to stumbling and discords. This did not exactly seem like a church on the move.

I shall never forget that first Sunday morning offering: $85. The church's monthly mortgage payment was $232, not to mention the utility bills or having anything left over for a pastoral salary.

I shall never forget that first Sunday morning offering: $85. ❧

When the first mortgage payment rolled around at the end of the month, the checking account showed something like $160 in hand. We were going to default right off the bat. How soon would it take to lose the building and be tossed out into the street? That Monday, my day off, I remember praying, "Lord, you have to help me. I don't know much—but I *do* know that we have to pay this mortgage."

I went to the church on Tuesday. *Well, maybe someone will send some money out of the blue,* I told myself, *like what happened so often with George Mueller and his orphanage back in England—he just prayed, and a letter or a visitor would arrive to meet his need.*

The mail came that day—and there was nothing but bills and fliers.

Now I was trapped. I went upstairs, sat at my little desk, put my head down, and began to cry. "God," I sobbed, "what can I do? We can't even pay the mortgage." That night was the midweek service, and I knew there wouldn't be more than three or four people attending. The offering would probably be less than ten dollars. How was I going to get through this?

I called out to the Lord for a full hour or so. Eventually, I dried my tears—and a new thought came. *Wait a minute! Besides the mail slot in the front door, the church also has a post office box. I'll go across the street and see what's there. Surely God will answer my prayer!*

With renewed confidence I walked across the street, crossed the post office lobby, and twirled the knob on the little box. I peered inside . . .

Nothing.

As I stepped back into the sunshine, trucks roared down Atlantic Avenue. If one had flattened me just then, I wouldn't have felt any lower. Was God abandoning us? Was I doing something that displeased him? I trudged wearily back across the street to the little building.

As I unlocked the door, I was met with another surprise. There on the foyer floor was something that hadn't been there just three minutes earlier: a simple white envelope. No address, no stamp—nothing. Just a white envelope.

With trembling hands I opened it to find . . . *two $50 bills.*

I began shouting all by myself in the empty church. "God, you came through! You came through!" We had $160 in the bank, and with this $100 we could make the mortgage payment. My soul let out a deep "Hallelujah!" What a lesson for a disheartened young pastor!

To this day I don't know where that money came from. I only know it was a sign to me that God was near—and faithful.

BREAKDOWN

THE HECTIC SCHEDULE, of course, was wearing us out, and Carol and I soon realized we should cast our lot with one church or the other. Oddly enough, we began to feel drawn to Brooklyn, even though our only salary came from the Newark church. Remarkably, God put it into both our hearts to commit ourselves, for better or worse, to the fledgling Brooklyn Tabernacle. We somehow knew that was where we belonged.

Both of us quickly took second jobs—she in a school cafeteria, I as a junior high basketball coach. We had no health insurance. Somehow we put food on the table and bought gas for the car, but that was about it.

I didn't know whether this was a normal experience in the ministry or not; I had no preconceived ideas from Bible college or seminary by which to judge, because I hadn't been there. We were just blundering along all by ourselves. Even Carol's father didn't offer a lot of advice or perspective; I guess he thought I would learn more in the school of hard knocks. He often told me, "Jim, you're just going to have to find your own way, under God, of ministering to people."

On one of those Sunday nights early on, I was so depressed by what I saw—and even more by what I felt in my spirit—that I literally could not preach. Five minutes into my sermon, I began choking on the words. Tears filled my eyes. Gloom engulfed me. All I could say to the people was "I'm sorry ... I ... I can't preach in this atmosphere.... Something is terribly wrong.... I don't know what to say—I can't go on.... Carol, would you play something on the piano, and would the rest of you come to this altar? If we don't see God help us, I don't know...." With that, I just quit. It was embarrassing, but I couldn't do anything else.

The people did as I asked. I leaned into the pulpit, my face planted in my hands, and sobbed. Things were quiet at first, but soon the Spirit of God came down upon us. People began to call upon the Lord, their words motivated by a stirring within. "God, help us," we prayed. Carol played the old hymn "I Need Thee, Oh, I Need Thee," and we sang along. A tide of intercession arose.

Suddenly a young usher came running down the center aisle and threw himself on the altar. He began to cry as he prayed.

When I placed my hand on his shoulder, he looked up, the tears streaming down his face as he said, "I'm sorry! I'm sorry! I won't do it again! Please forgive me." Instantly I realized that he was apologizing for taking money from the offering plate. I stood speechless for a moment, bewildered by his unexpected confession.

It was our first spiritual breakthrough. I had not had to play detective, confront the culprit with his misdeed, or pressure him to confess. Here in a single night, during a season of prayer, Problem Number One (out of seemingly thousands) was solved.

That evening, when I was at my lowest, confounded by obstacles, bewildered by the darkness that surrounded us, unable even to continue preaching, I discovered an astonishing truth: God is attracted to weakness. He can't resist those who humbly and honestly admit how desperately they need him. Our weakness, in fact, makes room for his power.

> **I discovered an astonishing truth: God is attracted to weakness. He can't resist those who humbly and honestly admit how desperately they need him.** ❧

In a parallel vein, people are not put off by honesty, either. I didn't have to keep up a ministerial front. I could just preach God's Word as best I knew and then call the congregation to prayer and worship. The Lord would take over from there.

How I treasure those early humblings. Those experiences showed me that I didn't need to play the preacher. Jesus called fishermen, not graduates of rabbinical schools. The main requirement was to be natural and sincere. His disciples had to depend totally upon the Lord and his power. In the same way, I had to stop trying to act ministerial—whatever that was. God could only use Jim Cymbala the way he is. What a breakthrough that was for me as I learned to trust in God to use my natural personality. God has always despised sham and pretense, especially in the pulpit. The minute I started trying to effect a posture or pose, God's Spirit would be grieved.

What I could do, however, was to get even more serious about studying. I began building a biblical library and giving many hours during the week to digging into God's Word. But another John Wesley or G. Campbell Morgan I would never be—that was obvious. I had to find my own style and stay open and dependent on God.

On the Ragged Edge

Every week seemed to carry with it a new challenge. The burner went out on the heating system and would cost $500 to repair. Unfortunately, my impassioned efforts as a fundraiser mustered only $150 in pledges from the people. I thought more than ever about quitting. *I'm not cut out for this,* I told myself. *I don't have that ministerial flair. I don't have a pastoral voice. I'm not an orator. I look too young. I'm so tired....*

Neither Carol nor I knew where to turn for support. My parents lived in another part of Brooklyn, but my father was battling alcoholism at that point, and my mother was consumed with the struggle. So we couldn't rely much on her for encouragement.

The mother of one of Carol's friends heard what we were doing and dropped by one Sunday. She didn't say it, but you could tell what she was thinking: *What's a nice young couple like you doing down here?* It didn't take long to discover that most middle-class white Christians in other parts of the city did not find our location or congregation very attractive.

Some of the members we inherited were so out of step with the flavor of the church, so set on their own agenda, that I actually began to pray they would leave. One man informed me that he, too, was ordained and should be allowed to preach on Sunday nights. What I observed in his spiritual life, however, indicated just the opposite.

Confrontation came hard because we could ill afford to lose people. But if these members were to stay, the result would be ongoing discord—and I knew the Lord would never bless that kind of a mess with the spiritual power we so desperately needed. One by one, these people made their exit. On a couple of occasions I even had to help answer my own prayers by suggesting that members consider another church. I was learning that in pastoral work, as in basketball, sometimes you have to confront.

In time, despite these defections, the congregation was no longer twenty; it grew to forty or forty-five. The finances remained touch-and-go. Friends sometimes left bags of groceries on our doorstep, for which we were grateful. My first year in Brooklyn we received a total of $3,800 in salary. (The national average income for a household our size was $14,000!) The second year we climbed all the way to $5,200.

On more than one wintry Saturday night, I would think about the fact that attendance the next morning would probably be low because of the snow—most of our people couldn't afford cars. This would mean an even smaller offering. At such times I wondered how I could possibly face another Sunday. I even hoped that by some miracle the sun wouldn't come up the next morning.

Carol started a little choir with a grand total of nine voices. But problems soon arose there, too. No sooner did the choir begin to sing in the meetings than one of the girls in it got pregnant out of wedlock. In a small congregation everyone notices everything; everyone *talks about* everything.

After we had some Sunday night times of prayer around the altar, when people got into the habit of calling on the Lord, our attendance grew to fifty or sixty. But I knew God wanted to do much more ... and he would, if we provided good soil in which he could work. I was tired of the escapist mentality I had witnessed since childhood—always glorifying what God did way back in some revival, or else passionately predicting "the coming great move of God" just ahead. The truth is, I knew there were countless churches across the city and the nation that had not baptized a hundred truly converted sinners in a year, and most not in several years. Any growth came simply through transfers from one church to another. New York City was a hard mission field, but transfer growth was not what God had in mind for us.

What we needed instead was a fresh wind and fresh fire. We needed the Holy Spirit to transform the desperate lives of people all around us. Alcohol and heroin dominated the neighborhood; LSD was also a problem, and cocaine was starting its wicked rise. Prostitutes were working a couple of street corners within three blocks of the church. Urban decay had clearly set in. Anybody who could make any money was trying to get *away* from our area.

I despaired at the thought that my life might slip by without seeing God show himself mightily on our behalf. Carol and I didn't want merely to mark time. I longed and cried out for God to change everything—me, the church, our passion for people, our praying.

> **I despaired at the thought that my life might slip by without seeing God show himself mightily on our behalf.** 🌿

One day I told the Lord that I would rather die than merely tread water throughout my career in the ministry . . . always preaching about the power of the Word and the Spirit, but never seeing it. I abhorred the thought of just having more church services. I hungered for God to break through in our lives and ministry.

THE PROMISE

ABOUT THAT TIME, I came down with a cough that would not go away. I hacked and hacked for six weeks, to the point that Carol could hardly get any sleep at night. I was spitting up phlegm every day.

My in-laws became so concerned that they paid my airfare to come down to their home near St. Petersburg, Florida, and get some rest in the warm sunshine. Gratefully, I headed their way. The only bad part was leaving Carol and two-year-old Chrissy behind.

One day I went out on a party fishing boat with twenty or thirty tourists. The sky was an azure blue, and the warm waters of the Gulf of Mexico lapped soothingly against the sandy shore. Seagulls swooped and squawked overhead. The sun felt good for my congested lungs.

As we launched out toward deep water, the others laughed and talked about the fish they hoped to catch that afternoon. I held a pole in my hands, too . . . but my mind wasn't on fishing. I moved down toward the end of the boat, away from the crowd, and stared at the far horizon.

I began mulling over the many ideas and strategies I had heard or read on church growth. One Christian leader had told me, "Forget about the institutional church *building*; home meetings are where it's at these days. You might as well sell your building; God is doing a new thing."

A once-large and historic Baptist church a few blocks away had invested heavily in a fleet of buses, trying to bring in large numbers of children. The only results were high insurance rates, chronic vandalism, and an unchanged church.

I had attended larger churches that seemed to center on bringing in popular speakers and singers, whoever was hot at the moment. This helped market the church . . . at least to other Christians. As one pastor told me with a smile, "I don't 'steal sheep' from other churches, but I do like to leave my gate wide open."

The embarrassing truth is that sometimes even *I* didn't want to show up for a service—that's how bad it was. ❦

Whether that was a valid approach or not, it took money, so forget it—nobody would come to downtown Brooklyn for the little honorarium we could afford. Moreover, Carol and I had frankly admitted to each other that unless God broke through, the Brooklyn Tabernacle was doomed. We couldn't finesse it along. We couldn't organize and market and program our way out. The embarrassing truth was that sometimes even *I* didn't want to show up for a service—that's how bad it was.

We *had* to have a visitation of the Holy Spirit, or bust.

"Lord, I have no idea how to be a successful pastor," I prayed softly out there on the water. "I haven't been trained. All I know is that Carol and I are working in the middle of New York City, with people dying on every side, overdosing from heroin, consumed by materialism, and all the rest. If the gospel is so powerful . . ."

I couldn't finish the sentence. Tears choked me. Fortunately, the others on the boat were too far away to notice as they studied their lines in the blue-green water.

Then quietly but forcefully, in words heard not with my ear but deep within my spirit, I sensed God speaking:

If you and your wife will lead my people to pray and call upon my name, you will never lack for something fresh to preach. I will supply all the money that's needed, both for the church and for your family, and you will never have a building large enough to contain the crowds I will send in response.

I was overwhelmed. My tears intensified. I looked up at the other passengers, still occupied with their fishing. Nobody glanced in my direction.

I knew I had heard from God, even though I had not experienced some strange vision, nothing sensational or peculiar. God was simply focusing on the only answer to our situation—or anybody else's, for that matter. His word to me was grounded in countless promises repeated in the Scriptures; it was the very thing that had produced every revival of the Holy Spirit throughout history. It was the truth that had made Charles G. Finney, Dwight L. Moody, A. B. Simpson, and other men and women mightily used of God. It was what I already knew, but God was now drawing me out, pulling me toward an actual experience of himself and his power. He was telling me that my hunger for him and his transforming power would be satisfied as I led my tiny congregation to call out to him in prayer.

As the boat docked later that afternoon, I felt wonderfully calm. A few days later I flew back to New York, still the same young pastor I had always been. But all the modern trends and new ideas about church growth were now irrelevant. God had promised to provide, to respond to our cries for divine help. We were not alone, attempting the impossible in a heartless world. God was present, and he would act on our behalf.

A holy excitement came over me. I actually looked forward to the next Sunday morning on Atlantic Avenue.

TWO

❦

Catching Fire

Welcome back, Pastor Cymbala," people said when they saw me that morning. "Did you have a good rest in Florida? How's your cough?"

I told them my cough was much better, but inside, I couldn't wait to tell them something far more important. Early in the service I said, "Brothers and sisters, I really feel that I've heard from God about the future of our church. While I was away, I was calling out to God to help us—to help *me*—understand what he wants most from us. And I believe I've heard an answer.

"It's not fancy or profound or spectacular. But I want to say to you today with all the seriousness I can muster: *From this day on, the prayer meeting will be the barometer of our church. What happens on Tuesday night will be the gauge by which we will judge success or failure because that will be the measure by which God blesses us.*

"If we call upon the Lord, he has promised in his Word to answer, to bring the unsaved to himself, to pour out his Spirit among us. If we don't call upon the Lord, he has promised nothing—nothing at all. It's as simple as that. No matter what I preach or what we claim to believe in our heads, the future will depend upon our times of prayer.

"This is the engine that will drive the church. Yes, I want you to keep coming on Sundays—but Tuesday night is what it's really all about. Carol and I have set our course, and we hope you'll come along with us."

A minister from Australia (or perhaps it was New Zealand) happened to be present that morning—a rare occurrence. I introduced him and invited him to say a few words. He walked to the front and made just one comment:

"I heard what your pastor said. Here's something to think about:

"You can tell how popular a church is by who comes on Sunday morning.

"You can tell how popular the pastor or evangelist is by who comes on Sunday night.

"But you can tell how popular Jesus is by who comes to the prayer meeting."

And with that, he walked off the platform. That was all. I never saw him again.

THE NEW BEGINNING

IF MY ANNOUNCEMENT to that congregation sounds strange and overbearing, consider that it was not a whole lot different from what Charles Haddon Spurgeon, the great British pulpiteer, had said in a sermon almost exactly a hundred years before:

> The condition of the church may be very accurately gauged by its prayer meetings. So is the prayer meeting a grace-ometer, and from it we may judge of the amount of divine working among a people. If God be near a church, it must pray. And if he be not there, one of the first tokens of his absence will be a slothfulness in prayer.[1]

That first Tuesday night, fifteen to eighteen people showed up. I had no agenda or program laid out; I just stood up and led the people in singing and praising God. Out of that came extended prayer. I felt a new sense of unity and love among us. God seemed to be knitting us together. I didn't preach a typical sermon; there was new liberty to wait on God's presence.

In the weeks that followed, answers to prayer became noticeable. New people gradually joined, with talents and skills that could help us. Unsaved relatives and total strangers began to show up. We started to think of ourselves as a "Holy Ghost emergency room" where people in spiritual trauma could be rescued. In most hospitals, the ER isn't decorated as beautifully or fashionably as the rest of the building, but it's very efficient in saving lives.

> **We began to think of ourselves as a "Holy Ghost emergency room" where people in spiritual trauma could be rescued.** ✤

We were a prime example of what the great Scottish devotional writer Andrew Bonar wrote in 1853: "God likes to see His people shut up to this, that there is no hope but in prayer. Herein lies the Church's power against the world."[2]

So week after week, I kept encouraging the people to pray. And of course, as Samuel Chadwick said long ago, the greatest answer to prayer is more prayer.

We were not there to hear one another give voice to eloquent prayers; we were too desperate for that. We focused vertically, on God, rather than horizontally on one another. Much of the time we called out to the Lord as a group, all praying aloud in concert, a practice that continues to this day. At other times we would join hands in circles of prayer, or various people would speak up with a special burden to express.

The format of a prayer meeting is not nearly as important as its essence—touching the Almighty, crying out with one's whole being. I have been in noisy prayer meetings that were mainly a show. I have been with groups in times of silent prayer that were deeply spiritual. The atmosphere of the meeting may vary; what matters most is that we encounter the God of the universe, not just each other.

I also began to ease up in the Sunday meetings and not control them so tightly with a microphone. The usual format—two songs, then announcements, special music by the choir, the offering, then the sermon, finally a benediction—was gradually laid aside as God began to loosen me up. I didn't have to be so nervous or uptight—or phony. I had only been protecting myself out of fear.

After all, people weren't hungry for fancy sermons or organizational polish. They just wanted love. They wanted to know that God could pick them up and give them a second chance.

....

People weren't hungry for fancy sermons or organizational polish. They just wanted love. ❦

....

In those early days on Atlantic Avenue, as people drew near to the Lord, received the Spirit's fullness, and rekindled their first love for God, they naturally began to talk about it on their jobs, in their apartment buildings, at family gatherings. Soon they were bringing new people.

From that day to the present, more than two decades later, there has never been a season of decline in the church, thank God. By his grace we have never had a faction rise up and decide to split away. God has continued to send people who need help; often I can't even find out how they learned of us.

The offerings improved to the point that we could make some building repairs. We replaced the tumbledown pews with fiberglass chairs that locked together. More important, however, people began to sense the presence of the Lord in that humble place. They felt loved. Hardened people would come in and break down even during the singing. The choir began to grow.

SOUNDS OF REJOICING

CAROL HAD LOVED MUSIC from the time she was a teenager. She came by it honestly—her father had been an opera singer before his conversion, and her grandmother was a pianist.

Growing up around the city meant that she had absorbed the sounds of many cultures. Inside her head, the classics blended with black gospel, traditional Scandinavian hymns with contemporary worship choruses and Caribbean rhythms. At the age of only sixteen or seventeen, a dream had entered her heart of directing a large choir someday—not a stiff, formal choir, but a choir of the common people.

Carol did not have a competent accompanist at the church, so she had to play the piano and lead the group simultaneously. She doesn't know how to read music, so she figured out the songs in her head and then taught the group by rote. Even so, the number of singers began to climb, eventually reaching fifty or so. The platform was not nearly large enough to hold them; they would just stand all across the front and sing, overwhelming the small building with their sound.

Practices were held on Friday nights. That may surprise readers who find that other weekend events would be too stiff a competition for people's time. But the urban schedule is different; people are too rushed during the week with their jobs and the long commutes on trains, buses, and subways. They finally relax when Friday evening comes, knowing they don't have to get up early the next day.

Carol would begin with a half hour of prayer. Often a spirit of worship fell on the group. Someone might volunteer a testimony or feel impressed to read Scripture. Carol might offer a short exhortation. Many nights there was more prayer and worship than there was practicing; sometimes the choir never got around to singing at all.

This experience put people in a whole different frame of mind. The choir wasn't just coming up with two "specials" to sing before the sermon; rather, the members were engaged in full-scale ministry.

The band members were as untrained as Carol. Joey Vazquez, who became the bass player, learned the instrument "on the job." He had been plunking around on a bass at a friend's house one day; at choir practice the next night, his friend jokingly said that Joey knew how to play. Carol assumed the friend was serious and put Joey to work. That was the beginning of his career as a bass player; he is still with the church today.

Our drummer, Michael Archibald, a man from Trinidad, has likewise never had lessons. Jonathan Woodby, our organist (and one of the best in America, we think), cannot read music. Yet these two have performed on two Grammy Award-winning albums.

The choir played a crucial role when we started hosting monthly rallies in cooperation with Teen Challenge, a ministry to drug addicts and gang members that was started in Brooklyn in 1958 by David Wilkerson. Together with Teen Challenge, we rented a big Baptist church. For the first rally we advertised the film *The Cross and the Switchblade*, which tells the conversion story of the notorious gang leader Nicky Cruz.

The crowd was so large we had to show the film three times that night so that everyone would get a chance to see it.

For the next rally, Nicky himself came to speak. It was amazing; here he was, preaching in the very building where years before, out on the steps, he had knocked out some Italian guy, ready to kill him if the cops hadn't showed up.

Nicky's story was a great inspiration to me. He was a symbol of things to come in our church: God taking hopeless, even crazy people and changing them. I knew that a lot of churches gave lip service to the idea that God can do anything. But we needed to have real faith that anyone who walked in, regardless of his or her problems, could become a trophy of God's grace. Ever since that night, Nicky has been a close friend of mine and a frequent guest at the Tabernacle.

As more churches got involved in the rallies, Carol formed a multiracial "New York Challenge Choir" made up of people from the Tabernacle plus any others who wanted to sing—eighty or more voices altogether.

It was about this time also that Carol wrote her first song. She took the Christmas carol "Joy to the World" and created a new melody for it. Again, she didn't know how to write it down, but simply taught it to the choir by rote.

A COMMUNITY OF LOVE AND PRAYER

WE NEVER KNEW WHO might come to Christ at the Brooklyn Tabernacle. There were junkies, prostitutes, and homosexuals. But lost lawyers, business types, and bus drivers turned to the Lord there, too. We welcomed them all.

There were Latinos, African Americans, Caribbean Americans, whites—you name it. Once people were energized by the Holy Spirit, they began to see other races as God's creation. Instead of railing at homosexuals, we began to weep over them. People began driving thirty or forty minutes from Long Island. The one—and perhaps only—advantage of our location in downtown Brooklyn is that excellent mass transit was available, which meant that people from Manhattan, Queens, the Bronx, and elsewhere could reach us easily on the subways and buses. By the time we grew to 150 or 175 on Sunday morning, the prayer meeting was up to 100. There was life, joy, a sense of family, and love. When a meeting ended, people weren't in a hurry to leave; they lingered and prayed and talked to one another.

There was no air-conditioning, so on hot summer nights we would have all the windows open and people even sitting on the sills. One Sunday night in August, when it was 90 degrees outside and probably 100 degrees in the building, I felt oddly impressed to lead "Silent Night, Holy Night" as an expression of love to Jesus. A drunk was passing by and stopped to listen. In his confused brain, he said to himself, *This drinking problem of mine is getting totally out of hand. Now I'm hearing Christmas carols. I'd better go in this church and get some help!* The ushers were there to meet him and minister to him.

The mentally disturbed could drop by as well. A fellow named Austin, recently released from an institution, started coming to church. One Sunday he said something vulgar to one of our women. When I called him on Tuesday and warned him that this wouldn't be tolerated, he said, "Oh yeah? I'm going to come take care of you with my 'boys.'" He was a huge man, so I didn't laugh.

I replied, "Austin, you might take care of me, but not with your 'boys'—the way you act, I doubt you have any 'boys.'"

I alerted the ushers that if he showed up again, they should call me—and also immediately call the police. That very night, Austin came back. I left the prayer meeting and went out to talk with him, stalling for time. Soon the police burst through the door and took him away. They wanted me to press charges, but I declined. Instead, I went back in and rejoined the prayer meeting. Episodes as strange as this became a regular part of ministering in this section of the city.

> **Because I had been a basketball player, it never dawned on me to evaluate people on the basis of color. In America it would appear that there is more openness in the gym than in the church of Jesus Christ. 🌿**

The offerings, as one might expect, were never great because of the kind of community we served, characterized by single mothers, people on public assistance, people seeking to become free of drugs. But people who were settled and secure were coming, too, who didn't mind the socioeconomic mix.

Because I had been a basketball player, it never dawned on me to evaluate people on the basis of color. If you could play, you could play. In America it would appear that there is more openness, acceptance, and teamwork in the gym than in the church of Jesus Christ.

SPACE PROBLEMS

BY 1977 MORE PEOPLE were trying to fit into the pews on Sunday morning and Sunday night than there was room for. Down the block was a YWCA with an auditorium that could seat 400 to 500 people. We were able to rent it on Sundays and began lugging our sound equipment and other supplies down there every week. The windows were painted shut, and there was no air-conditioning. Often we had to sweep out the place on Sunday morning before we could set up chairs for church.

But at least we had space to use. We rented the YWCA for two years. Some of the earliest memories of church for our two younger children, Susan and James, are in that building. I remember glancing up during the singing one Sunday and seeing, to my horror, my acrobatic preschool daughter turning 360-degree flips on some parallel bars over on the edge of the hall. So much for the "perfect pastor's kids"!

When Lanny Wolfe, a well-known gospel singer and songwriter, visited a service, he was captivated by the choir's sound, now up to one hundred voices. He encouraged Carol to write more. "You have an eclectic feel that's totally different," he said. "The songs you write are unlike anything I would do, or Bill Gaither, or anyone else." Lanny's encouragement meant a great deal to both of us.

Since then, of course, Carol's music has gone far and wide across the country and is sung in all kinds of churches, whatever the style of their worship. After selling one million units of Brooklyn Tabernacle sheet music, Word Music gave Carol an award in 1994. Ironically, the Tabernacle has not bought a single piece of her music—it wouldn't do any good for a choir that doesn't read music.

Meeting in the YWCA was a temporary solution, at best, to the overcrowding. We purchased a lot across the street in the hope of erecting a real church building one day. It required a big step of faith, but God provided the funds.

We scheduled a groundbreaking ceremony, excited about starting a new building, a permanent home. Would you believe that on that special Sunday, it rained so hard we couldn't go outdoors to put a shovel in the ground? Disappointed, we packed ourselves back into the Y auditorium that evening.

But in that meeting God clearly spoke to us that it wasn't the ground across the street he wanted to break. Instead, he would break our hearts and build his church on that foundation.

The downpour, as it turned out, was providential. A few months later, a large 1,400-seat theater on Flatbush Avenue, the main north-south artery of Brooklyn, became available for only $150,000.

We were able to sell the lot at a profit. We needed to sell the run-down Atlantic Avenue building as well in order to buy the theater. Some pastors came to look at our old place and appeared serious about buying it. We agreed on a price—only to find out later they hadn't even tried to secure a mortgage. By then we were in danger of losing our option on the theater.

All our dreams were about to come crashing down. At a Tuesday night prayer meeting we laid the problem before God, weeping and pleading for a last-minute rescue of some kind.

On Wednesday afternoon the doorbell at the church rang. I went downstairs to answer. There stood a well-dressed stranger, who, it turned out, was a Kuwaiti businessman. He walked in and looked around while I held my breath lest he look too closely at crooked walls, dingy bathrooms, and questionable plumbing. The basement ceiling was so low I feared he would hit his head on one of the pipes that hung down.

"What are you asking for this building?" he said at last.

I cleared my throat and answered weakly, "Ninety-five thousand."

He paused a moment and then said, "That's fair."

I was shocked!

He continued, "We have a deal."

"Uh, well, how long will it take you to make arrangements at the bank?" I was still worried that our option on the Flatbush property would expire before we could close this deal.

"No bank, nothing," he answered abruptly. "Just get your lawyer to call my lawyer—here's the name and phone number. Cash deal." And with that, he was gone.

Once again, our prayer had been answered in a surprising way.

God had formed a core of people who wanted to pray, who believed that nothing was too big for him to handle. No matter what roadblock we faced, no matter what attack came against us, no matter how wild the city became in the late seventies—as cocaine arrived on top of heroin, and then crack cocaine on top of that—God could still change people and deliver them from evil. He was building his church in a tough neighborhood, and as long as people kept calling out for his blessing and help, he had fully committed himself to respond.

THREE

❧

A Song for the Desperate

Although the theater on Flatbush seemed a treasure to us, it was in wretched shape. We spent more than $250,000 fixing it up before we could move in, in January 1979. That was when things really began to take off spiritually.

We had been in the Flatbush building less than a year when someone with connections to a Manhattan recording studio came along and suggested that the choir do what is called a "custom album"—a low-budget production for our own use. We did that in 1980, with Carol composing three or four of the ten works.

Somehow copies made their way to Nashville, and music companies began to approach us. Word Music repackaged the first album and offered it for sale across the country. They soon asked us to do two more. The choir ended up recording with everyone from Larnelle Harris to Babbie Mason to Wayne Watson to the Talleys to West Coast praise and worship leader Morris Chapman.

On Sundays it was not unusual for the choir to sing and testify with such anointing that a spirit of praise would descend on the people, changing the whole direction of the meeting. Once the choir had planned to do three songs. To introduce the second one, a former drug addict gave his testimony. There was such a powerful sense of God's love that I couldn't help walking up as the song was ending, putting one arm around the fellow, and making an invitation right then for people to receive Christ. The response was immediate and strong.

The choir never got around to singing the third song—but after all, why should we hang onto some order of service if people were willing to get saved? God could use the choir, or anyone else, to turn the whole service into a prayer meeting if he wished.

Back from the "Dead"

Among the many people whom the Lord touched in those days—initially through the choir but also through the Tuesday night prayer meeting—one who stands out was a slender, red-haired young woman named Roberta Langella. Her story is so amazing, I will let her tell it:

❧

I was born the fourth of six children in Brooklyn and raised on Staten Island. My father was a longshoreman who provided a good living and a Catholic education for all of us. I was happy to be part of what I thought was a stable, loving home.

But then, when I was only eleven, the wheels came off. All of a sudden, we were moving to Florida to be near my mother's parents. The only trouble was, Dad wasn't coming with us. I had failed to recognize the tension that had developed between my parents and had ruptured their marriage.

I just couldn't believe what was happening. Our family had always stuck together. If you couldn't rely on grown-ups to do the right thing, what was life all about anyway? I was shattered.

Within a year or two, I was acting out my unhappiness by drinking and smoking pot. My mom remarried, which only made matters worse as far as I was concerned. We fought all the time. At age sixteen I came back to New York to live with my dad for a year. That wasn't much better; I dropped out of school and took off to crisscross the country on my own.

A year later, I was back in New York living with a man twice my age. I just wanted somebody—anybody—to love me and take care of me. Unfortunately, this guy was an IV drug abuser. Before long, we were both on cocaine and then heroin. I ended up overdosing several times.

One terrible night in 1980 I shot up so many drugs that people said my heart actually stopped beating. My boyfriend took off, afraid that I had died and that he'd be left to answer incriminating questions. I was abandoned on that rooftop, turning blue ... but by God's grace someone discovered me and called 911. The paramedics came and revived me.

I felt so bad about myself, I was sure nobody thought I was worth anything. That led to one destructive relationship after another. Around 1982 my then current boyfriend and I rented a second-floor apartment above a florist shop next door to the Brooklyn Tabernacle. Of course, we hadn't the slightest interest in what went on there.

My boyfriend was abusive; he punched me out regularly. One day he beat me so badly he broke my eardrum. But every time it happened I would plead, "Don't leave me." It was so pathetic! But worse than being beaten, worse than being hated, was the terrifying thought of being left alone. I couldn't stand it.

I remember one Sunday afternoon when I was so distraught I threatened him. "I'm going to take my life," I said. Sprawled out on the couch, watching a football game, he didn't look up. "I'm watching the Jets now. Talk to me at halftime." He didn't even care!

I somehow kept functioning, working as a bartender in nightclubs. I was totally into the punk culture of the eighties—featuring the "dead look," where I didn't brush my hair for a month.

I remember frequenting "shooting galleries," where twenty or thirty people were getting high all at once, sharing needles. Although I was afraid of the consequences of sharing those needles, I was even more desperate for the drugs.

After the Greenwich Village bars closed in the early hours of the morning, I would proceed to the after-hours scene, which is crazy even to the crazy people. You really don't want to know the outrageous and violent things that go on in the clubs, lasting even past sunup.

Finally I would head home. As I would walk up out of the subway in my black leather jacket, there would be a sidewalk full of church people—all waiting to get into the Tabernacle. I would grit my teeth as I walked past. All their happy faces made me so angry!

Pushing through the crowd, I'd dash upstairs as fast as I could. The only trouble was, my bedroom window faced the alley toward the church, and I couldn't escape the music coming through the walls ... songs like "How Jesus Loves" and "I'm Clean." I'd listen to the melodies and sometimes break down. Something in the music would touch me, even though I didn't want to be touched.

But go inside the church? No way. I was sure Jesus could never love someone as strung out as I was.

Before long, my boyfriend and I split up—as usual—and I moved on to another relationship, another apartment on the Upper West Side of Manhattan. Sometimes I'd hear the woman one floor below singing in the shower. I met her in the hall one day and said, "I hear you singing sometimes. Are you a musician?"

"No, not really. I just sing in a choir at my church, and I like to practice the songs at home."

"What church is that?" I asked.

"The Brooklyn Tabernacle."

I had moved away, but that church kept moving in on me.

Meanwhile, the drug and alcohol abuse intensified. At times we had no food in the house; the phone was turned off. We started selling furniture in order to finance my drug habit. Somehow, though, I always held onto a job. All-night highs wouldn't keep me from getting up in the morning and going to work.

One evening at a friend's house, I broke down crying. For the first time in my life, I said, "You know, I think I might have a drug problem." That was the understatement of the decade, but an important first step for me.

Over the next few days I zeroed in on what I felt had to be the cause of my problems: my boyfriend. His drug use was a bad influence on me, right? So I kicked him out.

Within a few weeks, I had a new live-in boyfriend who didn't do drugs. Instead, he was a *dealer!* He'd bring pounds of cocaine into the house. Obviously, I kept using.

One night I called my mother in Florida, who by then had become a Christian. I started talking about my life—and couldn't stop. I don't know how she managed it, but she replied calmly to my agonized self-revelations by inviting me to come down and spend a couple of days with her.

Those few days in Florida stretched out to fourteen months. My mom got me into Narcotics Anonymous, and I went clean. I also managed, after all the years, to get my GED—my General Equivalency Diploma. Things were finally looking up, and I was sure I could conquer the world. But my newfound confidence came crashing down all too soon.

A visit to the doctor unveiled a horrible fact: I was HIV-positive. After all the needle-sharing over the years, I shouldn't have been surprised. But I became furious at this news, coming just as I was trying hard to get my act together. I was mad at myself and at God.

I returned to New York and started my own business. In the meantime, my brother Stephen had found the Lord and began witnessing to me, but I brushed him off. Finally I agreed to go with him to the Brooklyn Tabernacle, insisting on sitting in the balcony, arriving late and leaving early.

> **"Finally I hit bottom, at the end of a five- or six-day crack binge. It was a Tuesday night when I ran out of money. For some reason I drove to the church."—ROBERTA LANGELLA ❧**

It was only a matter of time until the siren call of drugs broke through my resolve. I lapsed back into the world of crack cocaine after two years of living clean. Inside, the old feelings of embarrassment and shame rose up again. But I just couldn't help it. I wanted the rush of drugs more than I wanted to keep struggling with life alone.

Finally I hit bottom, at the end of a five- or six-day crack binge. It was a Tuesday night when I ran out of money. For some reason I drove to the church—I don't know why. That night I found myself at the altar shedding tears I couldn't stop. "Oh, God, I need you in my life. Help me, please!" It was the moment of final surrender for me. From that point on, I began to believe God loved me. And with this newfound faith came hope and a slowly growing confidence.

A year later, I was actually singing in the very same choir I had so resented! My life was on steady ground after so much turmoil. I knew—I really knew down deep—that God loved me and accepted me and I could relax in his love. I was free of the chains that had bound me for so many years.

✺

WE DIDN'T DISCOVER THIS wonderful miracle of God's grace until Roberta quietly sent Carol a seven-page letter. It was Easter time, and we were in the thick of planning a concert. Carol sat down to read this letter one evening and within minutes was weeping. "Jim—you have to stop and read this," she insisted, handing me the first page and then the next and the next. Soon I was in tears along with her.

When we finished, we looked at each other and said, "This is amazing. She *has* to tell her story at the Easter concert." Roberta had never spoken in public before, but she gamely agreed to try.

The day came, and the building was jammed. She had invited all her family. Many of them, including her father in the third row, didn't know the half of what they were about to hear.

After four choir numbers, Roberta came out of the choir, nervously picked up a microphone, and began to speak. "Hi, my name is Roberta Langella . . . and I want to tell you what the risen Jesus means to me."

We had coached her to leave out a few of the most lurid details, but even so, her story was powerful. As she got to the toughest parts, she couldn't help stopping to say, "Daddy . . . I know this is hard for you to hear. But I have to say it, because it shows how Jesus can forgive the worst in a person's life." The emotion was so incredible it took your breath away. People were on the edge of their seats.

The choir then sang the final song, and I brought the meeting to a close. The first person to the altar was Roberta's father, sobbing profusely. Then came her uncle, her aunt, and the rest of the clan.

Today Roberta Langella heads up our ministry called "New Beginnings," a weekly outreach to drug abusers and the homeless. She now has a hundred workers involved, riding the subway every Sunday afternoon to the shelters and rehab centers to escort people to our church for a meal and the evening meeting. The love of the Lord just exudes from her life.

Roberta is a real trooper these days, even when she doesn't feel well. As she sits in the balcony on Sunday nights with all the homeless she has brought with her, there's nobody too dirty, too far gone for her to care about. She sees herself in them. She is a living example of the power of God to pick up the downtrodden, the self-loathing, the addicted, and redeem them for his glory.

SECRET "FORMULA"

PROVIDING SPACE FOR PEOPLE such as Roberta and the scores of homeless she brings our way has turned out to be a perennial problem for us. In 1985 the overall growth of the church forced us to add an afternoon service at 3:30, and in early 1996, a fourth service—each of them two to two-and-a-half hours long. We have always felt we had to give the Holy Spirit time to work; we couldn't rush people through some kind of assembly line. The worship times are now 9:00 A.M., 12:00 noon, 3:30 P.M., and 7:30 P.M.

This makes a grueling schedule, but we have no choice until we can get into a larger facility. I simply cannot abide turning people away at the door, which is what has had to happen often.

With people in the overflow room plus the lobby sitting on stackable chairs and watching TV monitors, we can accommodate at least 1,600 per meeting. This increase has occurred in spite of the fact that around 1985 we began to send groups of people out to start churches in other parts of the city: the Glendale section of Queens, the Lower East Side of Manhattan, the South Bronx, Coney Island, Harlem, and so forth. The present count stands at seven churches in the greater New York area, plus another ten elsewhere, from New Hampshire to San Francisco and even overseas.

> **Each service is two to two-and-a-half hours long. We have always felt we had to give the Holy Spirit time to work; we couldn't rush people through some kind of assembly line.** ✿

The first groups were launched with the help of the choir through public concerts. Actually, that first concert was something of an accident. A minister in Manhattan called me one day to ask a favor. He had booked the famous Carnegie Hall, which seats 2,100, on a Wednesday night for a Christian concert—and the artist had canceled with only forty-five days to go. Was there any way our choir could fill in and somehow prevent the financial loss that would otherwise occur, since Carnegie Hall was not about to let him out of his contract?

We had never done anything like that, and we didn't know how to go about it. Should we sell tickets? We elected to sing with no admission charge, taking an offering instead. The hall management was not happy about this arrangement but reluctantly agreed.

We began passing the word throughout the city that the Brooklyn Tabernacle Choir would premiere some of its new songs at a free concert. On the appointed day we got the shock of our lives when people began lining up outside the hall before noon! The line stretched from the door on West 57th Street up to the corner, down a full block on Seventh Avenue, around another corner along West 56th—3,500 people in all.

The next thing I knew, the New York Police Department was there with crowd-control barricades and officers on horseback. I was so embarrassed about my mishandling of the whole situation that I went inside and hid in a basement room. A stern-faced sergeant came looking for me to ask, "What's going on here? Who caused all this?" I sheepishly admitted it was my fault.

The concert was a wonderful success. Near the end I gave a brief presentation of the gospel the choir had been singing about, then I closed with a public invitation. People readily came forward to accept Christ. We prayed with them right there and collected their names and addresses for follow-up.

A few weeks later I received a phone call from someone at Radio City Music Hall. "Why don't you book with us next time? We seat six thousand."

Carol and I were honored by the invitation, but there was, of course, the small matter of the charges: more than $70,000! We took a deep breath and decided to make the plunge, understandably selling tickets this time in order to cover the expense. We promoted the night as the premiere of a new album.

The tickets sold out in three days.

The next time we released a choir album, we did two nights. For the *Live . . . With Friends* album, we ventured for three nights—and sold out all three. Each choir member was committed to trying to sell fifty tickets to people at work who didn't attend church. When a member would say, "Hey, I'm singing at Radio City Music Hall next month—would you like to buy a ticket?" people usually reacted with amazement—and an affirmative response.

Church planting became an important motive for the events. We would give away free tickets in whatever section of the city we wanted to start a church. Then during the concert we would announce, "This coming Sunday, services will begin at such-and-such a place; please join us there."

The biggest distributor of Christian choral music in America got acquainted with us, liked the music, and sat down with Carol one day to ask: "So what's the formula here? What makes this work?"

She began talking about the choir prayer meeting. The visitor said to himself, *She didn't understand my question. I want to know what makes the music so inspirational.*

It was months before he realized that the life in the music comes from prayer. That's the formula.

Prayer cannot truly be taught by principles and seminars and symposiums. It has to be born out of a whole environment of felt need. If I say, "I *ought* to pray," I will soon run out of motivation and quit; the flesh is too strong. I have to be *driven* to pray.

Yes, the roughness of inner-city life has pressed us to pray. . . . But is the rest of the country coasting along in fine shape? I think not. ❦

Yes, the roughness of inner-city life has pressed us to pray. When you have alcoholics trying to sleep on the back steps of your building, when your teenagers are getting assaulted and knifed on the way to youth meetings, when you bump into transvestites in the lobby after church, you can't escape your need for God. According to a recent Columbia University study, twenty-one cents of every dollar New Yorkers pay in city taxes is spent trying to cope with the effects of smoking, drinking, and drug abuse.

But is the rest of the country coasting along in fine shape? I think not. In the smallest village in the Farm Belt, there are still urgent needs. Every congregation has wayward kids, family members who aren't serving God. Do we really believe that God can bring them back to himself?

Too many Christians live in a state of denial: "Well, I hope my child will come around someday." Some parents have actually given up: "I guess nothing can be done. Bobby didn't turn out right—but we tried; we dedicated him to the Lord when he was a baby. Maybe someday . . ."

The more we pray, the more we sense our need to pray. And the more we sense a need to pray, the more we *want* to pray.

CHECK THE VITAL SIGNS

PRAYER IS THE SOURCE of the Christian life, a Christian's life-line. Otherwise, it's like having a baby in your arms and dressing her up so cute—but she's not breathing! Never mind the frilly clothes; *stabilize the child's vital signs.* It does no good to talk to someone in a comatose state. That's why the great emphasis on teaching in today's churches is producing such limited results. Teaching is good only where there's life to be channeled. If the listeners are in a spiritual coma, what we're telling them may be fine and orthodox, but unfortunately, spiritual life cannot be taught.

Pastors and churches have to get uncomfortable enough to say, "We are not New Testament Christians if we don't have a prayer life." This conviction makes us squirm a little, but how else will there be a breakthrough with God?

If we truly think about what Acts 2:42 says—"They devoted themselves to the apostles' teaching and to the fellowship, to the breaking of bread and to prayer"—we can see that prayer is almost a proof of a church's normalcy. Calling on the name of the Lord is the fourth great hallmark in the list. If my church or your church isn't praying, we shouldn't be boasting in our orthodoxy or our Sunday morning attendance figures.

In fact, Carol and I have told each other more than once that if the spirit of brokenness and calling on God ever slacks off in the Brooklyn Tabernacle, we'll know we're in trouble, even if we have 10,000 in attendance.

FOUR

❦

The Greatest Discovery
of All Time

DURING COUNTLESS TUESDAY NIGHT prayer meetings I find myself encircled by the sacred sounds of prayer and intercession filling the church, spilling into the vestibule, and overflowing from every heart present. As the meeting edges to a close, I overhear mothers petitioning for wayward children . . . men asking God to please help them find employment . . . others giving thanks for recent answers to prayer . . . tearful voices here and there. I can't help but think, *This is as close to heaven as I will ever get in this life. I don't want to leave here. If I were invited to the White House to meet some dignitary, it would never bring the kind of peace and deep joy I sense here in the presence of people calling on the Lord.*

The sound isn't forced, as if the crowd had been worked up into a religious frenzy. Rather, it is the sound of people freely expressing their hearts' needs, desires, and praises.

What I'm hearing on those Tuesday nights is not unusual or peculiar to our church. Far from being a new invention, this kind of prayer has ancient roots. It goes back before Christ, before David, even before Moses organized a formal worship system with the tabernacle. The first mention occurs all the way back in Genesis 4:25–26:

> Adam lay with his wife again, and she gave birth to a
> son and named him Seth, saying, "God has granted me

another child in place of Abel, since Cain killed him."
Seth also had a son, and he named him Enosh.

At that time men began to call on the name of the LORD.

Think about that. Until then, people had known God mainly as the Creator. He had made the Garden of Eden and the rest of the world as far as their eyes could see.

Now came the beginning of the first *collective relationship* with the Almighty. Before a Bible was available, before the first preacher was ordained or the first choir formed, a godly strain of men and women distinguished themselves from their ungodly neighbors by *calling on the Lord.* Cain and his posterity had gone their own way, independent of God. By contrast, these people affirmed their dependence on God by calling out to him.

In fact, God's first people were not called "Jews" or "the children of Israel" or "Hebrews." In the *very* beginning their original name was "those who call on the name of the LORD."

On some unmarked day . . . at some unnoted hour . . . a God-placed instinct in human hearts came alive. People sensed that if you are in trouble and you call out to God, he will answer you! He will intervene in your situation.

I can imagine one woman saying to another, "Have you heard about the God who answers when you call on him? He's more than just the Creator; he cares and responds to our needs. He actually understands what we're feeling."

"What are you talking about? God does whatever he pleases; people can't influence him one way or the other."

"No, no, you're wrong. When you call out to him, he doesn't turn a deaf ear. He listens! He responds. He acts."

"LORD, HELP!"

DAVID JEREMIAH, MY LONGTIME FRIEND from Shadow Mountain Community Church near San Diego, has preached several times at the Brooklyn Tabernacle. Immediately after being diagnosed with cancer, he called to ask us to pray. Several months later he returned to visit us during an outreach meeting we held at Madison Square Garden arena. Later he preached at one of our Sunday services. The whole congregation was delighted to see this wonderful Christian brother for whom we had all interceded.

> **God is not aloof. He says continually through the centuries, "I'll help you, I really will. When you're ready to throw up your hands— throw them up to me."** ❧

Moved by the love and thanksgiving his appearance produced, David later remarked about it from the pulpit:

"I called here as soon as I learned of my sickness because I knew of your emphasis on prayer. In fact, someone just greeted me in the lobby and remarked, 'Pastor Jeremiah, we really cried out to God on your behalf.' That is why I called you. I knew your praying wouldn't be just some mechanical exercise but a real calling out to God with passion for my need. And God brought me through the ordeal."

That is the literal meaning of the Hebrew word used countless times in the Old Testament when people *called* upon God. It means *to cry out, to implore aid.* This is the essence of true prayer that touches God.

Charles Spurgeon once remarked that "the best style of prayer is that which cannot be called anything else but a cry."[1]

Isn't that what God *invites* us to do all through the Bible? "Call to me and I will answer you and tell you great and unsearchable things you do not know" (Jer. 33:3). God is not aloof. He is not disconnected. He says continually through the centuries, "I'll help you, I really will. When you don't know where to turn, then turn to me. When you're ready to throw up your hands—throw them up to me. Put your voice behind them, too, and I'll come and help you."

After Moses came down from Mount Sinai, calling on God became an earmark of his people's successes. The patriarch spotlighted this most dramatically in his farewell address: "What other nation is so great as to have their gods near them the way the LORD our God is near us whenever we pray to him?" (Deut. 4:7). The other nations may have had better chariots, better weaponry, but that wouldn't matter in the end. They didn't have what Israel had: a God who would respond when they called upon him. And note that there was no promised help from God if Israel ceased calling out to him. Only defeat and humiliation would follow.

THE REAL FORCE

SATAN'S MAIN STRATEGY WITH God's people has always been to whisper, "Don't call, don't ask, don't depend on God to do great things. You'll get along fine if you just rely on your own cleverness and energy." The truth of the matter is that the devil is not terribly frightened of our human efforts and credentials. But he knows his kingdom will be damaged when we lift up our hearts to God.

Listen to David's confident assertion in Psalm 4:3. "Know that the LORD has set apart the godly for himself; the LORD *will hear when I call to him.*" That was David's whole posture, his instinct, and especially his approach to warfare. *It doesn't matter what the Philistine armies have. If we call out to God, he will give us the victory. If we backslide and don't call, then we can be defeated by a tiny army.*

I can almost hear David saying, "You can chase me, you can persecute me, you can do anything you want—but when I call on God, you're in trouble! The Lord will hear when I call to him."

> **The devil is not terribly frightened of our human efforts and credentials. But he knows his kingdom will be damaged when we begin to lift up our hearts to God.** 🌿

Notice how God defines wicked people in Psalm 14:4. "Will evildoers never learn—those who devour my people as men eat bread *and who do not call on the LORD?*" That is the divine definition of the ungodly. They will do many things, but they will not humble themselves and recognize God's omnipotence by calling on his name with all their hearts.

One of the great devotional writers said, "The main thing God asks for is our attention."

Salvation itself is impossible until a person humbly calls upon the name of the Lord (Acts 2:21), for God has promised specifically to be rich in mercy to those who call on his name (Rom. 10:12–13).

"Call upon me in the day of trouble," God says in Psalm 50:15. "I will deliver you, and you will honor me." God desires praise from our lives . . . but the only way fresh praise and honor will come is as we keep coming to him in times of need and difficulty. Then he will intervene to show himself strong on our behalf, and we will know that he has done it.

Are not we all prone to be a little cocky and think we can handle things just fine? But let some trouble come, and how quickly we sense our inadequacy. Trouble is one of God's great servants because it reminds us how much we continually need the Lord. Otherwise, we tend to forget about entreating him. For some reason we want to carry on by ourselves.

HOW REVIVAL STARTS

THE HISTORY OF PAST revivals portray this truth in full color. Whether you study the Great Awakening, the Second Great Awakening, the Welsh Revival, the 1906 outpouring on Azusa Street in Los Angeles, or any other period of revival, you always find men and women who first inwardly groan, longing to see the status quo changed—in themselves and in their churches. They begin to call on God with insistence; prayer begets revival, which begets more prayer. It's like Psalm 80, where Asaph bemoans the sad state of his time, the broken walls, the rampaging animals, the burnt vineyards. Then in verse 18 he pleads, "Revive us, and we will call on your name."

The Holy Spirit is the Spirit of prayer. Only when we are full of the Spirit do we feel the need for God everywhere we turn. We can be driving a car, and spontaneously our spirit starts going up to God with needs and petitions and intercessions right there in the middle of traffic.

If our churches don't pray, and if people don't have an appetite for God, what does it matter how many are attending the services? How would that impress God? Can you imagine the angels saying, "Oh, your pews! We can't believe how beautiful they are! Up here in heaven, we've been talking about them for years. Your sanctuary lighting—it's so clever. The way you have the steps coming up to the pulpit—it's wonderful. . . ."

I don't think so.

If we don't want to experience God's closeness here on earth, why would we want to go to heaven anyway? He is the center of everything there. If we don't enjoy being in his presence here and now, then heaven would not be heaven for us. Why would he send anyone there who doesn't long for him passionately here on earth?

I am not suggesting that we are justified by works of prayer or any other acts of devotion. I am not a legalist. But let us not dodge the issue of what heaven will be like: enjoying the presence of God, taking time to love him, listening to him, and giving him praise.

I have talked with pastor after pastor, some of them prominent and "successful," who have told me privately, "Jim, the truth is, I couldn't have a real prayer meeting in my church. I'd be embarrassed at the smallness of the crowd. Unless somebody's teaching or singing or doing some kind of presentation, people just won't come. I can only get them for a one-hour service, and that only once a week."

Is that kind of religion found anywhere in the Bible? Jesus himself can't draw a crowd even among his own people! What a tragedy that the quality of ministry is too often measured by numbers and building size rather than by true spiritual results.

As a preacher myself, let me be blunt here. Preaching itself can easily become just a subtle form of entertainment. When I stand at the Judgment Seat of Christ, he is not going to ask me if I was a clever orator. He is not going to ask me how many books I wrote. He is only going to ask whether I continued in the line of men and women, starting way back in the time of Adam's grandchildren, who led others to call upon God.

A PERSONAL TEST

ALL MY TALKING ABOUT prayer faced a severe test several years ago when Carol and I went through the darkest two-and-a-half-year tunnel we could imagine.

Our oldest daughter, Chrissy, had been a model child growing up. But around age sixteen she started to stray. I admit I was slow to notice this—I was too occupied with the church, starting branch congregations, overseeing projects, and all the rest that ministry entails.

Meanwhile, Chrissy not only drew away from us, but also away from God. In time, she even left our home. There were many nights when we had no idea where she was.

As the situation grew more serious, I tried everything. I begged, I pleaded, I scolded, I argued, I tried to control her with money. Looking back, I recognize the foolishness of my actions. Nothing worked; she just hardened more and more. Her boyfriend was everything we did not want for our child.

How I kept functioning through that period I don't know. Many a Sunday morning I would put on my suit, get into the car to drive to the Tabernacle early, ahead of Carol ... and cry for the next 25 minutes, all the way to the church door. "God, how am I going to get through three meetings today? I don't want to make myself the center of attention. The people have problems of their own—they're coming for help and encouragement. But what about me? I'm hanging by a thread. Oh, God, please ... my firstborn, my Chrissy."

Somehow God would pull my nerves together enough for me to function through another long Sunday. There were moments, however, as we were worshiping God and singing, that my spirit would almost seem to run away from the meeting to intercede for Chrissy. I had to control myself to stay focused on the people and their needs.

While this was going on, we learned that Carol needed an operation—a hysterectomy. As she tried to adjust afterward, the devil took the opportunity to come after her and say, *You might have this big choir, and you're making albums and doing outreaches at Radio City Music Hall and all the rest. Fine,*

*you and your husband can go ahead to reach the world for Christ—
but I'm going to have your children. I've already got the first one.
I'm coming for the next two.*

Like any mother who loves her children, Carol was smitten with tremendous fear and distress. Her family meant more to her than a choir. One day she said to me, "Listen, we need to leave New York. I'm serious. This atmosphere has already swallowed up our daughter. We can't keep raising kids here. If you want to stay, you can—but I'm getting our other children out." She wasn't kidding.

> **One day Carol said to me, "Listen, we need
> to leave New York. I'm serious. We can't
> keep raising our kids in this atmosphere."** ❧

I said, "Carol, we just can't do that. We can't unilaterally take off without knowing what God wants us to do."

Carol wasn't being rebellious; she was just depressed after the surgery. She elected not to pack up and run after all. And it was at that low point that she went to the piano one day, and God gave her a song that has touched more people than perhaps anything else she has written:

> In my moments of fear,
> Through every pain, every tear,
> There's a God who's been faithful to me.
> When my strength was all gone,
> When my heart had no song,
> Still in love he's proved faithful to me.
> Every word he's promised is true;
> What I thought was impossible, I see my God do.

He's been faithful, faithful to me,
Looking back, his love and mercy I see.
Though in my heart I have questioned,
Even failed to believe,
Yet he's been faithful, faithful to me.

When my heart looked away,
The many times I could not pray,
Still my God, he was faithful to me.
The days I spent so selfishly,
Reaching out for what pleased me;
Even then God was faithful to me
Every time I come back to him,
He is waiting with open arms,
And I see once again.

He's been faithful, faithful to me. . . .[2]

Were we calling on the Lord through all of this? In a sense we were. But I couldn't help jumping in to take action on my own, too. I was still, to some degree, the point guard wanting to grab the basketball, push it down the floor, make something happen, press through any hole in the defense I could find. But the more I pressed, the worse Chrissy got.

Then one November, I was alone in Florida when I received a call from a minister whom I had persuaded Chrissy to talk to. "Jim," he said, "I love you and your wife, but the truth of the matter is, Chrissy's going to do what Chrissy's going to do. You don't really have much choice, now that she's eighteen. She's determined. You're going to have to accept whatever she decides."

I hung up the phone. Something very deep within me began to cry out. "Never! I will never accept Chrissy being away from you, Lord!" I knew that if she continued on the present path, there would be nothing but destruction awaiting her.

Once again, as back in 1972, there came a divine show-down. God strongly impressed me to stop crying, screaming, or talking to anyone else about Chrissy. I was to converse with no one but God. In fact, I knew I should have no further contact with Chrissy—until God acted! I was just to believe and obey what I had preached so often—

Call upon me in the day of trouble, and I will answer you.

I dissolved in a flood of tears. I knew I had to let go of this situation.

Back home in New York, I began to pray with an intensity and growing faith as never before. Whatever bad news I would receive about Chrissy, I kept interceding and actually began praising God for what I knew he would do soon. I made no attempts to see her. Carol and I endured the Christmas season with real sadness. I was pathetic, sitting around trying to open presents with our other two children, without Chrissy.

February came. One cold Tuesday night during the prayer meeting, I talked from Acts 4 about the church boldly calling on God in the face of persecution. We entered into a time of prayer, everyone reaching out to the Lord simultaneously.

An usher handed me a note. A young woman whom I felt to be spiritually sensitive had written: *Pastor Cymbala, I feel impressed that we should stop the meeting and all pray for your daughter.*

I hesitated. Was it right to change the flow of the service and focus on my personal need?

Yet something in the note seemed to ring true. In a few minutes I picked up a microphone and told the congregation what had just happened. "The truth of the matter," I said, "although I haven't talked much about it, is that my daughter is very far from God these days. She thinks up is down, and down is up; dark is light, and light is dark. But I know God can break through to her, and so I'm going to ask Pastor

Boekstaaf to lead us in praying for Chrissy. Let's all join hands across the sanctuary."

As my associate began to lead the people, I stood behind him with my hand on his back. My tear ducts had run dry, but I prayed as best I knew.

To describe what happened in the next minutes, I can only employ a metaphor: *The church turned into a labor room.* The sounds of women giving birth are not pleasant, but the results are wonderful. Paul knew this when he wrote, "My dear children, for whom I am again in the pains of childbirth until Christ is formed in you . . ." (Gal. 4:19).

There arose a groaning, a sense of desperate determination, as if to say, "Satan, you will *not* have this girl. Take your hands off her—she's coming back!" I was overwhelmed. The force of that vast throng calling on God almost literally knocked me over.

When I got home that night, Carol was waiting up for me. We sat at the kitchen table drinking coffee, and I said, "It's over."

"What's over?" she wondered.

"It's over with Chrissy. You would have had to be in the prayer meeting tonight. I tell you, if there's a God in heaven, this whole nightmare is finally over." I described what had taken place.

Back from the Abyss

Thirty-two hours later, on Thursday morning, as I was shaving, Carol suddenly burst through the door, her eyes wide. "Go downstairs!" she blurted. "Chrissy's here."

"Chrissy's *here?*"

"Yes! Go down!"

"But Carol—I—"

"Just go down," she urged. "It's you she wants to see."

I wiped off the shaving foam and headed down the stairs, my heart pounding. As I came around the corner, I saw my daughter on the kitchen *floor*, rocking on her hands and knees, sobbing. Cautiously I spoke her name:

"Chrissy?"

She grabbed my pant leg and began pouring out her anguish. "Daddy—Daddy—I've sinned against God. I've sinned against myself. I've sinned against you and Mommy. Please forgive me—"

My vision was as clouded by tears as hers. I pulled her up from the floor and held her close as we cried together.

Suddenly she drew back. "Daddy," she said with a start, *"who was praying for me? Who was praying for me?"* Her voice was like that of a cross-examining attorney.

"What do you mean, Chrissy?"

"On Tuesday night, Daddy—who was praying for me?" I didn't say anything, so she continued:

"In the middle of the night, God woke me and showed me I was heading toward this abyss. There was no bottom to it—it scared me to death. I was so frightened. I realized how hard I've been, how wrong, how rebellious.

"But at the same time, it was like God wrapped his arms around me and held me tight. He kept me from sliding any farther as he said, 'I still love you.'

"Daddy, tell me the truth—*who was praying for me Tuesday night?"*

I looked into her bloodshot eyes, and once again I recognized the daughter we had raised.

Chrissy's return to the Lord became evident immediately. By that fall, God had opened a miraculous door for her to enroll at a Bible college, where she not only undertook studies but soon began directing music groups and a large choir, just like her mother. Today she is a pastor's wife in the Midwest with three wonderful children. Through all this, Carol and I learned as never before that persistent calling upon the Lord breaks through every stronghold of the devil, for nothing is impossible with God.

For Christians in these troubled times, there is simply no other way.

FIVE

❦

The Day Jesus Got Mad

LIKE MOST CHRISTIANS, I love the mental picture of Jesus the Good Shepherd putting the lamb on his shoulders and carrying it to safety.

I love the soft image of the Baby in the manger.

I love the story about Christ feeding the hungry multitudes with bread and fish.

When I think about Jesus dying on the cross to pay for my sin, I'm deeply moved.

I marvel at the sight of him bursting out of the tomb, alive on Resurrection morning.

But there is one picture of Jesus that, frankly, doesn't seem to fit. It is so stunning I wonder why God would even put it in the Bible ... not once, but twice. The second account is in Mark 11:15–18.

> On reaching Jerusalem, Jesus entered the temple area and began driving out those who were buying and selling there. He overturned the tables of the money changers and the benches of those selling doves, and would not allow anyone to carry merchandise through the temple courts. And as he taught them, he said, "Is it not written:
>
> "'My house will be called a house of prayer for all nations'?

But you have made it 'a den of robbers.'"

The chief priests and the teachers of the law heard this and began looking for a way to kill him, for they feared him, because the whole crowd was amazed at his teaching.

The twelve disciples were no doubt just as stunned as the crowd; nothing is said about their helping their Master clean house. All by himself Jesus started pitching over the tables, blocking people who were carrying things, and saying, "Get out of here with that! You can't bring that through the courts." He stormed over to the merchants of oxen and sheep and doves, saying, "Out! Get your business out of here!"

What happened to the loving Jesus? Anyone who gets that irate and physical surely must not be walking in the Spirit, right? But this was Jesus Christ. In fact, the first time he did this a couple of years before (see John 2), he even made a whip out of cords. He was physically thrashing people out of the temple!

What made God's Son so agitated?

His house was being prostituted *for purposes other than what was intended.*

As the feathers were flying and the coins were clattering to the pavement and the businessmen were shouting for the police, Jesus said above the roar, "This place looks and feels more like a mall than a temple. Whatever happened to Isaiah's word about the real point of this building—to be a house of prayer for all nationalities and races? Out! Get out, all of you!"

JUST DOING THEIR JOB

THE ODD THING ABOUT this event is that if Eyewitness News had interviewed any of the merchants that day, each would have vigorously defended the right to be there. "We provide an essential service to the worshipers," they would have said. "How else are people going to get the required animal to sacrifice? If you live any distance away, you can't be herding your sheep and cows through the streets of Jerusalem. We've got to help the program along. . . ." But, of course, they had added a gouging surcharge to the price.

> **Jesus is not terribly impressed with religious commercialism. He is concerned not only *whether* we're doing God's work, but also *how and why* we're doing it.** ❧

The money changers would have said the same. "Everybody has to pay the temple tax, and people can't be walking in here with Greek or Roman or Macedonian money. They've got to use the special coins minted here in Jerusalem. We help people with their currency problems." But once again, they were tacking on big-time profits.

For all of us involved in preaching the gospel, performing music, publishing Christian materials, and all the rest, there is an uncomfortable message here: Jesus is not terribly impressed with religious commercialism. He is concerned not only *whether* we're doing God's work, but also *how and why* we're doing it. At the Judgment Seat of Christ, his main questions for me will have to do not with the growth or the budget of the Brooklyn Tabernacle, but with *why* I pastored this church—in what spirit.

If you sing in a choir, the question is not just *if* you're on your note; it's *why* you are singing at all.

If you teach a class, are you doing it with a heart that radiates God's love for the students, or for some other reason?

I am dismayed at the contracts required by some contemporary Christian musical groups. To perform a concert at your church, the stated fee will be so much (in either four or five figures) plus round-trip airfare—often in first class, not coach. Every detail of the accommodations is spelled out, down to "sushi for twenty persons" waiting at the hotel, in one case. All this is done so that the group can stand before an inner-city audience and exhort the people to "just trust the Lord for all your needs."

Our forebears back in the camp meeting days used to say that if people left a meeting talking about what a wonderful sermon the preacher gave or how beautifully the singers sang, the meeting had failed. But if people went home saying things like "Isn't God good? He met me tonight in such a wonderful way," it was a good meeting. There was to be no sharing the stage with the Lord.

The first-century money changers were in the temple, but they didn't have the spirit of the temple. They may have played a legitimate role in assisting people to worship, but they were out of sync with the whole purpose of the Lord's house.

> **Does the Bible ever say anywhere from Genesis to Revelation, "My house shall be called a house of preaching"?** ❦

"The atmosphere of my Father's house," Jesus seemed to say, "is to be prayer. The aroma around my Father must be that of people opening their hearts in worship and supplication. This is not just a place to make a buck. This is a house for calling on the Lord."

I do not mean to imply that the Jerusalem temple, built by Herod the Great, is the direct counterpart of our church buildings today. God no longer centers his presence in one particular building. In fact, the New Testament teaches that *we* are now his dwelling place; he lives in his people. How much more important, then, is Jesus' message about the primacy of prayer?

> **I have seen God do more in people's lives during ten minutes of real prayer than in ten of my sermons. ❧**

The feature that is supposed to distinguish Christian churches, Christian people, and Christian gatherings is the aroma of prayer. It doesn't matter what your tradition or my tradition is. The house is not ours anyway; it is the Father's.

Does the Bible ever say anywhere from Genesis to Revelation, "My house shall be called a house of preaching"?

Does it ever say, "My house shall be called a house of music"?

Of course not.

The Bible does say, "My house shall be called a house of prayer for all nations." Preaching, music, the reading of the Word—these things are fine; I believe in and practice all of them. But they must never override prayer as the defining mark of God's dwelling. The honest truth is that I have seen God do more in people's lives during ten minutes of real prayer than in ten of my sermons.

THE CHURCH'S MAIN POINT

HAVE YOU EVER NOTICED that Jesus launched the Christian church, not while someone was preaching, but while people were praying? In the first two chapters of Acts, the disciples were doing nothing but waiting on God. As they were just sitting there ... worshiping, communing with God, letting God shape them and cleanse their spirits and do those heart operations that only the Holy Spirit can do ... the church was born. The Holy Spirit was poured out.

What does it say about our churches today that God birthed the church in a prayer meeting, and prayer meetings today are almost extinct?

> **What does it say about our churches today that God birthed the church in a prayer meeting, and prayer meetings today are almost extinct?** 🌾

Am I the only one who gets embarrassed when religious leaders in America talk about having prayer in public schools? We don't have even that much prayer in many churches! Out of humility, you would think we would keep quiet on that particular subject until we practice what we preach in our own congregations.

I am sure that the Roman emperors didn't have prayer to God in their schools. But then, the early Christians didn't seem to care what Caligula or Claudius or Nero did. How could any emperor stop God? How, in fact, could the demons of hell make headway when God's people prayed and called upon his name? Impossible!

In the New Testament we don't see Peter or John wringing their hands and saying, "Oh, what are we going to do? Caligula's bisexual ... he wants to appoint his horse to the Roman Senate ... what a terrible model of leadership! How are we going to respond to this outrage?"

Let's not play games with ourselves. Let's not divert attention away from the weak prayer life of our own churches. In Acts 4, when the apostles were unjustly arrested, imprisoned, and threatened, they didn't call for a protest; they didn't reach for some political leverage. Instead, they headed to a prayer meeting. Soon the place was vibrating with the power of the Holy Spirit (vv. 23–31).

The apostles had this instinct: When in trouble, pray. When intimidated, pray. When challenged, pray. When persecuted, pray.

The British Bible translator J. B. Phillips, after completing his work on this section of Scripture, could not help reflecting on what he had observed. In the 1955 preface to his first edition of Acts, he wrote:

> It is impossible to spend several months in close study of the remarkable short book ... without being profoundly stirred and, to be honest, disturbed. The reader is stirred because he is seeing Christianity, the real thing, in action for the first time in human history. The newborn Church, as vulnerable as any human child, having neither money, influence nor power in the ordinary sense, is setting forth joyfully and courageously to win the pagan world for God through Christ. ...
>
> Yet we cannot help feeling disturbed as well as moved, for this surely is the Church as it was meant to be. It is vigorous and flexible, for these are the days before it ever became fat and short of breath through prosperity, or muscle-bound by overorganization. These men did not make 'acts of faith,' they believed; they did not 'say their prayers,' they really prayed. They did not hold conferences on psychosomatic medicine, they simply healed the sick. But if they were uncomplicated

and naive by modern standards, we have ruefully to admit that they were open on the God-ward side in a way that is almost unknown today.[1]

Open on the God-ward side ... doesn't that stir your spirit? That one brief phrase sums up the secret of power in the early church, a secret that hasn't changed one bit in twenty centuries.

No One Too Tough

A FASCINATING FOOTNOTE APPEARS in Acts 9 when Saul of Tarsus, the violent persecutor of the church, was converted, and God needed a believer to minister to him. Naturally, no Christian wanted to get within five blocks of the man. Yet God coaxed Ananias along by saying, "Go ... ask for a man from Tarsus named Saul, for he is praying" (v. 11). This was the proof, it seems, that everything had changed. "It's okay, Ananias ... calm down ... you don't have to be afraid now, it's safe: He's praying."

At the Brooklyn Tabernacle a few years ago, we saw the Lord break through to an equally tough sinner in answer to believing prayer. The whole outreach that touched Ricardo Aparicio was born in prayer.

Most ministries in our church have *not* begun with a bright idea in a pastors' meeting. We usually don't say, "Let's start a street outreach," and then go recruit laypeople to staff it. We have learned over the years to let God birth something in people who are spiritually sensitive, who begin to pray and feel a calling. Then they come to us. "We want to start such-and-such," they say—and the ministry gets going and lasts. Discouragement, complications, and other attacks by the enemy don't wash it out.

A fellow named Terry and some others grew concerned for the subculture of male prostitutes that flourishes on the Lower West Side of Manhattan in a place called the "salt mines," where the city keeps salt for deicing streets in the winter. This sick subculture ranges up to a couple of hundred men when the weather is warm. Living in abandoned vehicles or subterranean cavities, many dress in drag and offer themselves to customers who come by—some of them wealthy professionals in stretch limousines.

Many of them, as boys, were raped by adult male relatives. At the "salt mines" they start as young as age sixteen but they don't last much beyond forty; after that, they are either in jail or dead from a sexually transmitted disease or a drug overdose. The neighborhood has many leather-and-chain bars. Some of the male prostitutes carry razor blades for protection.

Our outreach team began to bring food and blankets during the daylight hours on Saturday, when the men weren't distracted by their "work." Although the men made considerable money, they tended to squander it on drugs. That left them scavenging garbage cans and dumpsters for food.

To feel compassion for these guys, to understand their wretched life, was extremely difficult. We prayed fervently on Tuesday nights for love, compassion—and protection.

My teenage daughter Susan became part of the team, and more than once she told me, "Daddy, it was so frustrating last night! I was talking to this drag queen about Jesus, and he was really listening to me. And just when I thought I was getting somewhere with him—up rolls this limo, the rear door opens a crack, a hand beckons—and he's gone. 'Sorry, Susan—gotta take care of business now,' he says to me."

All was not in vain, however. One Sunday afternoon about half an hour before the afternoon service, Terry knocked on my office door. "Pastor Cymbala! We've got twenty-seven guys here today from the 'salt mines.' Isn't that great!"

"How did that happen?" I asked.

"We got a bunch of vans and brought them. For many of them, this is going to be their first time ever in church."

I learned later that one of them had a machete inside the sleeve of his raincoat just "in case" he felt he needed to use it.

The congregation took their presence in stride, even though the men didn't exactly look—or smell—All-American. At the end of the service some of them responded to give their hearts to the Lord. Others sat stunned as church members greeted them with smiles and handshakes.

Walking down the center aisle, I bumped into an attractive woman in a black dress, with blond, shoulder-length hair, nicely done nails, black stockings, and high heels. "Excuse me, ma'am," I said.

She turned . . . and this low voice with a heavy Spanish accent replied, "No, that's okay, man."

My heart skipped a beat. This was not a woman after all. But neither was it a sloppy transvestite. This was a knockout of a "woman"—bone-thin, no body hair thanks to hormonal treatment. As I took closer notice, the only visual giveaway was the Adam's apple.

I edged toward my wife. "Carol, you're not going to believe this," I whispered, "but that's a *guy* standing over there."

"Don't fool me," she said.

"I'm not kidding. That *is* a guy—trust me."

His name was Ricardo, known on the street as "Sarah." Terry reported later, "He was the main troublemaker of all. He introduced all the young kids to crack cocaine and prostitution." Ricardo had been plying his trade for at least ten years, and the dreariness was finally starting to get to him. Imagine the despair of hustling most of the night to make

$400 or $600, immediately blowing that money on cocaine, falling asleep under a bridge . . . and waking up the next morning to pick through garbage cans looking for some breakfast. The next night, as evening draws near, you start all over again.

Ricardo sat in the meetings, and it dawned on him that maybe he *could* be different. This Jesus could actually set him free from crack. Perhaps this Jesus could even change him into a true man, not this half-and-half person he assumed was his nature. He had been teased from childhood about being effeminate. His mother had pleaded with him to forsake homosexuality, and he had tried, to no avail. His willpower had failed him countless times.

But the idea that God was stronger, that God could in fact change him on the inside . . . that was a new thought. Ricardo kept listening, and after about a month, he gave his heart to the Lord. It was not a dramatic conversion; I am not even sure when it happened. But it was real on the inside.

I will never forget the Tuesday night we introduced him to the congregation. He stood before us, a bit shy, in male clothing. His blond hair had been cut, and dark roots were now growing out. His nail polish had been chipped off. Subconscious habits were being overhauled with instruction from Terry and the others: "No, Ricardo, don't cross your legs like that. Put your ankle all the way up on your other knee. . . ." It sounds humorous, but they had to start all the way back at "square one" with how a man sits and walks.

The congregation couldn't help but cheer and praise God for this miracle. Ricardo stood there perplexed at the noise. Why were all these people applauding him?

In the months that followed, Ricardo made great progress in his spiritual life. It took three months to get him straight enough even to be accepted in a drug rehabilitation program. Nevertheless, his commitment to follow Christ was solid. The old had gone, the new had definitely come.

Ricardo had come out of pitch blackness and into the light. Charles Spurgeon once said that when a jeweler shows his best diamonds, he sets them against a black velvet backdrop. The contrast of the jewels against the dark velvet brings out the luster. In the same way, God does his most stunning work where things seem hopeless. Wherever there is pain, suffering, and desperation, Jesus is. And that's where his people belong—among those who are vulnerable, who think nobody cares. What better place for the brilliance of Christ to shine?

Ricardo eventually moved to Texas. I was in Dallas one summer and ran into him. It was great to see the transformation. He had gained weight and was every inch a real man. I hugged him, and then he delivered a new shock:

"Pastor, I wish you could come back in two weeks. I'm getting married!"

"You're what?" My mind flashed back to the first time I had met him dressed in drag.

"Oh, yes," he said. "I've met a Christian woman named Betty, and we love each other deeply. We're getting married."

The fact that Ricardo had AIDS made the situation complicated. But with proper guidance and counseling, he and Betty established a new home together.

A Legacy to Leave

A few years later, at Christmastime, while I was in my office just as the Sunday afternoon service was beginning, I received a message that said Ricardo was dying. He wanted to talk to me.

I slumped in my chair, and as I picked up the phone, Betty's voice greeted me. "Hello, Pastor. . . . When I put my husband on the phone, you won't be able to hear much, because he's very weak. But he still remembers all that you and the church did for him."

In a moment I heard a fragile, wispy voice say, "Pastor—Cymbala—so—glad—to—hear—you."

I choked up.

Ricardo continued, forcing out the breathy syllables: "I—never—forgot—how—you—all—loved—me—and—took—me—in.—Thank—you—so—much."

My ministerial instincts then revived, and I prepared to make a comforting little speech, to tell him he would be going to heaven soon, that he would get there before me but I would see him on the other side for all eternity. . . .

The Holy Spirit stopped me. *No!* a voice seemed to say. *Fight for him! Cry out to me!*

I changed course. "Ricardo, I'm going to pray for you right now. Don't try to pray along with me; save your strength." I began to intercede with intensity, fighting against the death that loomed before him. "O God, touch Ricardo with your power! This is *not* his time to die. Restore him, for your glory, I pray." I remember even hitting my desk a couple of times with my fist.

When I finished, I marched directly into the meeting and stopped it. "I've just gotten off the phone with Ricardo, whom most of you know," I said. People looked up expectantly all across the building. "He's very sick with AIDS—but I want us to pray for his recovery."

That unleashed a torrent of prayer as people cried out to God for Ricardo.

I called Betty two days later. "Pastor Cymbala, it's incredible!" she reported. "He went to sleep after the two of you talked—and the next day, all his vital signs had done a U-turn. He began to eat, after taking almost nothing for days."

Within three weeks, Ricardo actually flew to New York and came walking unannounced into a Tuesday night prayer meeting. The crowd gasped with joy.

In my heart I felt that God spared him for a reason: To get his testimony onto video so that others could know his remarkable story. This eventually became a gripping eight-minute segment of the Brooklyn Tabernacle Choir's concert video called *Live at Madison Square Garden* (Warner Alliance). The power of his testimony, shot on the streets in the "salt mines," is riveting. It may partly explain why the video surprised us all by staying on *Billboard*'s national best-seller list for months.

The last time I saw Ricardo, a year later, his weight had dropped again. "I'm so tired," he said. "I've fought this disease long enough; I just want to go to Jesus. I can go now, because you have me on film, and everybody will know in years to come what Jesus did in my life." He passed away not long afterward.

The Secret of Grace

Ricardo's story is evidence of what God will do in response to fervent prayer. No one is beyond his grace. No situation, anywhere on earth, is too hard for God.

The apostle Paul, having benefited from that grace in his own life, preached and wrote about it ever after. He outlines in Romans 10:13–15 a chain of events that describes New Testament salvation:

> "Everyone who calls on the name of the Lord will be saved." How, then, can they call on the one they have not believed in? And how can they believe in the one of whom they have not heard? And how can they hear

without someone preaching to them? And how can they preach unless they are sent?

Churches often refer to this passage in connection with overseas missionary work. "We need to give a good offering today in order to send out preachers," they say—which is true. But that is just the beginning of Paul's sequence.

Sending leads to *preaching*.
Preaching leads to *hearing*.
Hearing leads to *believing*.
Believing leads to *calling on the name of the Lord*.

Notice that believing is not the climax. Even the great Protestant Reformers who taught us the principle of *sola fide* ("faith alone") also preached that intellectual assent alone does not bring salvation. There is one more step for demonstrating a real and living faith, and that is calling out to God with all of one's heart and soul.

The clearest instructions about church life come in the Pastoral Letters, where Paul tells young pastors such as Timothy how to proceed. The apostle couldn't be more direct than in 1 Timothy 2:1:

"*I urge then, first of all*, that requests, prayers, intercession and thanksgiving be made for everyone."

Why? Why first of all, before anything else? *Well, Timothy my son, we've got to remember that God's house is to be called a house of prayer.*

Later in the same chapter (v. 8), Paul says, "I want men everywhere to lift up holy hands in prayer, without anger or disputing." That is the sign of a Christian church.

The book of Revelation says that when the twenty-four elders eventually fall at the feet of Jesus, each one will have a golden bowl—and do you know what's in the bowls? What is this incense that is so fragrant to Christ? "The prayers of the saints" (Rev. 5:8).

Just imagine ... you and I kneel or stand or sit down to pray, really opening our hearts to God—and what we say is so precious to him that he keeps it like a treasure.

In the community where you live, what church do you know that takes a prominent night of the week, with all the leaders present, and says that because prayer is so great, so central to Jesus' definition of the church, they're going to concentrate on prayer?

Americans designate one day a year as a National Day of Prayer. Do we have any right to ask mayors and senators to show up for a special event, with the television cameras rolling, if we don't have regular prayer meetings in our churches? If praying is that important, why don't we do it every week?

How is it that Christians today will pay $20 to hear the latest Christian artist in concert, but Jesus can't draw a crowd?

For myself, I have decided that the Tuesday night prayer meeting is so crucial that I will never be out of town two Tuesdays in a row. If that means I can't accept certain speaking invitations across the land, so be it. Why would I prefer to be anywhere else?

The Bible has all these promises:

"Ask and it will be given to you; seek and you will find; knock and the door will be opened to you" (Matt. 7:7).

"You will seek me and find me when you seek me with all your heart" (Jer. 29:13).

"You do not have, because you do not ask God" (James 4:2).

Isn't it time to say, "Stop! We're going to pray, because God said that when we pray, he will intervene."

The sad truth is, in the city where I live—as in Chicago and Philadelphia and Houston and right across to L.A.—

more people are turning to crack than to Christ. More people are dipping into drugs than are getting baptized in water. What is going to reverse this tide? Preaching alone will not do it; classes aren't going to do it; more money for more programs won't do it. Only turning God's house into a house of fervent prayer will reverse the power of evil so evident in the world today.

> **More people are turning to crack than to Christ. More people are dipping into drugs than are getting baptized in water.** ❦

THE MISSING LINK

OVER THE LAST 30 years, more books have been written about marriage than in all the preceding 2,000 years of church history. But ask any pastor in America if there aren't proportionally more troubled marriages today than in any other era. We have all the how-to's, but homes are still falling apart.

The couple that prays together stays together. I don't mean to be simplistic; there will be difficult moments in any union. But God's Word is true when it says, "Call upon me, and I will help you. Just give me a chance."

The same holds true for parenting. We may own stacks of good books on child rearing and spending "quality time" with our children. Yet we have more problems per 100 young people in the church today than at any previous time. This is not because we lack knowledge or how-to; it is because we have not cried out for the power and grace of God.

What if, in the last 25 years, we had invested only half the time and energy in writing, publishing, reading, and discussing books on the Christian family ... and put the other half into praying for our marriages and our children? I am certain we would be in far better shape today.

Again, J. B. Phillips points out with great insight:

> The Holy Spirit has a way of short-circuiting human problems. Indeed, in exactly the same way as Jesus Christ in the flesh cut right through the matted layers of tradition and exposed the real issue; ... so we find here [in Acts] the Spirit of Jesus dealing not so much with problems as with people. Many problems comparable to modern complexities never arise here because the men and women concerned were of one heart and mind in the Spirit. ... Since God's Holy Spirit cannot conceivably have changed one iota through the centuries, ... He is perfectly prepared to short-circuit, by an inflow of love, wisdom and understanding, many human problems today.[2]

That is why the writer to the Hebrews nails down the most central activity of all for Christians: "Let us then approach the throne of grace with confidence, so that we may receive mercy and find grace to help us in our time of need" (Heb. 4:16). It doesn't say, "Let us come to the sermon." We in America have made the sermon the centerpiece of the church, something God never intended. Preachers who are really doing their job get people to come to the throne of grace. That's the true source of grace and mercy.

To every preacher and every singer, God will someday ask, "Did you bring people to where the action could be found ... at the throne of grace? If you just entertained them, if you just tickled their ears and gave them a warm, fuzzy moment, woe unto you. At the throne of grace, I could have changed their lives. Jim Cymbala, did you just dazzle people with your cleverness, or did you make them hungry to come to me?"

If a meeting doesn't end with people touching God, what kind of a meeting is it? We haven't really encountered God. We haven't met with the only One powerful and loving enough to change our lives.

I am well aware that we don't get everything we ask for; we have to ask according to God's will. But let us not use theological dodges to avoid the fact that we often go without things God wants us to have right now, today, because we fail to ask. Too seldom do we get honest enough to admit, "Lord, I can't handle this alone. I've just hit the wall for the thirty-second time and *I need you.*"

The words of the old hymn ring true:

> Oh, what peace we often forfeit,
> Oh, what needless pain we bear,
> All because we do not carry
> Everything to God in prayer.

God has chosen prayer as his channel of blessing. He has spread a table for us with every kind of wisdom, grace, and strength because he knows exactly what we need. But the only way we can get it is to pull up to the table and taste and see that the Lord is good.

Pulling up to that table is called the prayer of faith.

In other words, God doesn't tell us to pray because he wants to impose some sort of regimen on us. This is not a system of legalism. E. M. Bounds wrote,

> Prayer ought to enter into the spiritual habits, but it ceases to be prayer when it is carried on by habit only.... Desire gives fervor to prayer. The soul cannot be listless when some great desire fixes and inflames it.... Strong desires make strong prayers....

The neglect of prayer is the fearful token of dead spiritual desires. The soul has turned away from God when desire after him no longer presses it into the closet. There can be no true praying without desire.[3]

God says to us, "Pray, because I have all kinds of things for you; and when you ask, you will receive. I have all this grace, and you live with scarcity. Come unto me, all you who labor. Why are you so rushed? Where are you running *now?* Everything you need, I have."

If the times are indeed as bad as we say they are . . . if the darkness in our world is growing heavier by the moment . . . if we are facing spiritual battles right in our own homes and churches . . . then we are foolish not to turn to the One who supplies unlimited grace and power. He is our only source. We are crazy to ignore him.

PART 2

Diversions from God's Best

SIX

❧

A Time for Shaking

IMAGINE YOURSELF AT MADISON Square Garden for a college basketball game on a January night back in the mid-1960s. The Rhode Island Rams, my team, have come down to New York to play, say, Fordham or St. John's. You take your seat down close to the floor a few minutes before the opening tip-off.

After eight or nine minutes, the Rams are losing 23 to 7. We're committing foolish turnovers, we're not rebounding aggressively, we're giving up fast breaks.

The coach calls a time-out. We huddle, and one player says, "Isn't this fun? We get to play in Madison Square Garden!"

Another says, "I really like the gold trim here on the uniforms. Looks sharp against the white, doesn't it?"

A third is waving to his Aunt Nellie up in the mezzanine seats, while a fourth runs over to plant a quick kiss on his girlfriend's cheek.

If this had actually happened, what do you think Coach Calverley would have said to us? "Hey! Would you guys please look at the scoreboard? We're getting killed! When you go back out there, I want you to go into a tight man-to-man press, in the backcourt as well as up front. No more sleepwalking! This game is going to get away from us if you guys don't wake up!"

Actually, he wouldn't have said it that politely.

As a team we couldn't fantasize or make believe we were doing well. The scoreboard was the inescapable signal that we had to change our game plan.

The Christian world today is not playing nearly as well as we think. We are often confusing faith with fantasy. Although Hebrews 11:6 declares that "without faith it is impossible to please God," we seem to have grown adept at putting a positive spin on every conceivable situation. "These are wonderful days!" some preachers exult. "What a great time of blessing for God's people."

Meanwhile, Christian researcher George Barna reports that 64 percent of "born-again" Americans and 40 percent of "evangelical" Americans say there is no such thing as absolute truth. In other words, the Ten Commandments may or may not be valid, Jesus Christ isn't necessarily the only way to God, and so forth. With this kind of sloppy thinking, what does "born again" even mean anymore? In the rush for "success" and "growth," we have revised and distorted the very essence of the gospel.

More than three-fourths of current church growth, Barna adds, is merely "transfer growth"—people moving from one church to another. Despite all the Christian broadcasting and high-profile campaigns, the Christian population is not growing in numbers nationally. In fact, church attendance in a given week during 1996 was down to 37 percent of the population, a ten-year low ... even though 82 percent of Americans claim to be Christians.

Yet everyone agrees that the culture is becoming more promiscuous, more violent, and more hateful by the day. So what has happened to the church as light and salt in the earth? What do spin doctors in the body of Christ make of these things?

WELCOME TO LAODICEA

I SAY WE ARE in trouble. It is high time to wake up and look at the scoreboard.

With some exceptions, we are like the church at Laodicea. In fact, we have so institutionalized Laodiceanism that we think lukewarm is normal. Any church winning more than a few people to Christ is considered "outstanding."

....

We are like the church at Laodicea. In fact, we have so institutionalized Laodiceanism that we think lukewarm is normal. ❧

....

The stern words of Jesus apply to us as much as to Christians at the end of the first century: "You are neither cold nor hot. I wish you were either one or the other! So, because you are lukewarm—neither hot nor cold—I am about to spit you out of my mouth. You say, 'I am rich; I have acquired wealth and do not need a thing'" (Rev. 3:15–17). In other words, they were voicing a wonderful "positive confession." They were proclaiming victory and blessing. The only trouble is, Jesus was unimpressed. He responded:

"But you do not realize that you are wretched, pitiful, poor, blind and naked. . . . Those whom I love I rebuke and discipline. So be earnest, and repent" (Rev. 3:17, 19).

Strong language, to be sure. Jesus always deals strongly, however, with those he loves. "What son is not disciplined by his father?" asks the writer of Hebrews (12:7).

Notice that the Laodiceans were saints of God, with all the promises to claim. They were part of Christ's body— singing hymns, worshiping on Sunday, enjoying physical benefits, and no doubt viewing themselves as more righteous than their pagan neighbors. Yet they were on the verge of being vomited out. What a wake-up call!

THE FIRST FACE-OFF

WHENEVER THE BODY OF Christ gets into trouble—whether through its own negligence, as in Laodicea, or through some special attack of Satan—strong action is required. We cannot merely sit by and hope the problem will resolve itself.

We can benefit from studying what the early church did when it got into trouble.

The disciples had enjoyed three years of teaching from Jesus. They had been discipled by the Master Discipler. But mere teaching is never enough, even if it comes directly from Jesus. Because they did not have the empowerment of the Holy Spirit, the disciples acted like cowards on the night of Jesus' arrest.

Once they were empowered on the Day of Pentecost, however, they became the church victorious, the church militant. With the gracious manifestation of God's Spirit in the Upper Room, the disciples encountered their first audience. Peter, the biggest failure of them all, became the preacher that day. It was no homiletical masterpiece, to be sure. But people were deeply convicted—"cut to the heart," according to Acts 2:37—by his anointed words. Three thousand were gathered into the church that day.

Which church? Baptist? Presbyterian? Pentecostal? There were no such labels at that time—and in God's view of things, there still aren't. He ignores our categories. All he sees when he looks down is the body of Christ, made up of all born-again, blood-washed believers. The only subdivisions he sees are geographical—local churches. Other distinctions are immaterial.

I find it curious that we Christians will vigorously defend what Ephesians 4 says about "one Lord" (no polytheism) and "one faith" (salvation through Christ alone) … but then grow strangely silent regarding "one body" (vv. 4–6). At that point we start making excuses, historical and otherwise, for the shameful divisions within the church.

The early Christians began dynamically in power. They were unified, prayerful, filled with the Holy Spirit, going out to do God's work in God's way, and seeing results that glorified him. The hour seemed golden. This was truly the church overcoming the gates of hell, as Jesus described.

One day a public miracle occurred—the healing of the lame man, as related in Acts 3—which drew another crowd, and another sermon from Peter. Thousands more believed in Christ.

Then came the first attack. The priests, Sadducees, and captain of the temple guard broke in on them "greatly disturbed because the apostles were teaching the people and proclaiming in Jesus the resurrection of the dead. They seized Peter and John, and because it was evening, they put them in jail until the next day" (Acts 4:2–3).

Jesus had warned that difficult days would come. Now they were here. Although the attacks later on would come in the form of false teaching or internal division, this blow was physical and frontal.

A surprise awaited the Jewish leaders, however. "When they saw the courage of Peter and John and realized that they were unschooled, ordinary men, they were astonished and they took note that these men had been with Jesus" (4:13). These fishermen seemed guileless, sincere—quite the opposite of what we so often see today, which results in a great deal more polish in the pulpit, and a great deal less power.

The apostles were released on the condition that they not speak further in the name of Jesus. How did they respond? What did they do?

They didn't petition the government. They didn't wring their hands about how unfair this was. They didn't complain about losing their freedom of speech, although they could have made a solid case that the Roman Empire, with its panoply of other gods, shouldn't mind their speaking about the god named Jesus. The apostles could have done any number of things to sway public opinion. But to their minds this was not a political problem—it was spiritual. They quickly joined a meeting of the believers and began to pray. They immediately turned to their primitive power source.

This is how they prayed:

> "Sovereign Lord, . . . you made the heaven and the earth and the sea, and everything in them. . . . Now, Lord, consider their threats and enable your servants to speak your word with great boldness. Stretch out your hand to heal and perform miraculous signs and wonders through the name of your holy servant Jesus" (Acts 4:24, 29–30).

This is precisely what the prophets, down through the centuries, had told them to do: When under attack, when facing a new challenge, in all seasons, in all times, call on the name of the Lord, and he will help you.

It sounds as if things got rather energetic, perhaps even a little noisy: "They raised their voices together in prayer to God" (v. 24). When we read such passages, it is important not to force them into the context of our particular tradition. Would you or I have felt comfortable in the room that day? It doesn't matter. This is the church on the move, giving us a Spirit-inspired model for today.

This is the only prayer longer than a sentence or two that is quoted in the entire book of Acts. No doubt it is only a summary of what the group prayed in a variety of words that day. Yet it offers a unique glimpse at the prayer life of the early church. As seriously as we revere and study the long prayer of Jesus in the garden (John 17), we should also examine what is said here.

Isn't it strange that the group prayed for boldness? We might have expected them to pray, "Lord, help us find a safe shelter now. We need to 'lie low' for a few weeks until the heat goes away. We'll stay out of sight, and if you could just make the Sanhedrin sort of forget about us . . ."

Not at all. If anything, they prayed against backing down. They asked God to help them press on. Retreat was the furthest thing from their minds.

And how did God react?

"After they prayed, the place where they were meeting was shaken. And they were all filled with the Holy Spirit and spoke the word of God boldly" (v. 31).

The first time vocalist Steve Green came to sing at the Brooklyn Tabernacle, we gathered in my office with the associate pastors to pray just before the meeting began. We prayed in unison that God would come among us that day.

When we opened our eyes, Steve had an odd look on his face. "What was that vibration I just felt?" he asked. "Is there a train that runs near here, or was that really . . . ?"

I explained that, as far as I knew, the rumble wasn't caused by the power of the Holy Spirit—would to God it was! Rather, it was the passing of the "D" train in the subway that runs directly beneath our building.

For the early church that day in Jerusalem, however, the vibration was nothing short of Spirit-induced. In that prayer meeting God's power came in a fresh, new, deeper way.

These people had already been filled with the Holy Spirit on the Day of Pentecost (Acts 2), but here they sensed a new need. God met them with a new infusion of power.

I am well aware that Christians disagree today on whether the infilling (baptism, empowerment) of the Spirit is a part of the salvation "package" or a separate, subsequent experience. Long and intense discussions go on about that. Whatever you or I believe, let us admit that this passage shows bona fide Christians experiencing a fresh infilling. The apostles didn't claim they already had everything they needed. Now that they were under attack, they received fresh power, fresh courage, fresh fire from the Holy Spirit.

Our store of spiritual power apparently dissipates with time. Daily living, distractions, and spiritual warfare take their toll. We need, in the words Paul used in Ephesians 5:18, to "be always being filled with the Spirit" (literal translation).

Can anyone say with a straight face that the Laodiceans, at the time Jesus addressed them in the letter, had a Spirit-filled church? 🌿

Positional theology is good as far as it goes, such as "I am God's child regardless of how I feel at the moment." But if we stretch this idea to make statements such as "I am categorically Spirit-filled for the rest of my life," we deceive ourselves.

Can anyone say with a straight face that the Laodiceans, at the time Jesus addressed them in the letter, had a Spirit-filled church? They were Christians, to be sure. But they were in desperate need of an Acts 4-type prayer meeting.

Andrew Bonar wrote in his diary on December 13, 1880, "I long more and more to be filled with the Spirit, and to see my congregation moved and melted under the Word, as in great revival times, 'the place shaken where they are assembled together,' because the Lord has come in power."[1]

Whether we call ourselves classical evangelicals, traditionalists, fundamentalists, Pentecostals, or charismatics, we all have to face our lack of real power and call out for a fresh infilling of the Spirit. We need the fresh wind of God to awaken us from our lethargy. We must not hide any longer behind some theological argument. The days are too dark and dangerous.

STRAIGHT AHEAD

THE WORK OF GOD can only be carried on by the power of God. The church is a spiritual organism fighting spiritual battles. Only spiritual power can make it function as God ordained.

The key is not money, organization, cleverness, or education. Are you and I seeing the results Peter saw? Are we bringing thousands of men and women to Christ the way he did? If not, we need to get back to his power source. No matter the society or culture, the city or town, God has never lacked the power to work through available people to glorify his name.

> **Are you and I seeing the results Peter saw? If not, we need to get back to his power source.** ❧

When we sincerely turn to God, we will find that his church always moves *forward*, not *backward*. We can never back up and accommodate ourselves to what the world wants or expects. Our stance must remain militant, aggressive, bold.

That is what characterized General William Booth and the early Salvation Army as they invaded the slums of

London. It characterized the early mission movements, such
as the Moravians. It characterized Hudson Taylor in China
as well as revivalists on the American frontier. These Christians were not bulls in a china shop, but they did speak the
truth in love—fearlessly.

In the familiar story of David and Goliath, there is a
wonderful moment when the giant gets irked at the sight of
his young opponent. "Am I a dog, that you come at me with
sticks?" he roars (1 Sam. 17:43). Goliath is genuinely
insulted. "Come here, . . . and I'll give your flesh to the birds
of the air and the beasts of the field!" (v. 44).

Does David flinch? Does he opt for a strategic retreat
behind some tree or boulder, thinking maybe to buy a little
time?

Absolutely not.

"As the Philistine moved closer to attack him, *David ran
quickly toward the battle line to meet him*" (v. 48).

That is the picture of what God wants for us today: *running toward the fray!*

David's weaponry was ridiculous: a sling and five stones.
It didn't matter. God still uses foolish tools in the hands of
weak people to build his kingdom. Backed by prayer and his
power, we can accomplish the unthinkable.

The Brooklyn Tabernacle Choir sings a song that cap-
tures God's penchant for using the weak to shame the strong.
It goes, "If you can use anything, Lord, you can use me."
Kenneth Ware, one of the associate pastors, has shown this
kind of faith more than once. Years ago, this godly, gray-
haired African American started all-night prayer meetings on
Friday nights in the church. Then he organized a Prayer
Band—a group of people committed to calling on the Lord
at the church on a continuing schedule.

Soon the members of the Prayer Band were praying five nights a week, from 11 P.M. to 6 A.M. Today they are in the church seven days a week, twenty-four hours a day, praying in three-hour shifts or longer. Every request we receive is written on a little card and lifted to the Lord for the next thirty days.

I remember the day Pastor Ware said to me in a fatherly tone (he's at least fifteen years older than I am), "Pastor, you know, we're still not seeing God do all he wants to do. You're preaching with all your heart, but we need to see more conviction of sin, more of God's manifest presence in our services."

I agreed and listened, wondering what he would say next.

"I'm serious," Pastor Ware continued. "We probably have half a dozen HIV-positive people in every meeting. We've got crack addicts. We've got marriages on the rocks, brokenhearted moms, young people hardened by the city. They really need the Lord.

"I want to have the Prayer Band start praying somewhere about this *during* the actual meetings, while you're preaching. We need to see God break through among us."

I gave Pastor Ware my blessing, and to this day he has twenty or so people closed in a room to pray during each of the four meetings—a total of eighty intercessors each Sunday. They start by praying with the pastors fifteen minutes before the meeting and keep going even after everything ends. Sometimes, in leaving the building at ten or ten-thirty at night, I have heard them still praying.

The first or second Sunday of this effort, I was in my office getting ready for the afternoon service when I heard, through the heating ducts, a noise from the room upstairs ... the sound of people praying. The worship had just begun, and the Prayer Band was already calling on God.

Someone must have been kneeling at a chair directly beside a vent, because I distinctly heard a woman's voice say: "God, protect him. Help him, Lord. Use him to proclaim your Word today. Convict of sin; change people, Lord!"

My heart started to beat faster. My spirit began to rise toward the throne of grace along with theirs. In a few minutes I left my office wondering what God might have in store for us that afternoon.

The place was packed as usual. The choir sang, and I preached with all my heart about the love of God. "How desperately God wants you to come to him," I pleaded near the end. "What damns a soul in the end and sends you off into a terrible eternity is rejecting the love of God. He chases you, tries to hem you in, tries to get your attention. This love, this passion for you, is so real. He desires the death of no one. He wants everyone to come to a knowledge of the truth. Don't reject God's love! Don't go there! That's what will seal your doom."

As I reached the end of my message, I moved to the side of the pulpit and closed my eyes. I kept urging people to come to the front and respond to God's love. I kept talking, lost in my passion for those who didn't know Christ. . . .

> **What I didn't see, because I had my eyes shut, was the steel-gray 38-caliber revolver in the man's right hand, leveled right at me.** ❧

A Jewish man about 25 years old, wearing beige chinos and a light green sport shirt, stood up in the back row of the lower auditorium and began edging toward the center aisle. What I didn't see, because I still had my eyes shut, was the steel-gray 38-caliber revolver in his right hand, leveled at me!

Down the aisle he came, the gun pointed right at my chest. Many in the congregation didn't notice because their eyes, like mine, were closed. The ones who saw him froze in terror. Even the ushers seemed paralyzed. By the time they sprang into action, it was too late—the man was coming up the steps onto the platform. All the while, I continued to implore the crowd to yield to God's love, having no idea that my life seemed in imminent danger.

Carol was playing the piano behind me, and her eyes were wide open. In panic she screamed my name twice: "Jim! Jim!" I didn't hear her. I was busy urging people to come to Jesus— and seemingly, I was on my way to Jesus myself right then.

Carol was sure she was about to witness the cold-blooded murder of her husband—and then what? Would the fellow turn on her next?

He did neither. Instead, he walked up right beside me and tossed the weapon onto the pulpit. Suddenly I heard a crash, my eyes flew open—*and there's a gun on my pulpit!*

The man started to run back across the platform, down the steps, and up the aisle again. My only instinct was to chase after him and call, "No, no—don't go! It's okay. Wait!—"

He fell into a heap and began to weep as he cried out in a pitiful moan, "Jesus, help me! I can't take it anymore!"

By then the ushers were on top of him, not to harm him but to control the situation and also to begin to pray for him. Meanwhile, the church was in pandemonium. Some people were crying, others were praying aloud, still others sat in stunned silence.

In a moment I walked back up to the pulpit. I took a deep breath, then held up the gun—not realizing it was loaded—and said just one sentence, more to myself than to the audience:

"Look what the love of God can make somebody give up."

Suddenly, from all over the building, people began to race to the altar. God had attached the final point to my message. A great harvest of needy souls came to the loving Christ that day.

As I watched the response, my mind went back to the woman's prayer a couple of hours earlier: "Lord, protect him today. Convict of sin; change lives...."

The man, somewhat unbalanced in his mind, said he had never intended to hurt me. He was planning to hurt somebody who had meddled with his girlfriend ... and he had just stopped by our meeting on the way. He became so convicted of the hate in his heart that he said to himself, *I have to get rid of this gun. I must give it to the preacher.*

As a result of the Prayer Band's praying straight into the face of danger, a life was spared. A great victory for God's kingdom was won; we baptized more than a dozen people as a result of that one meeting. The power of God was evident, and his work went forward.

THE FALLOUT

WHILE MOST PEOPLE WERE relieved and rejoicing at the outcome, my wife was in shock. She said very little the rest of that Sunday. The next morning, as we were having coffee, she let go of her feelings.

"Is that the way it's going to end for us someday, Jim? Is that how we're going to go out—somebody's just going to walk up and kill you in a meeting?

"We have no protection up there! Where were the ushers? Where were the security people? We could easily have been killed yesterday."

I tried to console her and reason with her. "No, Carol—the Lord protected us this time, and he will in the future.

The ushers had no chance to stop him anyway." But my words fell flat.

All week long, Carol suffered. The fear was oppressive. She had trouble sleeping. I would find her staring into space, replaying the awful moments of Sunday afternoon in her mind, again and again.

That Friday night Carol made herself lead the choir practice as usual. Following their custom, the members began with a half hour or more of prayer and worship before ever singing a note.

The Holy Spirit spoke to one of the choir members. She came out of her section to stand beside Carol, took the microphone, and said, "You know what? I believe God just showed me that we should lift up Carol in prayer. Would you all join me?"

They gathered around, laid hands on my wife, and began to pray with intensity. In that moment, something happened that five days of her brooding and my consoling had not achieved. Carol was free of fear once again.

When we get serious about drawing upon God's power, remarkable things will happen. Even if we grow listless and lukewarm, still Christ says, "Here I am! I stand at the door and knock. If anyone hears my voice and opens the door, I will come and eat with him, and he with me. . . . He who has an ear, let him hear what the Spirit says to the churches" (Rev. 3:20, 22).

Those gentle words, quoted often by evangelists to those who do not know Christ, were addressed to the Laodicean Christians whom Jesus had just scolded. Although he was grieved by their lethargy, he nevertheless offered his renewing love and power to any who would open the door. Will we?

SEVEN

The Lure of Novelty

IN THE WORLD OF advertising, every copywriter knows the power of two magic words: "Free!" and "New!" We see them in the supermarket, in the newspaper, on billboards. And consumers respond.

In the church today, we are falling prey to the appeal of "New!" The old truths of the gospel don't seem spectacular enough. We're restless for the latest, greatest, newest teaching or technique. We pastors in particular seem to search for a short-cut or some dynamic new strategy that will fire up our churches.

The prayer of the early believers recorded in Acts 4 highlights three fundamentals from which we are in danger of sliding away: "Enable your servants to speak your word ... with great boldness ... Stretch out your hand to heal and perform miraculous signs and wonders" (vv. 29–30).

I want to probe the first of these: "Enable your servants to speak your word...."

There was no confusion in the minds of the first Christians about *what* to proclaim. There was no searching for new and novel messages. The plain gospel that they heard from Jesus their Lord was considered entirely adequate.

I received a surprise at a large conference not long ago when, between sessions, I sat casually talking with a number of the other speakers. The conversation led to various emphases in the church today. Soon I found myself wondering what religion they were discussing.

One man said how important it is for all believers to find out if any of their ancestors had ever attended a séance, even centuries ago. Unless that "generational curse" was removed we could not expect to prosper as Christians. Even our children and grandchildren would continue to be at risk, he claimed. Imagine being saved, a new creation in Christ, "rescued ... from the dominion of darkness and brought ... into the kingdom of the Son" (Col. 1:13)—yet somehow still under a curse of Satan!

I thought of the numerous Haitians at the Brooklyn Tabernacle who have come to New York from a land where the main religion is voodoo. If this man's teaching is true, these Haitians have a lot of homework to do, finding out which of their great-grandmothers had dabbled in the occult, then taking steps to break this long-standing bondage.

Why, I wondered, didn't Paul speak about this more clearly in his letters? The first century saw plenty of witchcraft. Did the believers in Corinth and Galatia and Rome have to explore their family trees for traces of an evil spell?

In one of the teaching sessions another speaker said, "There are three levels of spiritual warfare: battles with ordinary demons every day, confrontations with the occult such as astrology or New Age, and then strategic-level territorial warfare against the spirits in charge of a whole region. And even the apostle Paul never understood this third level or exercised this kind of ministry." Imagine this clever teacher transcending the great apostle of the New Testament!

I couldn't help wondering, what is the name of the demon over Brooklyn? The effects of evil are obvious enough on every street corner. Could I really knock the evil out with one rebuke of the territorial power over the whole borough?

Where does the New Testament portray this strategy? Did Peter bind the spirit over Joppa or Caesarea? Paul spent three years in Ephesus, a center of idol worship, yet there is no mention of "binding the spirit of the goddess Diana," whose temple in that city was one of the Seven Wonders of the Ancient World. In Acts 4, the apostles did not ask for the name of the evil spirit over Jerusalem.

Carol and I returned to the hotel sad and depressed. How tragic that young ministers were feverishly writing down all these exotic teachings in the vain hope of igniting their struggling churches back home with techniques and teachings nowhere found in Scripture.

I could find no evidence that these speakers were implementing their concepts at the local church level. Their books and tapes were selling well, but I wondered why they hadn't come to Brooklyn or other dark places and put their teachings into practice.

> **What we have today is the work of "technicians"**
> **or "revisionists" or "idea men" who feel the need**
> **to innovate, to devise novelties in order to help**
> **God's kingdom along.** ❧

I fear that what we have here is the work of "technicians" or "revisionists" or "idea men" who feel the need to innovate, to devise novelties in order to help God's kingdom along. Unfortunately, America's moral climate and the church's spiritual temperature prove these novelties to be impotent.

THE DEVIL IS STILL IN BUSINESS

IF PRESENT-DAY TEACHERS AND authors have in fact discovered something new under the theological sun, I have a question to ask:

Why is there still so much evil rampant in the earth if the devil has indeed been "bound" so many times by Christians today? One well-known preacher went to San Francisco a few years ago, rented a stadium, and did "spiritual warfare" for the night, claiming to bind and rebuke every evil spirit and principality in the city. The next day he and his entourage flew home again. Is San Francisco a more godly place today as a result?

The Bible speaks more about *resisting* the devil than it does about *binding* him. First Peter 5:8–9 says, "Your enemy the devil prowls around like a roaring lion looking for someone to devour. Resist him, standing firm in the faith, because you know that your brothers throughout the world are undergoing the same kind of sufferings." Why didn't the apostle Peter just *bind* that roaring lion and be done with the problem?

The Bible speaks more about *resisting* the devil than it does about *binding* him. ❦

Jesus did talk in Matthew 12:29 about binding the strong man in order to rob his house. He used this metaphor immediately after casting a demon out of a blind and mute man. The meaning is that one person had been set free; nothing more cosmic in scope is mentioned. The text conveys that a strong man, Satan, had been evicted by a stronger one, Christ.

A similar truth can be applied to the practice of seeking to know a demon's name. Out of Jesus' dozens of encounters with Satan during his ministry, he asked for a name only *once* (Mark 5:9). Again, this had to do with one man's problem, not that of a whole province or territory. Moreover, the apostles never told young ministers such as Timothy or Titus to inquire about demons' names.

Please don't misunderstand: I fully believe that the devil invades people's lives today and has to be confronted. I have had to confront him a number of times in my ministry. One Tuesday night two members of the church brought a teenager to the prayer meeting who, they said, was on drugs and needed to be delivered. That's all they told me. I didn't think too much about it; this kind of thing happens often. (Our wonderful members don't know better than to bring the unconverted to a prayer meeting!)

About a half hour into the meeting, after we had been worshiping for a while, I said, "There's a girl here who's been brought by some members, and they'd like her to be prayed for; she's hooked on drugs."

These members began walking toward the front with a short Hispanic girl. She seemed in a daze—the effect of drugs, I assumed. Her name was Diana.

I was standing, as I usually do on Tuesday nights, on the ground level with the people, at the head of the center aisle. All of a sudden, I began to tense up; alarm bells seemed to be going off in my spirit signifying that something was wrong— something was about to happen.

I noticed off to my right a visiting evangelist I knew. I said to her, "Amy, it's good to see you here tonight. Would you come help me pray for this young lady?" As she moved out of her seat, the Holy Spirit came upon her, and she sensed the same anticipation. We were suddenly both on "red alert" for some unknown reason.

One of the associate pastors joined us, and we laid hands on Diana and began to pray. "O Jesus, help us," I said quietly.

Like a shot, the mention of Jesus' name brought an explosion of rage and screaming. The five-foot-one-inch girl lunged for my throat, throwing back the two friends who had guided her up the aisle. Before I knew what was happening,

I had been body-slammed against the front edge of the platform. Diana ripped the collar right off my white shirt as if it
were a piece of tissue. A hideous voice from deep inside her
began to scream, "You'll never have her! She's ours! Get away
from her!" The language then turned obscene.

> **The five-foot-one-inch girl lunged for my
> throat. Before I knew what was happening, I
> had been body-slammed backward against the
> platform.** ❦

Some in the congregation stood and began to pray aloud.
Others gasped. Some covered their eyes. Meanwhile, several
deacons jumped up and tried to pull her off of me. Despite
her size, she fought all of us with tremendous strength.

We finally managed to subdue her. Amy, the evangelist,
began to pray fervently. I leaned over the girl to address the
spirits: "Shut up! In the name of Jesus, come out of her!" I
demanded.

Diana's eyes rolled back in her head, and twice she spit
directly into my face, no more than a foot away. The church
kept earnestly calling out to God for his help. Clearly, we
were not battling some imaginary "spirit of anger" or whatever. This was a classic case of demon possession.

Within a few minutes, the girl was set totally free. She
stopped cursing; her body relaxed. We relaxed our grip on
her, and she gently stood up to raise her hands and begin
praising the Lord. Soon she was singing, with the rest of us,
"Oh, the blood of Jesus! It washes white as snow," as tears
streamed down her cheeks, ruining her makeup.

Diana has been serving the Lord for ten years now in the
Brooklyn Tabernacle. Recently she married a young man, and

both of them gave strong testimonies of their faith in front of mostly unbelieving relatives. She is a wonderful Christian today who loves the Lord and wants to serve him alone.

Diana has allowed me to tell her story to make the point that I believe in confronting satanic activity. Was her experience unique or weird? Not by New Testament standards. This was just "mere Christianity," the kind of thing Jesus and the apostles did on a regular basis.

But we should not expect to discover new shortcuts in the spiritual realm. Have we forgotten that when Jesus sent out his twelve disciples, he specifically "gave them authority to drive out evil spirits" … yet he also told them that some towns would not welcome them. "They will hand you over to the local councils and flog you in their synagogues" (Matt. 10:1, 17). If the twelve, with one sweep of the hand, could have bound the opposing spirit in that city, wouldn't Jesus have explained this? It would have spared Christians a lot of conflict.

Instead, Jesus addressed the various churches in the book of Revelation with somber warnings about the opposition they were facing:

To Smyrna: "I tell you, the devil will put some of you in prison to test you, and you will suffer persecution for ten days. Be faithful, even to the point of death" (Rev. 2:10). Christ warns that they are in a hostile environment and there are no quick fixes.

To Pergamum: "I know where you live—where Satan has his throne." The next sentence does not read: *Kick him out! Bind him!* No. Jesus calmly continues, "Yet you remain true to my name. You did not renounce your faith in me, even in the days of Antipas, my faithful witness, who was put to death in your city—where Satan lives" (Rev. 2:13).

The all-knowing King of kings and Lord of lords, who holds the keys of death and hell, tells the Christians to battle through. In both these letters Jesus describes what Satan was permitted to do, within the limits of some sovereign plan of God that we don't fully comprehend. Nevertheless, the believers are to press ahead with old-fashioned spiritual endurance.

The trouble with today's man-made novelties is that they simply don't produce the impressive results that are often advertised. They do not, so far as I know, result in masses of people being converted, being baptized in water, or forming strong, prayerful churches. Where is the city anywhere in the world that has been "taken for God," as the rhetoric often claims? Wouldn't it be wiser, as Paul said, to "not boast beyond proper limits" (2 Cor. 10:13) but rather let the Spirit produce results that speak for themselves?

Just as some say the powers of evil are attached to certain locales, others are proclaiming certain centers of God's "new anointing." Certain cities are said to be chosen for a unique outpouring of the Holy Spirit. Where do we find this in Scripture?

It is totally unbiblical to insinuate that people must travel to a particular church anywhere to receive what God has for them. There is no special anointing from the Brooklyn Tabernacle or any other church that can be passed on by the laying on of hands. Nowhere in the book of Acts do people travel to Jerusalem or any other city to be "where the action is."

All we find in the New Testament is the admonition to "come near to God and he will come near to you" (James 4:8). The responsibility lies with us. If enough people in New York City or San Francisco call out to God with all their hearts, those cities can become world-famous for revival. God is no respecter of geography.

We are too easily distracted from the call to simply wait on the Lord. We get pulled away from the simplicity of the gospel. In Acts 4, the apostles only wanted to preach the Word. It sounds too minimal to modern ears, doesn't it—

isn't there something more, something greater, something newer?

In the face of a world ignoring Christ's offer of salvation, we can either humble ourselves before God and return to his basics ... or we can go on dancing with ourselves. The potential to see local churches explode with the life of God rests in the balance.

NO HOCUS-POCUS

THERE IS NO BETTER example of God's moving mightily in a city than the account told in Acts 11:20–21: "... men from Cyprus and Cyrene, went to Antioch and began to speak to Greeks ... telling them the good news about the Lord Jesus. The Lord's hand was with them, and a great number of people believed and turned to the Lord."

Such a harvest occurred that Barnabas was dispatched from Jerusalem to check things out. "When he arrived and saw the evidence of the grace of God, he was glad.... And a great number of people were brought to the Lord" (vv. 23–24).

Who were these men who launched such a mighty church that it eventually surpassed the mother church in Jerusalem? We don't know their names. We don't know their methodology. We don't know whether they were premillennial or postmillennial or amillennial. But we do know a couple of things: They spread "the good news about the Lord Jesus," and "the Lord's hand was with them" (vv. 20–21).

This turned out to be the first truly multicultural church, with multicultural leaders, according to Acts 13:1—Simon the Black, some Jewish leaders, some Greeks, Manaen the boyhood friend of Herod (which would have made him suspect to everyone!), and others. Yet they worked together in a powerful model of cross-cultural unity.

The Jewish-Gentile hatred of the first century was even greater than our racial strife today. God met this problem head-on, for he was building his church his way.

Racial feelings in New York City are worse now than they were ten years ago. A harsh spirit prevails in many churches. We desperately need the love of God to override these tensions, as it did in Antioch long ago.

No novel teaching is going to turn the trick. There are no trendy shortcuts, no hocus-pocus mantras that can defeat Satan.

One man told me, "You know, you ought to think about getting a topographical map of Brooklyn so you could figure out the highest point in the borough. Then you could go there and pray against the territorial spirits."

I wanted to say, "Brother, that is nothing but Old Testament sorcery. The idolaters of Elijah's time were into 'high places,' remember?" They somehow thought they could get a better angle on the demons, I guess. I don't care if I led my whole congregation over to the eighty-sixth-floor observation deck of the Empire State Building—we would get a wonderful view of Brooklyn, but we wouldn't impress God. Or the devil, for that matter.

Others are saying, "The key to releasing God's power is to *sing* through the streets of your city. Put on a march, make banners, and declare God's sovereignty in a big parade." While Christians may enjoy such an outing, does it really make a measurable difference in a community?

Still others say, "Rebuke the devil, face the north, and stamp your feet when you do it. That will bring victory."

On vacation, Carol and I watched a Sunday morning church service on television in which the pastor was emphasizing spiritual warfare. He was in the pulpit *dressed in military fatigues!* This was supposed to scare the devil, I guess. We weren't sure whether to laugh or cry.

Can someone show me where the New Testament attaches any promise to the movement of our bodies or how we clothe them? When bizarre physical manifestations become the official sign of a supposed new awakening, we have abandoned our biblical roots. Only trouble lies ahead.

Let's forget the novelties. If we prevail in prayer, God will do what only he can do. How he does things, when he does them, and in what manner are up to him. The name of Jesus, the power of his blood, and the prayer of faith have not lost their power over the centuries.

When Charles Finney preached in Rochester, New York, in the 1820s, more than 100,000 people came to Christ within a year. "The whole community was stirred," according to one eyewitness. "Grog [liquor] shops were closed; the Sabbath was honored; the sanctuaries were thronged with happy worshipers. . . . Even the courts and the prisons bore witness to [the] blessed effects. There was a wonderful falling off in crime. The courts had little to do, and the jail was nearly empty for years afterward."[1]

I can assure you that Finney didn't "bind the spirit of alcohol" or anything else; he just did God's work in God's way, and a whole city was affected.

During the Welsh revival around 1904, according to historian J. Edwin Orr, a police sergeant told the local newspaper, "There are seventeen churches in our town, and we have quartets of policemen ready to provide music to any church that wants it." That was because the cops had little else to do with their time. Even the criminals were apparently in church, where a young coal miner named Evan Roberts led most of the meetings by praying rather than preaching.

When G. Campbell Morgan and other distinguished churchmen came from London to observe the revival, they could not get into the building; they were reduced to peering over other people's heads out in the vestibule. Did they hear Roberts calling for a march to the high places of the Welsh mountains? In fact, the opposite: Roberts was often overheard to pray, "Lower, Lord—take us lower." He would fall on his knees and begin to groan out his intercession for Wales, following the biblical pattern of humbling oneself in prayer (see James 4:9–10 and 1 Peter 5:6).

There was also a wave of bankruptcies in Wales during those years—mostly taverns.

THE BIBLE IS ENOUGH

AS A MINISTER I firmly believe that I am not allowed to preach what is not in the Bible. It is an exciting enough book as it stands. It is not something dull that we need to spice up. If we do and teach all that Jesus did and taught—and no more—we will have plenty of thrills. Otherwise, let us be silent where the Bible is silent.

> **As a minister I firmly believe that I am not allowed to preach what is not in the Bible. It is an exciting enough book as it stands.** ❧

The apostle Paul put it plainly in his letter to the church at Corinth, which had gotten itself into several messes. He was trying to move the people back on track, so he urged them to "learn from us the meaning of the saying, 'Do not go beyond what is written'" (1 Cor. 4:6). Apparently Paul thought that a scriptural foundation was essential, and beyond that lay little more than trouble.

Meanwhile, he told the Galatians, "Even if we or an angel from heaven should preach a gospel other than the one we preached to you, let him be eternally condemned!" (Gal. 1:8).

I love what William J. Seymour wrote—the one-eyed, marginally educated African-American elder at the Azusa Street Mission in Los Angeles, where the modern Pentecostal movement took shape in 1906. "We are measuring everything by the Word," he wrote in the September 1907 issue of *Apostolic Faith* magazine. "Every experience must measure up with the Bible. Some say that is going too far [in other words, being too strict!], but if we have lived too close to the Word, we will settle that with the Lord when we meet Him in the air."

> **No one has the right to adjust the gospel or revise God's plan for his church. ❦**

No one has the right to adjust the gospel or revise God's plan for his church. Those precious things are not yours or mine; they are God's. We need to stop fussing with them. We need to submit to the heavenly design laid down long ago.

DEEPER, NOT WIDER

THE THINGS OF GOD have a circumference. They are preserved in a written body of truth. It is like a well—and no one has ever fathomed the depth of God's truth.

To go into the power of the gospel, or of prayer, or the Holy Spirit, or divine love is to plunge ever deeper and deeper into God's well. Every man or woman used by God has gone *down* into this vast reservoir.

The tendency today, however, is merely to splash around in truth for a while ... and then jump *outside* the well to the surrounding soil. "Look at this—God is doing a new thing!" people proclaim. In six months or so, of course, the novelty wears off, and they jump again to a new patch of grass. They spend their whole lives hopscotching from one side of God's well to another, never really probing the depth of the living waters inside.

Inside the well there is no cause for leaving or jumping out. Who will ever fathom the fullness of the love of God? Who will ever exhaust the richness of his mercy to fallen human beings? Who will ever understand the real power of prayer?

Especially since the 1960s, fads have come and gone in the North American church, only to be replaced by newer fads. Leonard Ravenhill, the revival-minded preacher and author from Britain, told me shortly before he died, "People say the church today is 'growing and expanding.' Yes, it's ten miles wide now—and about a quarter-inch deep."

Deliverance from the dark powers has especially captured our fantasies. While Jesus and the apostles did indeed cast out demons from the unsaved, nowhere do we see this being done for the benefit of Christians. Nowhere do we find Paul saying, "You know, you Corinthians have a real mess there. You need to get the elders of the church together, have them go into earnest prayer, and then anoint the church members with oil to cast out the 'spirit of gossip' in your church. The folks who are overweight need to have the 'demon of fat' cast out of them. The immoral brother who's living with his stepmother needs to be delivered from the 'spirit of lust.' . . ."

Paul had a much more mundane explanation for these problems: They were simply "works of the flesh." He called for repentance, for dying daily to self—not flamboyant exorcism.

Just as our culture in general is taken up with a victim mentality, where everything is somebody else's fault, to be relieved by psychotherapy, government handouts, or litigation, so in the church people are saying, "It's the devil's fault. Don't blame me." No wonder there is little brokenness of spirit among us. Why pray and confess if your main problem is oppression (or possession) by an evil spirit that someone else needs to get off your back? Few Christians or sermons use the word "sin" anymore. Few sense the need to repent of their own wrongdoing. Rather, they look to the outside for a scapegoat.

When you work in the inner city, as I do, the victim mentality can be very strong. "I'm black, or brown, so it's hard for me to get anywhere in life.... I was molested as a child by my uncle, and I'm still dealing with the pain of that...."

I often reply, "Yes, those things are real—but God is greater. None of us can afford to blame the past indefinitely. My father, in fact, was an alcoholic for twenty-one years, to the point that he lost his career at Westinghouse. His weekend binges eventually stretched to entire weeks, then a full month. When he was drinking, he would call me every four-letter word I'd ever heard, and some I hadn't.... He even missed my wedding.

"So I should accomplish absolutely nothing in life, right?

"Not at all. I am still responsible. I have no license from God to lie down and vegetate. God can still hold me and put me to work in his service."

I usually go on to point out a wonderful detail in the life of Joseph, the young man whose brothers sold him into Egyptian slavery. After being framed by Potiphar's wife, thrown into prison, and forgotten ... when he finally married and had a son, he named him Manasseh, which means "to forget." He said, "It is because God has made me forget all my trouble and all my father's household" (Gen. 41:51). God is more powerful than anybody's past, no matter how wretched. He can make us forget—not by erasing the memory but by taking the sting and paralyzing effect out of it.

I am thankful that my father's life has been redeemed in recent times. He has been sober for more than thirteen years. Today he loves the Lord with all his heart, as does my mother. They are both faithful members and a tremendous support to the Brooklyn Tabernacle.

All Needs Already Supplied

If we venture into a gymnasium these days, we are likely to run into fellows who look like superstars in expensive Adidas sneakers, color-coordinated knee bands and all the rest. The only trouble is, they can't get the ball into the hoop. They have all the latest gear, but they still can't play.

We as God's people have all the equipment we need. It has been around for two thousand years. He has given us everything necessary to put points on the scoreboard and win victories in his name. So let us move forward with full confidence in what we have received.

Nothing about God will change. Tomorrow he will be no more anxious to help our lives, our families, and our churches then than he is right now. If we simply avail ourselves of his promises, we will see him do things we could never ask or think, just as he did in the New Testament. It is time to press on.

EIGHT

❧

The Lure of Marketing

Have you noticed that whenever you ask a fellow Christian these days about his or her church, the subject invariably goes to *attendance?*

Question: "Tell me about your church. How is the Lord's work coming along there?"

Answer: "Well, we have about three hundred on Sunday, I'd say."

When I ask fellow pastors the same question, I get the same answer—plus two others: "Membership is at five-fifty, we've just finished a new education wing, and our gross income this year will top out at about four hundred thousand."

Attendance, buildings, and cash. A-B-C: The new holy trinity.

How Big Was Antioch?

Such a thing would never have happened in Peter and Paul's day. For one thing, they had no buildings to call their own. They met in people's homes, in public courtyards, sometimes even in caves. As for budget, they seemed to have dispensed most of their funds in helping the poor.

Headcounts hardly appear after the Day of Pentecost. We notice a couple of large numbers in Acts 2:41 and 4:4. Later on, Acts 19:7 says "about twelve men" in Ephesus were filled with the Holy Spirit under Paul's ministry. Beyond that, we know nothing. In 1 Corinthians 1:14–16, Paul can't even remember whom he baptized, let alone the total count.

How large was the attendance in the Antioch church? Berea? Philippi? Rome? We have no idea.

How large was the congregation at Philadelphia, one of the seven churches addressed in the book of Revelation? Apparently, not very big. The Lord says, "I know that you have little strength." Yet he proceeds to give them a glowing review (Rev. 3:7–13).

No church, including the one I pastor, should be measured by its attendance.

By contrast, how large was the congregation at Laodicea? One can get a hint from the fact that the church was "rich and in need of nothing." For all we know, it may have drawn 7,000 on a Sunday. Their bills were certainly paid—yet they received a scathing spiritual rebuke.

Nowhere in the epistles do we find Paul saying, "I hear your attendance was down last quarter—what's the problem? What are you going to do about it?"

This leads me to say that no church, including the one I pastor, should be measured by its attendance. Although I am thankful for the crowds of people who come to the Brooklyn Tabernacle every week, that is not the sign of God's grace.

Beyond Popularity

Then what kind of spiritual things *do* matter in a book-of-Acts church? The apostles' prayer in Acts 4 provides our next benchmark: "Enable your servants to speak your word *with great boldness*" (v. 29). What the disciples wanted was not numbers but an essential quality that would keep them *being* the church God intended.

Boldness can only be imparted by the Holy Spirit. There is no such thing as "taught boldness." You cannot get it through a seminar. Second Timothy 1:7 says, "For God did not give us a spirit of timidity, but a spirit of power, of love and of self-discipline."

New Testament preachers were boldly confrontational, trusting that the Holy Spirit would produce the conviction necessary for conversion. They were not afraid.

Listen to Peter on the Day of Pentecost: "You, with the help of wicked men, put him to death by nailing him to the cross" (Acts 2:23). This was the *last* thing the crowd wanted to hear. If David Letterman had a Top Ten list of things *not* to say to a Jewish audience, number one would be "Guess what—with your own hands you just killed the Messiah, the one Israel has been expecting for centuries."

But Peter's boldness did not drive the people away. Instead, it stabbed their consciences. By the end of the day a huge group had repented of their sin and been converted.

In the next chapter, Peter was just as straightforward with the crowd that gathered after the healing of the cripple: "You disowned the Holy and Righteous One and asked that a murderer be released to you. You killed the author of life. . . . Repent, then, and turn to God, so that your sins may be wiped out, that times of refreshing may come from the Lord" (Acts 3:14–15, 19).

When Paul preached in Ephesus some years later, his confrontation with the pagan idolatry was so direct that a riot broke out. "They were furious and began shouting: 'Great is Artemis of the Ephesians!' Soon the whole city was in an uproar" (Acts 19:28–29). This doesn't sound very market-sensitive or user-friendly to me.

A strong church was established nonetheless. And when Paul bade them farewell, he could say, "I have not hesitated to proclaim to you the whole will of God.... Remember that for three years I never stopped warning each of you night and day with tears" (Acts 20:27, 31). Notice: "the *whole* will of God ... I never stopped *warning* you." This was at the heart of apostolic ministry.

The apostles realized that without a bold, aggressive attitude in proclaiming God's Word, they would not build the church Jesus intended. Any church in any city of the world must come to the same conclusion.

The apostles weren't trying to finesse people. Their communication was not supposed to be "cool" or soothing. They aimed for a piercing of the heart, for conviction of sin. They had not the faintest intention of asking, "What do people want to hear? How can we draw more people to church on Sunday?" That was the last thing in their minds. Such an approach would have been foreign to the whole New Testament.

> **The apostles weren't trying to finesse people.**
> **They had not the faintest intention of asking,**
> **"What do people want to hear? How can we**
> **draw more people to church on Sunday?"** ❧

Instead of trying to bring men and women to Christ in the biblical way, we are consumed with the unbiblical concept of "church growth." The Bible does not say we should aim at numbers but rather urges us faithfully to proclaim God's message in the boldness of the Holy Spirit. This will build God's church God's way.

Unfortunately, some churches now continually monitor how pleased people are with the services and ask what else they would like. One denominational specialist told a reporter, "We need to learn how to surf with changes."[1]

We have no permission whatsoever to adjust the message of the gospel. Whether it seems popular or not, whether it is "hip" to the times, we must faithfully and boldly proclaim that sin is real but Jesus forgives those who confess.

God nowhere asks anyone to have a large church. He only calls us to do his work, proclaiming his Word to people he loves under the anointing and power of the Holy Spirit to produce results that only he can bring about. The glory then goes to him alone—not to any denomination, local church, local pastor, or church-growth consultant. That is God's only plan, and anything else is a deviation from the teaching of the New Testament.

God told Ezekiel that if wicked people needed a warning and he failed to deliver it, their blood would be on the prophet's hands. The same holds true today for ministers of the Word.

Dwight L. Moody was haunted all his life by an occasion when he felt he got too clever in presenting the gospel. Six years before he died he recounted what had happened back in Chicago in the fall of 1871:

> I intended to devote six nights to Christ's life. I had spent four Sunday nights on the subject and had followed him from the manger along through his life to his arrest and trial, and on the fifth Sunday night, October 8, I was preaching to the largest congregation I had ever had in Chicago, quite elated with my success. My text was "What shall I do then with Jesus which is called the Christ?" That night I made one of the biggest mistakes of my life. After preaching . . . with all the power that God had given me, urging Christ upon the people, I closed the sermon and said, "I wish you

would take this text home with you and turn it over in your minds during the week, and next Sunday we will come to Calvary and the cross, and we will decide what we will do with Jesus of Nazareth."

Just at that moment, a fire bell rang nearby. Moody quickly dismissed the meeting and sent the people out of the building. It was the beginning of the Great Chicago Fire, which over the next 27 hours left 300 dead, 90,000 homeless, and a great city in ashes. Obviously, Moody never got to finish his sermon series.

He continued:

I have never seen that congregation since. I have hard work to keep back the tears today.... Twenty-two years have passed away ... and I will never meet those people again until I meet them in another world. But I want to tell you one lesson I learned that night, which I have never forgotten, and that is, when I preach to press Christ upon the people then and there, I try to bring them to a decision on the spot. I would rather have [my] right hand cut off than give an audience a week to decide what to do with Jesus.

No wonder the apostle James wrote, "Why, you do not even know what will happen tomorrow. What is your life? You are a mist that appears for a little while and then vanishes" (4:14). The gospel is too important to be left to tomorrow, or next week, or when the crowd seems friendlier.

Did John Wesley, preaching to hardened miners in the open fields of England in the 1700s, ever say to himself, *I had better not tell them they're sinners; they might leave?*

Today we have an anti-authority spirit in America that says, "Nobody can tell me I need to change. Don't you dare."

Both in the pulpit and in pastoral counseling we have too often given in to this mentality and are afraid to speak the truth about sin. We keep appealing to Paul's line about becoming "all things to all men" (1 Cor. 9:22), not noticing that in the very next paragraph he says, "Run in such a way as to get the prize" (v. 24). Adapting our style to get a hearing is one thing, but the message can never change without leaving us empty-handed before the Lord.

> **Today, we have an anti-authority spirit in America that says, "Nobody can tell me I need to change. Don't you dare." 🌿**

Do we still believe the truth of Proverbs 28:23, where it says, "He who rebukes a man will in the end gain more favor than he who has a flattering tongue"?

Jesus was confrontational. When Peter told him to avoid the cross, Jesus didn't reply, "You know, Peter, I'm really trying to understand where you're coming from. I appreciate how you care about me and don't want me to get hurt." Rather, he said to his number-one disciple, "Get behind me, Satan! You are a stumbling block to me; you do not have in mind the things of God, but the things of men" (Matt. 16:23).

What do *we* have in mind?

GETTING TO THE POINT

I HAVE FOUND THAT about 90 percent of the time, the problems people describe to me are not their real problems. Therefore the challenge in all preaching and counseling is to get to the bottom-line spiritual issue. A husband says, "She doesn't understand me." It is easy to reply, "Yes, that's too bad. I feel sorry for you." But what may be really going on is that he's acting like a brute.

Graciously but firmly, we have to speak the truth in love.

An attractive young couple, whom I will call Michelle and Steve, came forward for prayer at the end of a Sunday service. Both were nicely dressed—he in an expensive suit and $60 silk tie, she in a fashionable dress. I could tell by the moisture in her eyes that something had touched her during the service. By contrast, he seemed to hold back just a step, not looking me in the eye.

"Would you please pray for us?" she asked.

"Certainly," I said. "What would you like me to pray about?"

"That God will bless our relationship," she replied.

That line can mean anything, especially in New York City. I felt prompted to ask a few more questions.

"Uh, before I pray, help me with a little background, if you will. How long have you known each other?"

"A couple of years."

The next question wasn't exactly polite, but I felt the Spirit nudging me. So, without the slightest change in my voice level or inflection, I said, "Are you living together?"

The shock was instantaneous. Her eyelashes blinked; his head snapped up. We stood there frozen for a second, staring at each other. Finally she answered, "Well, uh ... yes, we are."

I nodded, then said, "Okay, that puts me in sort of a bind. You want me to ask God to bless something that he has already expressed his opinion about. He's already made it clear in the Bible that living together outside of marriage is wrong. So it looks to me like I'd be wasting everybody's time to ask his help in this situation, wouldn't I?"

They just stared at me. I pressed on.

"I tell you what—let's get on track with God's plan. Steve, how about you finding another place to live—right now? You say you want God's best for your relationship. Okay, this is step number one. This will open the door for many other good things."

I could tell Steve wasn't thrilled with the idea.

"Do you have family or friends in the city where you could stay tonight?"

No, he couldn't think of anyone.

"Listen, we'll get you a place to stay," I said. "If God is real and you truly want his help in your life, then go his way. Otherwise, do whatever you like! Of course, it will destroy you in the end; you can't change God's consequences any more than you can change the law of gravity."

He mumbled another excuse. I called one of the lay helpers over and requested that Steve be provided with a bed for the night.

Steve and Michelle still weren't sure. "How about if we stay where we are but just don't sleep together? That would be all right, wouldn't it?"

I replied, "If you both profess to be Christians, you have to avoid the obvious physical temptation. Besides, when you walk out of your apartment in the morning, what would a neighbor logically assume? Do this thing right, all the way, okay?"

They finally agreed to the plan.

Some couples in the same situation, I must tell you, have not agreed. They have said things like "Well, we'll get back to you about that" and walked out. But at least I could rest at night knowing I had told them the truth before God.

I have also received follow-up letters from women saying, "You know, I didn't like what you said to my boyfriend and me that day. You showed us what we needed to hear from the Bible, but we didn't want to accept it. Anyway, I thought

I should let you know that in time, he left me, just as you said. I was a piece of meat, nothing more. Now I'm alone again, and I wish I would have listened."

Steve and Michelle's situation turned out better. He immediately found another place to live. We kept working with them and gave them counseling. God opened their eyes to spiritual realities. Then something wonderful happened. On a Tuesday night, as the prayer meeting was drawing to a close, I said, "Before you all leave, I have a surprise for you tonight. Everybody stand, please."

The congregation rose ... and the organist began the stately octaves of Lohengrin's "Wedding March." The rear doors opened and the smiling bride, in a simple street-length dress and holding flowers, moved forward. The people broke into wild applause. Steve, who had been sitting near me on the front row all evening, stood for the ceremony. In front of 1,500 witnesses, they were united in Christ.

Several times during the proceedings, their quiet weeping for joy became so loud it could be heard through my microphone. They managed to say their vows nevertheless. After the recessional I said to the audience, "You know, that couple just recently came to the Lord." I didn't go into the unseemly details of their past, but most people could figure it out. They knew full well the grace and power of God to make crooked things straight.

This kind of thing has happened a number of times on Tuesday nights over the years. It is always a wonderful celebration.

PLEASING WHOM?

THE STAFF OF THE Brooklyn Tabernacle have taken a bold stand even in complicated cases, as when the couple who are living together have children. To ask the man to move out temporarily but keep on paying the bills is tough. Those who are earnest about repenting, however, have followed through just that way.

I often say to cohabiting couples, "You're probably wondering, *What's this preacher's angle? What is he trying to prove?* I have no angle other than to please God. As you can see, the church building is already full; we're not desperate for new members or your contributions in the offering. But we *are* desperate to please God and not be ashamed when we stand before him someday."

The apostle Paul expressed his conviction this way in 1 Thessalonians 2:4. "We are not trying to please men but God, who tests our hearts." God didn't ask Carol and me to build a big church. He told us to preach the gospel and love people in his name. Some listeners reject the truth while others open up. It has been this way throughout history, but the results are always more dynamic and glorious when we do things God's way.

> **God didn't ask Carol and me to build a big church. He told us to preach the gospel and love people in his name.** ❦

Just as the Israelites were warned not to mingle with the Canaanite gods called Baal or Asherah, we must beware a god in our time called Success. Bigger is not better if it comes at the expense of disowning the truth or grieving the Holy Spirit.

Imagine a basketball court with hoops five feet off the ground. The free-throw line is three feet away. I've just made 884 free throws in a row.

My wife walks out to watch and says, "What are you doing?"

"I'm playing basketball. See, here's the ball, and there's the hoop on a backboard. The lines are all marked and everything."

Carol would say, "No, the hoop is supposed to be ten feet high, and the line is supposed to be fifteen feet away. *That* is basketball. What you're doing is nothing more than a charade."

We have a lot of markings that look like Christianity these days, but we have drastically revised the parameters. People have lowered the standards in a vain attempt to make churches look more successful than they really are. The sermons have to be uniformly positive, and the services can't go longer than 60 minutes. Even then, church is inconvenient for some, especially during football season. Showing up at church is such a burden that soon people will be faxing in their worship!

Showing up at church is such a burden that soon people will be faxing in their worship! ❧

One minister told me recently that two families left for another church because his parking attendants didn't direct cars out of the lot fast enough. What would these people have done the night in Troas when Paul preached until midnight? (See Acts 20:7.)

Can you imagine someone handing Peter a microphone on Sunday morning and whispering, "Okay, now, you've got twenty minutes. We have to get the people out of here promptly because the chariot races start at one o'clock"?

The truth is that "user-friendly" can be a cover-up word for carnality. The same people who want sixty-minute worship services rent two-hour videos and watch NBA and NFL games that run even longer. The issue is not length, but appetite. Why the misplaced desire?

Seriously, what will our children and grandchildren grow up experiencing in church? Extended times of waiting on the Lord will be totally foreign to their experience. There will be no memory bank of seeing people reach out to God. All they will recall are professionally polished, closely timed productions.

One of our soloists recently went to sing in a church and was told in advance, "We want to ask you not to sing any song that mentions the blood of Christ. People feel uncomfortable with that, and our goal here is to be user-friendly."

If people really don't appreciate the word *blood* in the sense of sacrifice, why are we so open to Fourth of July speakers referring to the sacrifice of the brave men and women who fought to defend America? Should we avoid mentioning the blood that was shed for political liberty? If not, how much more should we honor the blood of the Lamb of God, no matter what others think?

The message of the cross will always be foolishness to some, a stumbling block to others. But if our attention is on the market reaction, we move away from the power of the gospel. This fearfulness to talk about the blood of Christ is an overreaction. Worse than that, it borders on heresy, distorting and deflating the power of the Good News.

What has become of standing unashamed for the gospel of Christ? No one is smarter than God. When he says to do his work in his way, we can be assured that he will produce his results for his glory. We don't need to get "creative" on him. God knows exactly what we need to do and expects us to trust and obey him in childlike simplicity.

God does not ask us to be clever in appealing to those who want a worldly type of wisdom. It is not by might, not by power, not by computers, not by cleverness, but by my Spirit, says the Lord (see Zech. 4:6).

These days we are so programmed that God couldn't break in if he wanted to. During times of worship in many churches, the schedule of songs and hymns is so rigid that nothing, not even God's Spirit, can interrupt. The worship leaders have the musical key changes memorized and everything. If God could lead the Israelites for 40 years in the wilderness, can't he lead us through one meeting, one praise-and-worship time, without a lineup? A basic sign of revival is that the wind is allowed to blow where it will.

We don't need technicians and church programmers; *we need God.* He is not looking for smart people, because he's the smart one. All he wants are people simple enough to trust him.

According to 1 Corinthians 14, if meetings are governed by the Holy Spirit, the result for the visitor will be that "the secrets of his heart will be laid bare. So he will fall down and worship God, exclaiming, 'God is really among you!'" (v. 25). This should be our goal. When a visitor comes in, there should be such a mixture of God's truth and God's presence that the person's heart is x-rayed, the futility of his life is exposed, and he crumbles in repentance.

Are we longing for this? Are we praying for this? Are today's church leaders aiming for this? Are church members encouraging their pastors to act on the Lord's prompting no matter the cost?

Alexander Whyte, after observing the 1859 awakening in Scotland, made this marvelous statement: "In revival, the congregation does the preaching." What he meant was that, beyond the presence of preachers, musicians, and other ministries, what speaks to the heart is that God is dwelling in close communion with his people.

THE REAL TEST

AT A MUSIC CONFERENCE where I spoke, a gentleman approached me with tears in his eyes. "We've just gotten a new pastor," he said. "And his instructions to me, as the minister of music, are: 'Please discontinue "church music." I want you to look for choral music from Broadway, from the pop scene, for the Sunday meetings.'

"What am I going to do? I want to relate to people the same as he does—but does that mean I can't honor the Lord's name in our music, as I always have?"

I told him he had no choice but to go back to his pastor and open his heart. They needed to have a long talk.

There will come a day, Paul says, when all our "work will be shown for what it is, because the Day will bring it to light. It will be revealed with fire, and the fire will test the quality of each man's work" (1 Cor. 3:13). The gold, silver, and precious stones will endure while the wood, hay, and straw will go up in smoke.

Paul doesn't say that the *quantity* will be tested. He says nothing about attendance totals. Everything will focus on *quality*.

Warren Wiersbe made an interesting observation about this passage to the Brooklyn Tabernacle staff. "What's the difference between these materials, besides the obvious—that one group is fireproof while the other isn't?

"I think it's significant that wood, hay, and straw are abundant ... right outside your door, or only a few miles away at most. Any forest, any farmer's field has an abundance of these.

"But if you want gold, silver, and costly stones, you have to *dig* for them. You have to pursue with great effort. They're not just lying around everywhere. You have to go deep into the earth."

To me, these words are profound. Spiritual "construction" that uses wood, hay, and straw comes easy—little work, little seeking, no travail, no birthing. You just slap it up and it will look adequate—for a while. But if you want to build something that will endure on Judgment Day, the work is much more costly.

On that day it won't matter what your fellow Christians thought of you. It won't matter what the marketing experts advised. You and I will stand before the One whose eyes are "like fire." We won't soften him up by telling him how brilliant our strategy was. We will face his searing gaze.

He will only ask whether we were boldly faithful to his Word.

NINE

❦

The Lure of Doctrine
Without Power

I HAVE NOT MEANT to portray New York City as totally god-less and pagan, because in fact, Brooklyn has historically been known as "the borough of churches." We have countless buildings that once housed active, vibrant congregations. Unfortunately, they are almost empty today. As the neighborhoods "changed," as drugs became more prevalent, the momentum faded.

Many parishioners died or moved into the suburbs but generously left large endowments. Today these churches may have pitifully few people in the pews on Sunday but they can still pay a pastor's full-time salary and keep the enterprise going. One of the most famous is a downtown church we used to rent for special outreach events. The sanctuary, which seats 1,400, was packed in the 1930s and 1940s, but it has not been used for regular Sunday worship since the 1960s. The congregation currently meets in the basement.

Inner cities have thus become a forgotten mission field. Church buildings are empty in places where they should be crowded. Sin is abounding—but contrary to Romans 5, grace is *not* abounding more.

Is this because the pulpits are not declaring truth?

In some cases, yes—but in many cases, no. That may surprise you if you have assumed that the decline is always due to theological liberalism or false doctrine. But many groups who own these silent sanctuaries are as orthodox as a church could be. If you quizzed them about the divinity of Christ, the Virgin Birth, or their adherence to the Apostles' Creed, they would pass with flying colors.

So what is missing?

Beyond Head Knowledge

The absent element is what is expressed in the final sentence of the prayer recorded in Acts 4: "Stretch out your hand to heal and perform miraculous signs and wonders" (v. 30). What gains unbelievers' attention and stirs the heart is seeing the gospel expressed in power.

It takes more than academic rigor to win the world for Christ. Correct doctrine alone isn't enough. Proclamation and teaching aren't enough. God must be invited to "confirm the word with signs following" (see Heb. 2:4). In other words, the gospel must be preached *with* the involvement of the Holy Spirit sent down from heaven.

> It takes more than academic rigor to win the world for Christ. Correct doctrine alone won't do it. ❦

The apostles prayed for God to do supernatural things. They wanted people to know their belief was more than positional or theoretical. There was *power* in this faith. "O God, stretch out your hand—work with us in this." They wanted a faith that was obviously alive, a faith based not just on the cross but also on the empty tomb. The cross, as poignant as it is, is understandable from a human perspective: an innocent man was murdered by crooked politicians and religious leaders. But the empty tomb—what can you say? Only a supernatural God could accomplish that.

In too many churches today, people don't see manifestations of God's power in answer to fervent praying. Instead, they hear arguments about theological issues that few people care about. On Christian radio and television we are often merely talking to ourselves.

What we are dealing with today is an Old Testament "vow religion" comprised of endless repetitions and commands to do all the right things. Modern preachers, like Moses, come down from the mount calling for commitment. Everyone says yes but then promptly breaks the vow within two days. There is little dependence on God's power to make an ongoing difference. There is little calling upon God to revolutionize us in a supernatural way.

Jesus is saying today, as he said to the church at Sardis, "You have a reputation of being alive, but you are dead. Wake up! Strengthen what remains and is about to die, for I have not found your deeds complete in the sight of my God. . . . But if you do not wake up, I will come like a thief. . . . He who has an ear, let him hear what the Spirit says to the churches" (Rev. 3:1–3, 6).

Isn't it remarkable that only two of the seven churches of Revelation (Pergamum and Thyatira) were scolded for false doctrine? Far more common was a lack of spiritual vitality, of fervency, of closeness to the Lord. These are what the glorified Christ wanted to talk about most.

I am not advocating melodrama or theatrics that work up emotion. But I am in favor, as were the apostles, of asking God to stretch out his hand and manifest himself.

> **When a new Christian stands up and tells how God has revolutionized his or her life, no one dozes off.** ❦

People pay attention when they see that God actually changes persons and sets them free. When a new Christian stands up and tells how God has revolutionized his or her life, no one dozes off. When someone is healed or released from a life-controlling bondage, everyone takes notice. These things bear witness to a God who is strong and alive.

WHO IS OUTSIDE THE FORT?

MAINTAINING DOCTRINAL PURITY IS good, but it is not the whole picture for a New Testament church. The apostles wanted to do much more than simply "hold the fort," as the old gospel song says. They asked God to empower them to move out and impact an entire culture.

In too many places where the Bible is being thumped and doctrine is being argued until three in the morning, the Spirit of that doctrine is missing. William Law, an English devotional writer of the early 1700s, wrote, "Read whatever chapter of Scripture you will, and be ever so delighted with it—yet it will leave you as poor, as empty and unchanged as it found you unless it has turned you wholly and solely to the Spirit of God, and brought you into full union with and dependence upon him."[1]

One way to recognize whether we suffer from this disconnection is to look at our concern for people who are dirty ... people who are "other" ... people who don't fit the core group's image. The idea that a church could be called just to serve yuppies or some other designated class is not found in the

New Testament. The ravages of sin are not pleasant—but they are what Jesus came to forgive and heal. "The Son of Man came to seek and to save what was lost" (Luke 19:10). The Spirit of God is a Spirit of mercy, of compassion, of reaching out.

> **In too many places where the Bible is being thumped and doctrine is being argued until three in the morning, the Spirit of that doctrine is missing.** ❧

Yet Christians often hesitate to reach out to those who are different. They want God to clean the fish before they catch them. If someone's gold ring is attached to an unusual body part, if the person doesn't smell the best, or if the skin color is not the same, Christians tend to hesitate. But think for a moment about *God* reaching out to *us*. If ever there was a "reach," that was it: the holy, pure Deity extending himself to us who were soiled, evil-hearted, unholy. God could have said, "You're so different from me, so distasteful, I would really rather not get too close to you." But he didn't say that. It was our very differentness that drew his hand of love.

Jesus didn't just speak the healing word to lepers from a distance of thirty yards. He *touched* them.

I shall never forget Easter Sunday 1992—the day that Roberta Langella gave her dramatic testimony, as I recounted in chapter 3. A homeless man was standing in the back of the church, listening intently.

At the end of the evening meeting I sat down on the edge of the platform, exhausted, as others continued to pray with those who had responded to Christ. The organist was playing quietly. I wanted to relax. I was just starting to unwind when I looked up to see this man, with shabby clothing and matted hair, standing in the center aisle about four rows back and waiting for permission to approach me.

I nodded and gave him a weak little wave of my hand. *Look at how this Easter Sunday is going to end*, I thought to myself. *He's going to hit me up for money.* That happens often in this church. *I'm so tired....*

When he came close, I saw that his two front teeth were missing. But more striking was his odor—the mixture of alcohol, sweat, urine, and garbage took my breath away. I have been around many street people, but this was the strongest stench I have ever encountered. I instinctively had to turn my head sideways to inhale, then look back in his direction while breathing out.

I asked his name.

"David," he said softly.

"How long have you been homeless, David?"

"Six years."

"Where did you sleep last night?"

"In an abandoned truck."

I had heard enough and wanted to get this over quickly. I reached for the money clip in my back pocket.

At that moment David put his finger in front of my face and said, "No, you don't understand—I don't want your money. I'm going to die out there. I want the Jesus that red-haired girl talked about."

I hesitated, then closed my eyes. *God, forgive me*, I begged. I felt soiled and cheap. Me, a minister of the gospel ... I had wanted simply to get rid of him, when he was crying out for the help of Christ I had just preached about. I swallowed hard as God's love flooded my soul.

David sensed the change in me. He moved toward me and fell on my chest, burying his grimy head against my white shirt and tie. Holding him close, I talked to him about

Jesus' love. These weren't just words; I felt them. I felt love for this pitiful young man. And that smell . . . I don't know how to explain it. It had almost made me sick, but now it became the most beautiful fragrance to me. I reveled in what had been repulsive just a moment ago.

The Lord seemed to say to me in that instant, *Jim, if you and your wife have any value to me, if you have any purpose in my work—it has to do with this odor. This is the smell of the world I died for.*

David surrendered to the Christ he heard about that night. We got him into a hospital detoxification unit for a week. We got his teeth fixed. He joined the Prayer Band right away. He spent the next Thanksgiving Day in our home. We invited him back for Christmas as well.

I will never forget his present to me. Inside a little box was . . . one handkerchief. It was all he could afford.

Today David heads up the maintenance department at the church, overseeing ten other employees. He is now married and a father. God is opening more and more doors for him to go out and give his testimony. When he speaks, his words have a weight and an impact that many ordained ministers would covet.

As Christians reach out to touch everyone, including the unlovely who are now everywhere in our society, God touches them, too—and revolutionizes their lives. Otherwise we would just be circling the wagons, busying ourselves with Bible studies among our own kind. There is no demonstration of God's power because we have closed ourselves off from the *need* for such demonstration.

Why do the greatest miracle stories seem to come from mission fields, either overseas or among the destitute here at home (the Teen Challenge outreach to drug addicts, for example)? Because the need is there. Christians are taking their sound doctrine and extending it to lives in chaos, which is what God has called us all to do.

Without this extension of compassion it is all too easy for Bible teachers and authors to grow haughty. We become proud of what we know. We are so impressed with our doctrinal orderliness that we become intellectually arrogant. We have the rules and theories all figured out while the rest of the world is befuddled and confused about God's truth ... poor souls.

Such an attitude takes the heart out of the very Word we preach. We end up with lots of doctrinal particulars, but very little happens that resembles the Bible we're teaching from. I am personally tired of hearing all the positions and teaching principles. Where are the crowds of new converts? Where are the joyful baptisms? Where are the vibrant prayer meetings?

Once again, William Law writes:

> We may take for a certain rule, that the more the divine nature and life of Jesus is manifest in us, and the higher our sense of righteousness and virtue, the more we shall pity and love those who are suffering from the blindness, disease, and death of sin. The sight of such people then, instead of raising in us a haughty contempt or holier-than-thou indignation, will rather fill us with such tenderness and compassion as when we see the miseries of a dread disease.[2]

Carol and I have found that unless God baptizes us with fresh outpourings of love, we would leave New York City *yesterday!* We don't live in this crowded, ill-mannered, violent city because we like it. Whenever I meet or read about a guy who has sexually abused a little girl, I'm tempted in my flesh to throw him out a fifth-story window. This isn't an easy place for love to flourish.

But Christ died for that man. What could ever change him? What could ever replace the lust and violence in his heart? He isn't likely to read the theological commentaries on my bookshelves. He desperately needs to be surprised by the power of a loving, almighty God.

If the Spirit is not keeping my heart in line with my doctrine, something crucial is missing. I can affirm the existence of Jesus Christ all I want, but in order to be effective, he must come alive in my life in a way that even the pedophile, the prostitute, and the pusher can see.

ART OR HEART?

IF WE DO NOT yearn and pray and expect God to stretch out his hand and do the supernatural, it will not happen. That is the simple truth of the matter. We must give him room to operate. If we go on, week after week, filling the time with religious lectures and nothing more, God has little opportunity in which to move.

So long as we are busy polishing our oratory, the stage is entirely ours. Listen to the reproof of the great prophet of prayer E. M. Bounds more than a hundred years ago:

> Among the things that hinder spiritual results, fine preaching must have place among the first. Fine preaching is that kind of preaching where the force of the preacher is expended to make the sermon great in thought, tasteful as a work of art, perfect as a scholarly production, complete in rhetorical finish, and fine in its pleasing and popular force.

> In true preaching, the sermon proceeds out of the man. It is part of him, flowing out of his life. Fine preaching separates between the man and the sermon.

Such sermons will make an impression, but it is not the impression that the Holy Ghost makes. Influence it may have, but the influence is not distinctly spiritual, if spiritual at all. These sermons do not reach the conscience, are not even aimed at it.[3]

God is not nearly as enamored with the performance of pulpiteering as he is with humble words that manifest his presence to the soul. Consider Paul and Barnabas's ministry in two adjacent towns, as related in Acts 14:

1. Iconium: "Paul and Barnabas spent considerable time there, *speaking boldly* for the Lord, who *confirmed the message of his grace by enabling them to do miraculous signs and wonders*" (v. 3, italics added).

2. Lystra: "A man crippled in his feet ... listened to Paul as he was speaking. Paul looked directly at him, saw that he had faith to be healed and called out, 'Stand up on your feet!' At that, the man jumped up and began to walk" (vv. 8–10). The crowd's reaction was immediate.

Message plus divine demonstration. Doctrine plus power. This is the New Testament way.

For a more sobering example, see what happened in the previous chapter when these two apostles were addressing a government official on the island of Cyprus who "wanted to hear the word of God" (Acts 13:7). A sorcerer named Elymas interrupted the proclamation of the truth. "Paul, filled with the Holy Spirit, looked straight at Elymas" (v. 9) and rebuked him, announcing that God would strike him blind.

It is not accidental that the writer mentions Paul's spiritual condition: he was filled with the Holy Spirit. Here was a man specially empowered that moment by the Spirit and ready for the satanic challenge. Paul's doctrine was immediately reinforced by God's overwhelming power. "When the proconsul saw what had happened, he believed, for he was amazed at the teaching about the Lord" (Acts 13:12).

Amazed at the *teaching?* Yes, for this was a teaching with power. People must not only hear but feel, see, and experience the grace of God we speak about.

Such an event was certainly unpredictable. As we open up our church meetings to God's power, they will not always follow a predetermined schedule or order. Who can outline what God might have in mind?

....

As we open up our church meetings to God's power, they will not always follow a predetermined schedule. Who can outline what God might have in mind? ✺

....

Some have said, "The miracles, signs, and wonders of the book of Acts were temporary. They served to authenticate the apostles until such time as the New Testament could be written. Now we have the completed Word of God, which erases the need for supernatural happenings."

My response is this: If we have a completed revelation in written form, are we seeing at least as much advance for God's kingdom, as many people coming to Christ, as many victories over Satan as those poor fellows who had to get along with just the Old Testament? If not, why not? Are we missing something valuable that they felt was essential?

I have met preachers who have punched up a computer file and proudly showed me what they would be preaching for nearly the next year. Everything was cut-and-dried. The pressure of having to seek God week by week had been removed. What if God has a different idea? What if the spiritual temperature of the congregation changes by next

October? Without an anointing and prophetic edge to declare something fresh from God's Word, church life can be reduced to little more than a lecture series.

Imagine that Carol and I invited you to our home for a cookout. When you arrive, I greet you at the door. As soon as I take your coat, I hand you a little piece of paper with the evening's outline. There you see that for the first seven minutes we will have light socializing: How was the traffic? What are your kids doing these days?

Then for the next four minutes I will give a quick tour of our home, the deck out back, and so forth. Following that will be twenty-two minutes for the meal. The blessing will be voiced by Carol; then we will pass the food. . . .

You would say to yourself, *This is weird! Why all the regimen? Can't we just relax and get to know one another? What if somebody has an idea or wants to talk about something that's not on the agenda?*

Too often a church service, which is meant to draw us toward God, is not all that much different. Spontaneity and the leading of the Spirit have been thrown out in the name of keeping things on schedule. However, there has never been a revival of religion so long as the order of service has been strictly followed.

Please understand: I am not campaigning for disorder. I am not saying "anything goes." I am asking us to remember that we are to be led by the Holy Spirit. Jesus said *he* would build his church, and we must not be so independent that we lose contact with the Master Planner. God the Holy Spirit does unusual things, and he does not always notify us in advance.

"Those who are led by the Spirit of God are sons of God," says Romans 8:14. Read the gospels and look for Jesus' daily agenda. It just isn't there. Scan the book of Acts to find the apostolic liturgy. You'll come up empty. What you will find are people moving in spontaneous obedience as they are propelled by the fresh wind of the Holy Spirit.

The prayer of the Jerusalem believers recorded in Acts 4 says in essence, "God, please don't send us out there alone just talking. Work with us; confirm your message in a supernatural way." What way and in what manner was left entirely (and rightly) to God alone.

Charles Finney, the lawyer turned evangelist, once said that as long as an audience kept looking at him while he preached, he knew he was failing. Only when their heads began to drop in deep conviction of sin did he know that God was working alongside him, producing a heart change inside. The words of sound doctrine alone were not enough.

In fact, revivals have never been dominated by eloquent or clever preaching. If you had timed the meetings with a stopwatch, you would have found far more minutes given to prayer, weeping, and repentance than to sermons. In the "Prayer Meeting Revival" of 1857–59 there was virtually no preaching at all. Yet it apparently produced the greatest harvest of any spiritual awakening in American history: estimates run to 1,000,000 converts across the United States, out of a national population at that time of only 30,000,000. That would be proportionate to *9,000,000 Americans today* falling on their knees in repentance!

How did this happen? A quiet businessman named Jeremiah Lanphier started a Wednesday noon prayer meeting in a Dutch Reformed church here in New York City, no more than a quarter mile from Wall Street. The first week, six people showed up. The next week, twenty came. The next week, forty ... and they decided to have daily meetings instead.

"There was no fanaticism, no hysteria, just an incredible movement of people to pray," reports J. Edwin Orr. "The services were not given over to preaching. Instead, *anyone* was free to pray."[4]

During the fourth week, the financial Panic of 1857 hit; the bond market crashed, and the first banks failed. (Within a month, more than 1,400 banks had collapsed.) People began calling out to God more seriously than ever. Lanphier's church started having three noontime prayer meetings in different rooms. John Street Methodist Church, a few doors east of Broadway, was packed out as well. Soon Burton's Theater on Chambers Street was jammed with 3,000 people each noon.

The scene was soon replicated in Boston, New Haven, Philadelphia, Washington, and the South. By the next spring 2,000 Chicagoans were gathering each day in the Metropolitan Theater to pray. A young 21-year-old in those meetings, newly arrived in the city, felt his first call to do Christian work. He wrote his mother back East that he was going to start a Sunday school class. His name was Dwight L. Moody.

Does anyone really think that America today is lacking preachers, books, Bible translations, and neat doctrinal statements? What we really lack is the passion to call upon the Lord until he opens the heavens and shows himself powerful.

THE LIMITS OF TEACHING

LET ME MAKE A bold statement: Christianity is not predominantly a teaching religion. We have been almost overrun these days by the cult of the speaker. The person who can stand up and expound correct doctrine is viewed as essential; without such a talent the church would not know what to do. As I said in an earlier chapter, the North American church has made the sermon the centerpiece of the meeting, rather than the throne of grace, where God acts in people's lives.

The Jewish faith in Jesus' day was dominated by rabbis—teachers of the law. Their doctrine was thorough. Jesus told them, "You diligently study the Scriptures because you think that *by them* you possess eternal life. These are the Scriptures that testify about me, yet you refuse to come to me to have life" (John 5:39–40, italics added). They knew the written word of God very well, but not the living Word, even as he stood before them.

> **Christianity is not predominantly a teaching religion. . . . The teaching of sound doctrine is a prelude, if you will, to the supernatural.** 🌿

The Scriptures are not so much the goal as they are an arrow that points us to the life-changing Christ.

Unfortunately, the rabbis never did realize who was among them. In the last few days before his crucifixion, Jesus wept over the city as he said, "You did not recognize the time of your visitation" (Luke 19:44 NASB).

It is fine to explain *about* God, but far too few people today are experiencing the living Christ in their lives. We are not seeing God's visitation in our gatherings. We are not on the lookout for his outstretched hand.

The teaching of sound doctrine is a prelude, if you will, to the supernatural. It is also a guide, a set of boundaries to keep emotion and exuberance within proper channels.

But as Paul said, "The letter kills, but the Spirit gives life" (2 Cor. 3:6). If the Holy Spirit is not given an opening among us, if his work is not welcomed, if we are afraid of what he might do, we leave ourselves with nothing but death.

Granted, extremists have done fanatical things in the name of the Holy Spirit that have frightened many sincere Christians away. Chaotic meetings with silly things going on and a lack of reverence for God have driven many to prefer a quiet, orderly lecture. But this is just another tactic of the enemy to make us throw out the baby with the bathwater. Satan's tendency is always to push us toward one extreme or the other: deadness or fanaticism.

Gordon D. Fee, a New Testament scholar whose heritage is Pentecostal, has said about corporate worship, "You really should have this incredible sense of unworthiness—'I don't really belong here'—coupled with the opposing sense of total joy—'It is all of grace, so I *do* belong here.' What bothers me about some within the Pentecostal and charismatic tradition is the joy without reverence, without awe." But in too many mainstream evangelical churches, Fee adds, there is neither "reverence *nor* joy."[5]

The old saying is true: If you have only the Word, you dry up. If you have only the Spirit, you blow up. But if you have both, you grow up.

We must not succumb to fear of the Holy Spirit. More than 200 years ago, William Law bluntly declared that the church of his day was "in the same apostasy that characterized the Jewish nation. . . . The Jews refused Him who was the substance and fulfilling of all that was taught in their Law and Prophets. The Christian church is in a fallen state for the same rejection of the Holy Spirit." He said further that just as the Jews refused Jesus and quoted Scripture to prove their point, "so church leaders today reject the demonstration and power of the Holy Spirit in the name of sound doctrine."[6]

What would the Englishman say if he were alive today?

A CRY FOR MORE

I DO NOT MEAN to imply that all is well-adjusted in the life and worship of the Brooklyn Tabernacle. As I said in the beginning, there are no perfect churches. I must be honest and tell you that I live with an almost constant sense of failure. When I think of what God could do for all the needs of this city and how little we are accomplishing, it makes me passionate to seek God's intervention in even more powerful ways.

North American Christians must no longer accept the status quo. No more neat little meetings, even with the benefit of 100 percent correct doctrine.

Are we hiding behind the doctrine of God's omnipresence, that he is everywhere around the globe, especially "where two or three are gathered together" . . . to the point that we don't seriously ask and expect to see him work with power in our lives *here and now?* Shouldn't we expect to *see* him in action once in a while? Shouldn't we implore him to manifest himself? Moses did. Joshua did. Elijah did. Elisha did. Peter did. Philip did. Paul did. Shouldn't we?

God will manifest himself in direct proportion to our passion for him. The principle he laid down long ago is still true: "You will seek me and find me when you seek me with all your heart" (Jer. 29:13). *O God, split the heavens and come down! Manifest yourself somehow. Do what only you can do.*

PART 3

The Road Ahead

TEN

❦

Too Smart for
Our Own Good?

Often WHEN OUR PASTORAL staff meets together, amid the flurry of busy days and what the world would term "church success"—a large membership, nearly twenty branch churches, the choir performing at Billy Graham crusades, our videos being televised nationwide, invitations to speak here and there—a nagging thought from the Lord spreads across the edges of our hearts: *Remember who has done all this. Your need for me hasn't lessened at all.*

If you have been a Christian for any length of time, the same is true for you individually. Your first rush of emotion at how God wonderfully saved you from sin has faded. Your desperate early days when you cried out to the Lord because you didn't know what you were doing (as I had to do back on Atlantic Avenue) have given way to a degree of confidence and assurance. You and I have learned a lot, seen and heard a lot, built a track record, and accumulated a fair storehouse of "wisdom."

That's why we are at great risk.

We discover what this means in the life of a man named Asa. You probably haven't thought about this Old Testament king in a long time—maybe never. Most readers of the Bible, unless they happen to be history buffs, doze off once they

157

finish the accounts of the famous monarchs Saul, David, and Solomon.

Asa was Solomon's great-grandson. God gave him three whole chapters of 2 Chronicles for a reason. I happen to think his biography is one of the most important in all of Scripture, especially for today.

Asa was not brought up to be a spiritual person. Solomon, as everyone knows, had wandered from God near the end of his life. Rehoboam, who came next, and then Abijah, Asa's father, let idol worship come right into the midst of what was supposed to be a godly society. Baal was welcomed as a help to the crops; Asherah poles, oversized carvings of the male sex organ supposed to bring fertility, were common; children were actually offered as sacrifices in the fires of Molech.

In such a spiritual climate, who was it who got through to young Asa and convinced him to seek the Lord? We don't know. Second Chronicles 14:2–4 tells us only that early in his reign Asa "did what was good and right in the eyes of the LORD his God. He removed the foreign altars and the high places, smashed the sacred stones and cut down the Asherah poles. He commanded Judah to seek the LORD, the God of their fathers, and to obey his laws and commands."

In essence, Asa was saying, "Time out! We have a mess on our hands. The foreign altars and immorality must go. We're going to clean house throughout this entire kingdom. We're going to start obeying the Lord's commands and call out to him with all our hearts. We must have him near us in order to receive his blessing."

These people were Israelites, sons and daughters of Abraham, living in a specially chosen land. But they were in a terrible spiritual condition nonetheless. Their heritage did not remove the consequences of displeasing God. No claim of special rank could exempt them. In fact, their elect status would bring God's correction even more quickly than it would to their enemies.

The first step in any spiritual awakening is *demolition.* We cannot make headway in seeking God without first tearing down the accumulated junk in our souls. Rationalizing has to cease. We have to start seeing the sinful debris we hadn't noticed before, which is what holds back the blessing of God.

I wonder if any government employee said, "Excuse me, King Asa, but your father built that particular shrine.... Your grandfather dedicated that incense altar. Are you sure you want them demolished?"

If they had, Asa would have replied, "Tear them down— now! They're wrong. This idolatry was borrowed from the Canaanites—but we're not Canaanites. God will never bless us as long as these things stand."

Anytime people get hungry to truly know the Lord, the Holy Spirit quickly puts a shovel and broom into their hands. Husbands and wives begin to deal with long-buried issues hurting their marriages. Adults take a closer look at their choice of TV programs and movies. Church members begin to see the damage wreaked by their gossip, their racial attitudes, their criticism.

> **Anytime people get hungry to truly know the Lord, the Holy Spirit quickly puts a shovel and broom into their hands.** ❧

I admit this sounds old-fashioned. I am out of step with the modern habit of "claiming" God's blessing regardless of how we live. But what does the Bible show us?

Sin grieves the Holy Spirit and quenches his power among us. Without his blessing we miss out on what God has for us and wants us to be, no matter what religious label we may be carrying.

One Sunday about 20 years ago, back in our days in the YWCA, I said something impromptu while receiving new members into the church that has stuck with us ever since. People were standing in a row across the front before me, and as I spoke, the Holy Spirit seemed to prompt me to add, "And now, I charge you, as pastor of this church, that if you ever hear another member speak an unkind word of criticism or slander against anyone—myself, another pastor, an usher, a choir member, or anyone else—you have authority to stop that person in midsentence and say, 'Excuse me—who hurt you? Who ignored you? Who slighted you? Was it Pastor Cymbala? Let's go to his office right now. He will get on his knees and apologize to you, and then we'll pray together, so God can restore peace to this body. But we will not let you talk critically about people who are not present to defend themselves.'

"New members, please understand that I am entirely serious about this. I want you to help resolve this kind of thing immediately. And meanwhile, know this: If *you* are ever the one doing the loose talking, we will confront you."

To this very day, every time we receive new members, I say much the same thing. It is always a solemn moment. That is because I know what most easily destroys churches. It is not crack cocaine. It is not government oppression. It is not even lack of funds. Rather, it is gossip and slander that grieves the Holy Spirit.

People nod their heads with understanding, and as a result, rumor and busybody talk are kept to a minimum. We have had to confront a few people along the way, of course, but the general concern to live with clean hearts and clean speech before the Lord prevents many problems from ever getting started.

Asa's early years were marked by a national housecleaning. God's blessing flowed upon the king and his people in response.

A GREAT CHALLENGE

UNFORTUNATELY, SEEKING THE LORD wholeheartedly does not exempt us from outside attack. After ten years of peace, Asa's corner of the world was suddenly invaded by a huge Cushite (Ethiopian) army for no apparent reason. Asa's godliness did not guarantee a smooth road for the rest of his life.

> **Unfortunately, seeking the Lord wholeheartedly does not exempt us from outside attack.** ❦

In such a moment, seekers after God have built up a reservoir of ready faith to meet new problems. They know exactly what to do:

"Asa called to the LORD his God and said, 'LORD, there is no one like you to help the powerless against the mighty. Help us, O LORD our God, for we rely on you, and in your name we have come against this vast army. O LORD, you are our God; do not let man prevail against you'" (2 Chron. 14:11).

Asa's faith was not some kind of instant cake mix stirred from a box on the pantry shelf. He and the people had already been calling out to God for a decade. Hence, there was no panic. They cried for the Lord to arise—and he did. The Cushites were decisively wiped out, despite their overwhelming numbers, "for the terror of the LORD had fallen upon them" (v. 14).

This is a classic example of a cardinal principle of God's dealing with humanity. Hebrews 11:6 expresses it best:

"Anyone who comes to [God] must believe that he exists and that *he rewards those who earnestly seek him*." I cannot say it strongly enough: When we seek God, he *will* bless us. But when we stop seeking him ... all bets are off, no matter who we are. It doesn't matter how much talent we have, how many diplomas hang on our walls, what word of prophecy was proclaimed over us, or anything else.

On Asa's way home from the battle, a prophet stopped him and his army along the road to reinforce what had just happened:

"Listen to me.... The LORD is with you when you are with him. If you seek him, he will be found by you, but if you forsake him, he will forsake you" (2 Chron. 15:2). The cause-and-effect relationship could not be clearer.

The more we seek God, the more we see our need to seek him. Asa, buoyed by this experience, began to look around ... and discovered things he had missed earlier. The altar in God's temple was broken down; he immediately ordered it repaired. He called a solemn assembly of the whole population, where he made a new covenant with God.

> **God did not call me to be a white middle-class Christian; he called me to be a Christian, period.** ❧

He was later shocked to find that his own grandmother, Maacah, still had "a repulsive Asherah pole" (15:16). He cut down the pole and deposed the elderly woman from her throne as queen mother. Can you believe that Asa had the nerve to bust his own grandmother! The people of the land could not help but say to one another, "This king is *serious* about pleasing God."

Imagine the social current he was up against. Imagine the emotional ties he had to sever. His whole sense of family allegiance was arrayed against God's will. But Asa was determined to be more than just "Maacah's grandson."

I see many churchgoers today who find family pressure too much to challenge. Others are caught up with being part of the middle-class scene, or with being white, or black. God did not call me to be a white middle-class Christian; he called me to be a Christian, period, and whatever he asks takes precedence over every other loyalty.

Even being an American is not of the same magnitude with being a seeker after God. Preserving the American culture cannot be allowed to compete with advancing God's kingdom. Whatever God approves of comes first. Whatever grieves him has to go.

We are always either drawing nearer to God or falling away. There is no holding pattern. 🌿

Asa understood who deserved his first loyalty. It was not his grandmother, his culture, his tradition, or anything else. It was God alone. What a wonderful example of single-hearted service to the Lord!

THE BLUNDER

I WOULD GIVE ANYTHING if Asa's story ended this way. It doesn't.

Twenty-five years went by. Somewhere along the way — as has happened to many churches, pastors, choir directors, and whole denominations — Asa *stopped feeling his need to seek the Lord*. We don't know why. We don't know whether the cares of life somehow made him spiritually soft. Maybe he thought he had reached a spiritual pinnacle and could relax. But the Bible teaches that we are always either drawing nearer to God or falling away. There is no holding pattern.

One day Asa received news that a *small* army from his northern neighbor was starting to build a blockade around his territory (see 2 Chron. 16). The opponent was not nearly the size of the Cushite horde of a quarter century earlier. What would Asa do now? How would he respond?

"Asa then took the silver and gold out of the treasuries of the LORD's temple and of his own palace and sent it to Ben-Hadad king of Aram, who was ruling in Damascus. 'Let there be a treaty between me and you,' he said" (vv. 2–3).

This is stranger than Ripley's Believe It or Not. The man who had built his whole success in life upon seeking after God was now dipping into the Lord's coffers for a secular buy-off!

And the king of Aram was willing to be bought. He sent his army to put pressure on Asa's enemy, who quickly backed away from attacking Jerusalem. Asa even got to capture some building materials that were left behind.

In other words, the plan "worked." Asa probably felt proud of himself. *I used my head and figured my way out of this one. I'm smart.*

The people realized they had a very clever leader. Many churches today are making the same assumption: Whatever "works" is the way to go. If a technique gets the building filled and the bills paid, it must be blessed by God. Visible results are the proof that a strategy is heaven-ordained. Such thinking is due for a rude awakening when we stand before the Lord.

While Asa's court officials were high-fiving each other on the brilliant maneuver just completed . . . in walked another prophet, named Hanani. He began to speak, and faces suddenly dropped.

"Because you relied on the king of Aram and not on the LORD your God, the army of the king of Aram has escaped from your hand...." (v. 7). In other words, there would be no way for Asa ever to oppose Aram in the future; he was locked into being cooperative with this pagan empire.

God's messenger pressed on:

"Were not the Cushites and Libyans a mighty army with great numbers of chariots and horsemen? Yet when you relied on the LORD, he delivered them into your hand. *For the eyes of the LORD range throughout the earth to strengthen those whose hearts are fully committed to him.* You have done a foolish thing, and from now on you will be at war" (vv. 8–9, italics added).

Today God's eyes are still running all across America, Canada, Mexico, the islands of the sea, the world . . . looking for someone—*anyone*—who will totally and passionately seek him, who is determined that every thought and action will be pleasing in his sight. For such a person or group, God will prove himself mighty. His power will explode on their behalf.

Day after day goes by, and God keeps looking, looking.... Doesn't anyone want to call out for his blessing? Upon whom can he pour his grace? Isn't anyone interested?

The less we look for God, the more he has to go looking for us. Why not run in his direction? When Jesus cried out in the middle of the temple crowd in Jerusalem, he said, "If anyone is thirsty, let him come to me and drink. Whoever believes in me, as the Scripture has said, streams of living water will flow from within him" (John 7:37).

When we align ourselves with the channel of God's living grace, all kinds of marvelous things take place. His power energizes us to face any army, large or small, and win victories for him. We call upon him, and he sends us forth to accomplish what we could never do alone, regardless of our money, education, or track record.

Tough to the End

I wish I could tell you that Asa fell on his knees and begged God's forgiveness for straying, for thinking up his own political solution instead of calling upon the Lord. I wish I could say that Asa's heart melted in confession, resulting in a return to the fervent faith of his younger days.

In fact, the opposite happened.

"Asa was angry with the seer because of this; he was so enraged that he put him in prison. At the same time Asa brutally oppressed some of the people" (2 Chron. 16:10).

The young king who once led a whole nation in seeking God now became a coldhearted oppressor of that nation. Asa's story illustrates how people who stop seeking God tend to get crusty and arrogant. They think they know everything. A prophetic rebuke only irritates them.

Compare Asa with his great-great-grandfather, David, who in his later years made mistakes, too. In fact, David's blunders were even worse: a one-night stand with a married woman, a follow-up murder of her husband, later on, an unwise census. But when rebuked by prophets—Nathan in one case, Gad in the other—David broke down. "I have sinned greatly in what I have done," he confessed (2 Sam. 24:10). Psalm 51 is an eloquent, emotional outpouring of guilt before the Lord. No wonder he was called "a man after God's own heart."

People who have a seeking heart still make mistakes. But their reaction to rebuke and correction shows the condition of that heart. It determines what God is able to do with them in the future.

People who have a seeking heart still make mistakes. But their reaction to rebuke and correction shows the condition of that heart. ❧

If Asa, like David, had broken before God, who knows how his life would have ended? But he did not, and the closing picture of Asa is downright pitiful. As an old man he developed a painful case of foot trouble, probably gout. He hobbled around his palace, every step bringing a grimace to his face. "Though his disease was severe, even in his illness he did not seek help from the LORD, but only from the physicians. Then in the forty-first year of his reign Asa died" (2 Chron. 16:12–13).

Christendom, like Asa, is suffering from major illness today. Our vital signs are not good. Now we face a choice. We can stay hard and justify our backsliding by saying, "Don't tell me my spiritual life needs correction. I'm getting along; everything is still 'working,' isn't it? Leave me alone." Or we can be like David and admit the truth.

Anything and everything is possible with God if we approach him with a broken spirit. We must humble ourselves, get rid of the debris in our lives, and keep leaning on him instead of our own understanding. Your future and mine are determined by this one thing: seeking after the Lord. The blessings we receive and then pass along to others all hang on this truth: "He rewards those who earnestly seek him" (Heb. 11:6).

ELEVEN

❧

In Search of
Ordinary Heroes

THERE WILL COME A DAY when faith becomes sight, and then—only then—will our seeking of the Lord be finished at last. We will find ourselves in heaven, standing face-to-face with the One we have trusted and followed for so long. He himself will be what makes it truly heaven—not streets of gold or walls of jasper, but God alone in all his splendor. We will know him as he has known us from the beginning.

In addition, what a delight it will be to meet those heroes of the faith, both men and women, who fill the pages of the Bible. I can't wait to greet Paul the apostle, who penned so much of the New Testament and whose life has inspired so many Christians. I long to talk with Moses, who led Israel out of Egypt and did great exploits for God. Then I will soon move along to Abraham, Deborah, Joshua, Ruth, David, Helez, Sibbecai, Ahiam, Hezro, Zabad ... *Who? Did I wander off track a bit? You say you don't recognize those last few names?*

They are all carefully listed in 1 Chronicles 11, an amazing group of warriors known as David's "mighty men." God the Holy Spirit thought they were impressive enough to have every last one written down, because "they, together with all Israel, gave [David's] kingship strong support to extend it over the whole land, as the LORD had promised" (v. 10).

Such individuals are role models for us today—even if we can't pronounce their names. Some names are a bit strange, I admit: "Elhanan son of Dodo" (v. 26). I assume this father's name didn't mean the same thing in Hebrew as it does in English! While some young parents these days are enamored with choosing Old Testament names such as Seth or Caleb for their new baby boys, I doubt there will ever be a comeback for those in this list: Ithai, Hepher, Mibhar, Uzzia....

Nevertheless, these are people who applied their strength and courageous action toward what God had promised. It was not enough for them that the prophet Samuel had anointed David king-in-waiting back when he was a teenager. Much more recently the elders of Israel had gathered in Hebron to declare David the new monarch. But out in the villages, and especially on the borders of the land, not everyone was convinced. The picture was still unclear. The rule of God's king was yet to be established. Foreign enemies were still living inside the land promised to God's people.

These heroes did not just sit back, as many do today, saying, "Well, God promised, and I'm sure he'll fulfill his word." They stepped up and took action to make the promise become reality. They understood that God's work in the world is usually a joint project; he works with us as we yield ourselves to work with him.

So these men risked their lives. They left their families and headed for dangerous territory. The Bible uses a special word three times to describe what they did: *"exploits"* (vv. 19, 22, 24).

Similarly, the gospel of Jesus Christ will be planted today in hostile cities and territories and nations only by mighty men and women who dare to take risks. Apathetic churches across the land will be revived only by people of deep spirituality who refuse to accept the status quo. Wayward children and broken marriages will be touched by the hand of God only as someone stands in the gap and fights valiantly in the power of the Spirit.

Among the mighty warriors I have had the privilege of knowing, I count Delores Bonner, an African-American woman who lives alone in Bedford-Stuyvesant, one of Brooklyn's toughest neighborhoods. She has been a medical technician at Maimonides Hospital for more than thirty years. Carol and I met her one year at Christmastime while we were bringing gifts to some poor children in our congregation.

Delores had a full apartment that day—but these children were not hers. She had brought them from a nearby shelter to meet us. Their natural mother was too consumed with her own problems to be present even for an occasion such as this.

"How did you come to meet these children?" I asked.

She modestly mumbled something that didn't really answer my question. Only from others did I learn that right after her conversion in a prayer meeting at the church in 1982, she became concerned for children in the streets and in the crack houses. God touched her heart, and she started bringing the children to Sunday school. At first she packed them into taxis; later on someone heard what she was doing and bought her a car. Today she has a van so she can transport more children and teenagers to hear the gospel.

This is only part of Delores's story. On Sundays between services, she oversees the crew that cleans the sanctuary so it will be ready for the next crowd. On Saturdays she goes out with the evangelism teams, knocking on doors in the housing projects to share God's love. On weekdays I find her on her knees upstairs with the Prayer Band, taking a shift to intercede for people's needs. She did the same thing on a ministry trip to Peru, where she joined others in calling out to God on my behalf as I preached in an outdoor meeting.

When we honored Delores as the Brooklyn Tabernacle's "Woman of the Year," she was embarrassed and said little. But the whole church knows that living among us is a mighty woman of God whose fame transcends the world's shallow value system.

Delores is a woman of quiet determination, the kind shown in 1 Chronicles 12:18, where it says, "The Spirit came upon Amasai, chief of the Thirty, and he said: 'We are yours, O David! We are with you, O son of Jesse! Success, success [or "peace and prosperity"] to you, and success to those who help you, *for your God will help you.*" Once again, the merging of divine and human effort is clearly shown.

Oddly, two people on David's list weren't even Jewish. They would never have been allowed to worship at the holy tabernacle. Zelek the Ammonite (1 Chron. 11:39) and Ithmah the Moabite (v. 46) were definitely from the "wrong" nationalities. Their countrymen harassed the Israelites continually and tempted them toward idolatry. Yet Zelek and Ithmah ended up being honored because they fought and risked their lives for God's king.

All these were common people who did uncommon things for God. In that sense, they remind us of those "unschooled, ordinary" people of Acts 4:13, of whom we have already said much. David's thirty mighty warriors were not royalty. They were not graduates of West Point or Annapolis. They were just regular people from small places—Anathoth, Tekoa, Gibeah—who set their hearts to do exploits for God's anointed one.

What we desperately need in our own time are not Christians full of cant and posturing, railing at the world's problems of secular humanism, New Age, or whatever. We need men and women who will step out to turn back today's slide toward godlessness, prayerless churches, family breakup, and waning evangelistic fervor. They may not have been to seminary, but they have been schooled and trained by God for hand-to-hand warfare in the spiritual realm.

THE TELLING MOMENT

THE FIRST PERSON ON David's list, Jashobeam, "raised his spear against three hundred men, whom he killed in one encounter" (1 Chron. 11:11). That sounds impossible. There is no way he could pile up that kind of body count without the overshadowing presence and power of God. Human bravery alone is not enough when the odds are 300 to 1.

When it comes to spiritual matters, you and I will never know our potential under God until we step out and take risks on the front line of battle. We will never see what power and anointing are possible until we bond with our King and go out in his name to establish his kingdom. Sitting safely in the shelter of Bible discussions among ourselves, or complaining to one another about the horrible state of today's society, does nothing to unleash the power of God. He meets us in the moment of battle. He energizes us when there is an enemy to be pushed back.

> **You and I will never know our potential under God until we step out and take risks on the front line of battle.** 🌾

In verses 12–14 we meet Eleazar, who accompanied David into a major battle with the Philistines. We get an idea of how formidable the enemy was when the Bible says, "At a place where there was a field full of barley, the troops fled from the Philistines." This was no minor skirmish; this was all-out combat against a superior opponent. Many frightened Israelite soldiers saw the coming horde and ran for their lives.

But not Eleazar. He and David "took their stand in the middle of the field. They defended it and struck the Philistines down, and the LORD brought about a great victory." Once again we see the combination of human and divine efforts. God did not act alone. He didn't unleash a lightning strike from heaven to fry the Philistines. Instead, he was looking all across the horizon that day to see who would stay in the barley field and thus receive his supernatural aid. While others left in fear, these two—David and Eleazar—stood firm.

The account in 2 Samuel 23:10 adds even more detail about Eleazar. He "stood his ground and struck down the Philistines till his hand grew tired and froze to the sword." He swung his weapon with such grit, such adrenaline, that his muscles locked up on him; he couldn't let go. Talk about a mighty warrior for God!

What the world's situation cries out for today is this kind of determined and desperate faith that grips the sword of the Spirit, which is the Word of God, and won't let go until victory comes.

A man such as Eleazar brings to mind the little-known, seldom-seen partner of the great evangelist Charles Finney during the Second Great Awakening. His name was Daniel Nash, and he had had a lackluster record as a pastor in upstate New York. He finally decided, at the age of forty-eight, to give himself totally to prayer for Finney's meetings.

"Father Nash," as some called him, would quietly slip into a town three or four weeks before Finney's arrival, rent a room, find two or three other like-minded Christians to join him, and start pleading with God. In one town the best he could find was a dark, damp cellar; it became his center for intercession.

In another place, Finney relates,

> When I got to town to start a revival a lady contacted me who ran a boarding house. She said, "Brother Finney, do you know a Father Nash? He and two other men have been at my boarding house for the last three days, but they haven't eaten a bite of food. I opened the door and peeped in at them because I could hear them groaning, and I saw them down on their faces. They have been this way for three days, lying prostrate on the floor and groaning. I thought something awful must have happened to them. I was afraid to go in and I didn't know what to do. Would you please come see about them?"
>
> "No, it isn't necessary," I replied. "They just have a spirit of travail in prayer."[1]

Once the public meetings began, Nash usually did not attend. He kept praying in his hideaway for the conviction of the Holy Spirit to melt the crowd. If opposition arose—as it often did in those rugged days of the 1820s—Finney would tell him about it, and Father Nash would bear down all the harder in prayer.

One time a group of young men openly announced that they were going to break up the meetings. Nash, after praying, came out of the shadows to confront them. "Now, mark me, young men! God will break your ranks in less than one week, either by converting some of you, or by sending some of you to hell. He will do this as certainly as the Lord is my God!"

Finney admits that at that point he thought his friend had gone over the edge. But the next Tuesday morning, the leader of the group suddenly showed up. He broke down before Finney, confessed his sinful attitude, and gave himself to Christ.

"What shall I do, Mr. Finney?" he asked then. The evangelist sent him back to tell his companions what had changed in his life. Before the week was out, "nearly if not all of that class [group] of young men were hoping in Christ," Finney reported.[2]

In 1826 a mob in a certain town burned effigies of the two: Finney and Nash. These unbelievers recognized that one man was as big a threat to their wickedness as the other.

Shortly before Nash died in the winter of 1831, he wrote in a letter,

> I am now convinced, it is my duty and privilege, and the duty of every other Christian, to pray for as much of the Holy Spirit as came down on the day of Pentecost, and a great deal more.... My body is in pain, but I am happy in my God.... I have only just begun to understand what Jesus meant when He said, "All things whatsoever ye shall ask in prayer, believing, ye shall receive."[3]

Within four months of Nash's death, Finney left the itinerant field to become the pastor of a church in New York City. His partner in cracking the gates of hell was gone. If you want to see Father Nash's grave today, you will have to drive to northern New York, almost to the Canadian border. There, in a neglected cemetery along a dirt road, you will find a tombstone that says it all:

DANIEL NASH
Laborer with Finney
Mighty in Prayer
Nov. 17, 1775–Dec. 20, 1831

Daniel Nash was a nobody to the elite of his time. They would have found this humble man not worthy of comment because he lived on a totally different plane. But you can be sure that he was known all too well in both heaven and hell.

The Bible tells about another Daniel whose dedication made an impression in the courts of God. "A hand touched me and set me trembling on my hands and knees. He said, 'Daniel, *you who are highly esteemed . . .*'" (Dan. 10:10, italics added). Imagine being acclaimed by heaven itself!

God's mighty men and women lay aside the distractions of life to do exploits in the spiritual realm. Whether or not they become famous is beside the point. ❧

This is how it is with all God's mighty men and women. They are famous in heaven; they win crowns that make all earth's riches seem like cheap tinsel. They may witness, teach, lead, and pray in obscurity on earth, but they are the talk of heaven.

In every century, on every continent, warriors such as these are the ones who press forward the kingdom of God. They lay aside the distractions of life to do exploits in the spiritual realm. Whether or not they become famous on earth is beside the point. They are heroes and heroines nonetheless.

WHO, US?

THE LIST OF DAVID'S mighty warriors in 1 Chronicles 11:22 introduces us to Benaiah, whose exploits included overcoming two of Moab's best men. He also killed a lion in a snowy, slippery pit. Perhaps most amazingly, he took on an Egyptian tall enough to be a starting center for the Chicago Bulls. This seven-and-a-half-foot giant wielded a spear with a shaft as sturdy as a lead pipe while Benaiah had only a wooden club.

Even so . . . Benaiah "snatched the spear from the Egyptian's hand and killed him with his own spear. Such were the exploits of Benaiah son of Jehoiada. . . . He was held in greater honor than any of the Thirty" (vv. 23–25).

It was not a Ph.D. degree that brought honor to a person in those days. Honor did not necessarily flow to the person with money or leverage or media access. Honor came as a result of doing exploits for the king.

Who is doing exploits for God today? Where is the enemy being driven back? That is the great yearning of all spiritually minded people. They are not enchanted with polished sermons and slick organizational technique. Where are the mighty men and women anointed by God to truly make a difference?

....

Who is doing exploits for God today? Where is the enemy being driven back? ❦

....

I think I know at least one of God's mighty people. Rina Gatdula, a Filipino lady, is like a sister to Carol and me. God sent her in the early days of the Brooklyn Tabernacle with a valiant spirit that proved to be a tremendous blessing. When our ushers were intimidated by the occasional drunk or hostile person who would wander in, Rina would confront him or her head-on with a fearlessness granted by the Holy Spirit.

Although not especially gifted as a public speaker, she had a ministry of prayer and intercession that helped to carry us through many battles. Whether it is the need for a larger building or the need for a backslider to return to the Lord, she has the spirit of Benaiah. She will not let go of God when needy people come to the altar seeking help. She knows the fine art of "praying through" with people; many have found deliverance in Christ because she has stood with them at the throne of grace.

Her tenacity is so unique that when she moved to another part of the country, churches there almost didn't know what to make of her. They didn't understand her gifts; they saw only that her English was limited and that she didn't have certain clever skills. As a result, they didn't open up to her ministry.

Today Rina travels among the churches the Brooklyn Tabernacle has begun, both in this country and overseas, reminding them of the exploits they can do through God. She always seems to spark a spirit of prayer. Whether in Harlem, San Francisco, or Lima, Peru, she is a living example of a heroine of faith.

Consider how many gospel-preaching churches there are in the fifty states of America—200,000, if not more. If each of these churches, on average, brought only two converts to Christ a week—not robbing people from First Baptist or First Nazarene down the road, but winning new people for the kingdom of God—that would mean 100 new baptized believers in each church in a year's time, *or 20,000,000 nationwide.*

The population of the entire United States is about 270,000,000. By merely bringing eight or nine people a month to Christ in each church, America would be dramatically changed within two to three years. Can any serious Bible-preaching church not take on this modest goal in the name of its King?

God's plan for the local church has always centered in evangelism. Those brought to Christ are thus born into the very place where they can be nurtured and discipled. This avoids the slippage we often see when parachurch ministries try to do the work mainly assigned to the local church.

An evangelistic focus, of course, would force us back to serious prayer and an emphasis on the simple gospel of Jesus

Christ. God would prepare us as only he can for victorious spiritual warfare. Concerned believers wouldn't have time to watch as much television as they do now. A lot of other activities would have to give way. Living in the Bible, calling upon the Lord, fasting, and then reaching out to the unsaved would consume us. We would require God's anointing, whatever the cost.

Some churches in very small towns might have trouble reaching 100 people per year, but they would be offset by churches in urban areas, where the need and the opportunity are so great.

If the American church actually set out to do this "exploit" for God, bringing 20,000,000 to Christ this year, another 20,000,000 next year . . . in three or four years we wouldn't recognize our culture. Broadway and Hollywood would have to acknowledge the shift in audience preferences. Abortion clinics would wonder where all their customers went. Drug abuse would plummet.

Some will accuse me of idealistic dreaming, but isn't this plan the last thing Jesus told us to fulfill before his ascension? "Go and make disciples of all nations," he said, "baptizing them in the name of the Father and of the Son and of the Holy Spirit, and teaching them to obey everything I have commanded you" (Matt. 28:19–20). What will it take to shake denominational leaders, pastors, and laypeople, seeing that we all must answer to Christ at the Judgment Seat one day? Our sense of inadequacy is no excuse, given that he has promised to work with us as we set our hearts to the task of extending his kingdom.

BRAVE FOR GOD

THE MIGHTY WARRIORS OF 1 Chronicles 11 even helped David conquer a new capital for his kingdom, a story told in verses 4–9. The modern nation of Israel has made a big celebration of the 3,000th birthday of this city, Jerusalem, as the center of Jewish life.

It was not an easy prize. The Jebusites who lived in Jerusalem flatly told David, "No way. This is a tough, fortified city, and you won't get inside." In fact, 2 Samuel 5:6 records their insult: "Even the blind and the lame can ward you off."

So it is with every attempt to do something significant for God. It is never simple. Whenever God stirs us to establish his kingdom in a new place, the enemy is sure to taunt us. The devil always tries to convince us that we've tackled too much this time and we'll soon be humiliated.

But David and his warriors pressed on. They would not be turned back. In fact, David made an unusual offer: "Whoever leads the attack on the Jebusites will become commander-in-chief" (1 Chron. 11:6). This meant being the first to head uphill against well-armed soldiers perched atop thick walls, just waiting to rain down arrows and rocks. David's young nephew Joab, however, seized the opportunity to perform this exploit. He broke into the city first, and thus he became David's leading general for years to come.

That is not how we select leaders in the church today, is it? We go by resumes, seniority, image, education, and a half-dozen other human criteria. By contrast, David looked for bravery and boldness in the real world of battle.

If we are courageous enough to go on the spiritual attack, to be mighty men and women of prayer and faith, there is no limit to what God can accomplish through us. Some of us will turn out to be famous like King David and Catherine Booth and Charles Finney; the rest will remain obscure like Eleazar and Daniel Nash and Rina Gatdula. That doesn't matter. What counts is bringing God's power and light into a dark world, seeing local communities touched by God as churches turn back from perilous apathy to become Holy Spirit centers of divine activity.

The heroes of church history whom we now revere were not known for their cleverness; they were warriors for God. Moody was never ordained to the ministry. Finney never went to seminary. Yet whole cities were visited by God as a result of their anointed work.

THE TIME IS NOW

WHAT IS IT REALLY that stops us from becoming mighty warriors in the Lord? God has not changed. He is still superior to anything the enemy can throw against us.

No personal or church situation is too hopeless for the all-sufficient power of the Holy Spirit. God will be no more eager to act tomorrow than he is right now. He is waiting for us to take his promises seriously and go boldly to the throne of grace. He wants us to meet the enemy at the very point of attack, standing against him in the name of Christ. When we do so, God will back us up with all the resources of heaven.

Dear Father, thank you for your mercy and the salvation you have given us in Jesus Christ. Please forgive us for all our sins and shortcomings. Draw us to you, and begin a new work of grace in all of us.

Make us the people you want us to be. Fill our churches with your fresh wind and fresh fire. Break our pride, soften our hearts, and fill us to overflowing with your Holy Spirit.

O God, do all this so that the name of Jesus will be exalted throughout the earth.

Amen.

A Word to Pastors

I HAVE ALWAYS STRUGGLED with the notion of addressing pastors, because I am keenly aware of my lack of classical training. But in the school of practical experience, the main truths of the Bible have become evident, and that is what I try to share.

I mention the following out of my heart's concern that all of us fulfill God's calling on our lives:

1. Every real pastor is in the ministry today because, in the words of Ephesians 4:11, "it was he [Christ] who gave some to be . . . pastors and teachers." The ministry was not your idea or mine; it was God's plan from the beginning of time. He has entrusted us with a sacred privilege, and with that comes an awesome responsibility—one for which we will have to answer at the Judgment Seat of Christ.

Let us all lead our congregations with the desire for divine acceptance, rather than focusing so much on current trends or what is popular with our peers. Christ will one day assess the *quality* of our work. He will pay no attention to trends set by others in the pastoral profession. That is why we all need to go humbly before him with open hearts, letting him rearrange all we do in order to meet his approval.

2. We must face the fact that for our churches and ministries to be all God wants them to be, they *must* be saturated with prayer. No new revelation or church-growth technique will change the fact that spiritual power is *always* linked to

communion with God. If you and I are prayerless, if our churches have no appetite for God's presence, we will never reach our full potential in him.

3. Many visitors to our Tuesday night prayer meetings get inspired and want to go and do likewise back home. But it is very important to discern God's guidance as to the true spiritual temperature of a congregation and what the next step should be.

While some pastors have started prayer meetings similar to ours and have seen a wonderful response, others have been disappointed. Many times the spirit of prayer has been so absent in a church that a weeknight prayer meeting, no matter how biblical or laudable, meets with apathy and coldness. This discourages pastors even more, and they feel doubly defeated as fewer and fewer people come each week.

I often recommend that these pastors adjust the Sunday service instead. Preaching time can be shortened somewhat, and when the sermon is over, invite those who feel touched by the Word to come forward for prayer. Get your staff and the church's spiritual leaders around you and pray with them. What is an "altar service"? It's a mini prayer meeting.

After people find more freedom to bring their needs to God, the spirit of prayer can begin to take hold. Then God will lead you to the next step. We must always remember that prayer is a gift from the Holy Spirit, and we can't work it up. So give God time to work in people's hearts. After they have experienced the joy and power of his presence, God will be able to do even greater things.

4. Let us never accept the excuse that God cannot work in *our* situation ... that our particular people are too rich, or too poor ... too inner-city or too suburban ... too traditional or too avant-garde. This kind of thinking is never found in the Word of God. No matter what ethnic origin or geogra-

phy characterizes the local church, we *can* see God do things just as he did in the book of Acts, since he has *never* changed. The only changing that can occur is within us.

Let us purpose in our hearts to change in his direction and see him do incredible things to the praise of the glory of his grace.

NOTES

Chapter Two—Catching Fire

1. Tom Carter, comp., *Spurgeon at His Best* (Grand Rapids: Baker, 1988), p. 155: selections from the 1873 edition of the *Metropolitan Tabernacle Pulpit*, p. 218.

2. Andrew A. Bonar, *Heavenly Springs* (Carlisle, PA: Banner of Truth Trust, 1904), p. 15.

Chapter Four—The Greatest Discovery of All Time

1. Tom Carter, comp., *Spurgeon at His Best* (Grand Rapids: Baker, 1988), p. 145: selections from the 1901 edition of the *Metropolitan Tabernacle Pulpit*, p. 247.

2. Copyright © 1989 Carol Joy Music\ASCAP (admin. ICG)\Word Music\ASCAP. All rights reserved. Used by permission.

Chapter Five—The Day Jesus Got Mad

1. J. B. Phillips, *The Young Church in Action* (New York: Macmillan, 1955), p. vii.

2. Ibid., p. viii.

3. Lyle Wesley Dorsett, *E. M. Bounds, Man of Prayer* (Grand Rapids: Zondervan, 1991), p. 134.

Chapter Six—A Time for Shaking

1. Andrew A. Bonar, *Heavenly Springs* (Carlisle, PA: Banner of Truth Trust, 1904), p. 34.

188 🌢 Fᴙᴇsʜ Wɪɴᴅ, Fᴙᴇsʜ Fɪʀᴇ

Chapter Seven—The Lure of Novelty

1. Cited in V. Raymond Edman, *They Found the Secret* (Grand Rapids: Zondervan, 1984), p. 46.

Chapter Eight—The Lure of Marketing

1. Marc Spiegler, "Scouting for Souls," *American Demographics* (March 1996), pp. 42–49.

Chapter Nine—The Lure of Doctrine Without Power

1. William Law, *The Power of the Spirit* (Fort Washington, PA: Christian Literature Crusade, 1971), p. 19.
2. Ibid., p. 124.
3. E. M. Bounds, *Powerful and Prayerful Pulpits* (Grand Rapids: Baker, 1993), p. 55.
4. J. Edwin Orr, *America's Great Revival* (Elizabethtown, PA: McBeth Press, 1957), p.11.
5. Quoted by Wendy Murray Zoba, "Father, Son, and . . . ," *Christianity Today* (June 17, 1996), p. 21.
6. Law, *The Power of the Spirit*, p. 23.

Chapter Eleven—In Search of Ordinary Heroes

1. Cited by J. Paul Reno, *Daniel Nash: Prevailing Prince of Prayer* (Asheville, NC: Revival Literature, 1989), p. 8.
2. For a fuller account of this event, see Garth M. Rosell and Richard A. G. Dupuis, eds., *The Memoirs of Charles G. Finney: The Complete Restored Text* (Grand Rapids: Zondervan, 1989), pp. 119–20.
3. Reno, *Daniel Nash*, p. 160.

FRESH WIND, FRESH FIRE
STUDY GUIDE

CHAPTER ONE: THE AMATEURS

When Jim Cymbala, the new pastor of the Brooklyn Tabernacle, realized the church didn't have enough money to pay its mortgage, he prayed and asked God to provide. In what way(s) did God's faithful provision of a one-hundred-dollar anonymous donation help to prepare Jim and his wife, Carol, for what was to come in their ministry?

After a Sunday evening service that began with Pastor Cymbala being too depressed to preach, God helped him discover that "God is attracted to weakness. He can't resist those who humbly and honestly admit how desperately they need him. Our weakness, in fact, makes room for his power."

- In what way(s) have you seen these truths illustrated in your life?
- What effect(s) do you think pretense has on God's Spirit?
- How does God respond when we humble ourselves before him and seek to depend on him fully?

A Time to Share

If you feel comfortable doing so, share a time when you had to depend totally on the Lord and his provision. What happened?

While Pastor Cymbala was on a fishing boat recovering from a lung ailment, he sensed God saying to him, "If you and your wife will lead my people to pray and call upon my name, you will never lack for something fresh to preach." God then affirmed his commitment to provide vital funds.

Many times in the Bible, God uses the word *if* when talking about the way he wants to bless us: *if we* seek him, *if we* love one another, *if we*. Why does God sometimes make what he will do for us conditional on our hunger for him?

Throughout *Fresh Wind, Fresh Fire*, Pastor Cymbala emphasizes the importance of prayer. How would you describe the relationship between prayer and seeing the Holy Spirit work in our lives? In our churches?

CHAPTER TWO: CATCHING FIRE

"The format of a prayer meeting is not nearly as important as its essence—touching the Almighty, crying out with one's whole being," Pastor Cymbala writes. "What matters most is that we encounter the God of the universe, not just each other."

- What is it about encountering one another that sometimes seems sufficient for us?
- Why do we need to encounter God?

Which things begin to happen when people draw near to the Lord, receive the Holy Spirit's fullness, and rekindle their first love for God?

Why, as we seek to share the message of Jesus with hurting people, is it important for us to have faith in God's ability to transform anyone's life, regardless of his or her problems?

As people who attended the Brooklyn Tabernacle were energized by the Holy Spirit, what happened among the different races represented in the congregation?

Pastor Cymbala writes, "In America it would appear that there is more openness, acceptance, and teamwork in the gym [among people of different races] than in the church of Jesus Christ." Do you agree or disagree with this statement? Illustrate your answers whenever possible.

Personal Reflection

What might you, and/or members of your church, do within the next month to increase openness and respectful acceptance between races in your church? In your community?

Over and over again, Pastor Cymbala and members of the Brooklyn Tabernacle congregation have wept and pleaded before God for last-minute help. How do you approach God when you need his intervention in what otherwise would be an impossible situation?

Why is it important for us to want to pray and to continue to call out for God's blessing and help? What might be the result(s) if we stop praying and don't believe that God is big enough to meet our needs?

CHAPTER THREE: A SONG FOR THE DESPERATE

It is no secret that many church leaders rigidly schedule their services, including the songs and hymns, and leave little room for God's leading. Pastor Cymbala encourages those church leaders to trust God, long and pray for God's presence among them, and allow God's Spirit to govern the meetings. Sometimes, as the Brooklyn Tabernacle choir sings during a service, a spirit of praise descends on the people and the entire direction of the meeting changes.

- When you think about this happening in a service, how do you feel?
- What do you think the balance should be between spontaneity and the prepared order of service when the Holy Spirit is clearly at work within your congregation?

When she was delivered from the bondage of sin, Roberta Langella described how she finally knew "down deep" that God loved her and accepted her, so she could relax in his love. What is the difference between really experiencing God's love and just knowing it intellectually?

The four Sunday services at the Brooklyn Tabernacle are each at least two hours long. In Pastor Cymbala's words, "We have always felt we had to give the Holy Spirit time to work; we couldn't rush people through some kind of assembly line." In what way(s) is this approach to the Holy Spirit's working in a worship service different than the approach used in other churches?

What do you understand Pastor Cymbala to mean by the following comment? "Prayer cannot truly be taught by principles and seminars and symposiums. It has to be born out of a whole environment of felt need." In what way(s) does this perspective differ from what you have been taught concerning prayer?

Many of us would affirm, as Pastor Cymbala writes, that "prayer is the source of the Christian life, a Christian's lifeline." He then says that the greater emphasis on teaching in today's churches is producing limited results because many listeners do not have an active prayer life.

- What are some of the reasons many Christians spend little, or no, time in prayer each day?
- What effects does this lack of prayer create in their lives? In the churches they attend? In their outreach to non-Christians?

Personal Reflection

Would you describe yourself as a person who is devoted to prayer? Why or why not? How might a greater devotion to prayer change your life?

In Genesis 4:26, we read, "At that time men began to call on the name of the LORD." What would it mean for us to "call on" the name of the Lord with all of our heart and soul?

CHAPTER FOUR:
THE GREATEST DISCOVERY OF ALL TIME

Throughout *Fresh Wind, Fresh Fire*, Pastor Cymbala touches on God's commitment to listen to our prayers and respond to us. He writes that God is not aloof, that God says continually through the centuries, "I'll help you, I really will. When you don't know where to turn, then turn to me." And Pastor Cymbala shares how he and Carol had prayed for Chrissy, their daughter. In what way(s) does our view of God influence our desire and willingness to call on him in the day of trouble (Psalm 50:15)?

Personal Reflection

What difficulty are you or someone you know experiencing that you need to pray about? How is your view of God influencing your prayer life right now?

If you were to choose between attending a church in which the pastor uses preaching as a subtle form of entertainment and a church in which people really call on the name of the Lord and long to know him intimately, which would you choose? Why?

Pastor Cymbala writes, "The devil is not terribly frightened of our human efforts and credentials. But he knows his kingdom will be damaged when we lift up our hearts to God." Why is it so tempting for us to rely on our own cleverness and energy instead of humbling ourselves, calling on God's name with all our hearts, and depending on him to do great things?

Sometimes Pastor Cymbala changes the flow of a church service in order to pray for a specific need. If that happened in your church, what might the consequences be?

CHAPTER FIVE: THE DAY JESUS GOT MAD

Why is it important for those of us who are involved in Christian ministry—pastoring, preaching, singing in a choir, leading a small group—to look at *why* we are doing these things, to examine whether we do these things with hearts that radiate God's love or for some other reasons?

Pastor Cymbala writes, "I have seen God do more in people's lives during ten minutes of real prayer than in ten of my sermons." Do you agree that praying can be as, or even much more, beneficial than listening to great sermons? What results of real prayer have you seen?

A Time to Share

The Holy Spirit was poured out, as recorded in Acts 1–2, when the disciples were waiting on God. What do you think would happen if more Christians spent time waiting on God, letting him shape them, cleanse their spirits, and work in their hearts? If you feel comfortable doing so, describe a time when you experienced the fullness of God as a result of waiting on him.

If prayer is the key to strong churches and dynamic gospel outreach, what do you think is keeping more Christians from spending more time praying and calling on God's name?

Personal Reflection

What do you think will happen if you begin to pray that God will reveal his power in your life and lead you toward people whom he wants you to love?

If you don't already set aside time each day to pray and really talk with God about your troubles, your challenges, your persecutions, those around you who don't yet know him, what's stopping you from starting *today*? Set aside a few minutes today and talk to God about what's going on in your life and the lives of others.

Most ministries of the Brooklyn Tabernacle are birthed by spiritually sensitive people who pray about a need and feel a calling to start a ministry to meet that need. In what way(s) is this different from hatching an idea during a church staff or leadership meeting?

196 · FRESH WIND, FRESH FIRE

Often Pastor Cymbala describes people who come to the Brooklyn Tabernacle as being in desperate straits. What happens in your church when "unusual," desperate, or even very difficult people show up?

When we truly believe that God can change people from the inside out, regardless of how sinful or hopeless they may be, as opposed to viewing God as being somewhat powerless and uncaring, what changes occur in:

- Our response to God?
- Our prayer life?
- Our direct contact with desperate, needy people?
- Our congregations?

A Time to Share

Throughout *Fresh Wind, Fresh Fire*, Pastor Cymbala describes times when he and others have felt the Holy Spirit's prompting to pray for specific individuals who had specific needs. Then God responded in wonderful ways.

- What did you think when you read these stories?
- What does it mean to "listen" to God's voice?
- When do you believe you have "heard" God's voice?
- Why is it important for people to join together in fervent prayer, asking God to meet specific needs?

Revelation 5:8 reveals that "the prayers of the saints" are so precious to God that he keeps them like a treasure! How might that truth encourage us in our daily lives?

It is easy to be pessimistic when we look at the evil in the world around us. But Pastor Cymbala offers a solution: "Only turning God's house into a house of fervent prayer will reverse the power of evil so evident in the world today." Do you agree or disagree with this statement? Why?

Personal Reflection

Which area(s) of your life needs prayer? (Your marriage? Your children? Your business decisions?) How much are you willing to invest each day in crying out for God's grace and power?

Pastor Cymbala asks this question: "If a meeting doesn't end with people touching God, what kind of a meeting is it?" In answer to this question, how would you describe the purpose of a meeting where people do not meet God?

Pastor Cymbala repeatedly emphasizes the importance of realizing that prayer is God's channel of blessing—and then praying, not out of legalistic habit but out of strong desire. Where does this desire come from?

A Time to Share

Jesus' disciples acted like cowards following his arrest. In contrast, Pastor Cymbala describes some of the things they did after Jesus' resurrection:

- Received the Holy Spirit's infilling.
- Did not create labels for one another—denominational or any other kind—that might have created division.
- Were unified.
- Went out to "do God's work in God's way."
- Were guileless, sincere, and courageous.
- Often prayed together, calling on the Lord to help them.

  How do these observations relate to us in our daily lives?

Chapter Six: A Time for Shaking

In Ephesians 5:18, Paul writes that we need to "be always being filled with the Spirit" (literal translation). Why is it important for each of us—no matter whether we call ourselves evangelicals, fundamentalists, Pentecostals, or charismatics—to admit our lack of real power and be filled with God's fresh wind and fresh power?

Pastor Cymbala mentions that "God has never lacked the power to work through available people to glorify his name." What do you think it means, in practical terms, for us to be "available" to God?

Personal Reflection

In what way(s) have you accommodated yourself to what the world wants or expects from you? In what way(s) are you boldly, aggressively, and perhaps even militantly standing firm for Jesus? Even when you feel weak in your own strength, what might God be calling you to prayerfully and boldly accomplish for his kingdom? In your neighborhood? At work? In your family?

After a young man carried a pistol up to the pulpit while Pastor Cymbala was preaching, Carol Cymbala suffered from deep, oppressive fear that only went away after choir members joined together to pray after being prompted by the Holy Spirit.

- Why do you think Satan uses fear?
- How do Christians experience release from fear?

According to Revelation 3:20, God is ready to draw close to us and provide his love and power. Yet some of us refuse to open the door of our hearts and minds to him.

- Why do you think we do this?
- What are the real issues that keep us from turning to God?

CHAPTER SEVEN: THE LURE OF NOVELTY

A Time to Share

Pastor Cymbala writes, "In the church today, we are falling prey to the appeal of 'New!' The old truths of the gospel don't seem spectacular enough. We're restless for the latest, greatest, newest teaching or technique."

- In what way(s) has the emphasis on "New!" impacted churches in your community? Impacted the spiritual walk of people you know?
- What are the "old" truths that need to be shared and will make an impact in your community?
- Why do you think people are attracted to things other than the "plain gospel" Jesus proclaimed?

Personal Reflection

As you look back on your life, what impact has the basic gospel message had on you? Contrast this with the impact that nonscriptural teachings and techniques have had on you. In what way(s) are you strongly attracted to "innovations" and "new spiritual shortcuts" and tend to lose sight of the "plain gospel"?

Pastor Cymbala describes the importance of humbling ourselves before God and returning to God's "basics." Prayerfully reflect on your spiritual walk.

- To which of God's "basics" might he be calling you to return?
- Which step(s) will you take this coming week to move in this direction?

Pastor Cymbala writes, "The Bible speaks more about *resisting* the devil than it does about *binding* him [1 Peter 5:8–9]." Yet Christians in some circles emphasize "binding" rather than emphasizing their need to press on with old-fashioned spiritual endurance in their ongoing battle against Satan. Why is such endurance a vital part of our Christian walk?

A Time to Share

Pastor Cymbala explores Acts 11:20–24, which describes how God worked mightily in the city of Antioch.

- Which points stand out to you as you read these verses aloud? Why?
- How do these verses relate to what God wants to do through *us* today?

"Let's forget the novelties," Pastor Cymbala writes. "If we prevail in prayer, God will do what only he can do. How he does things, when he does them, and in what manner are up to him. The name of Jesus, the power of his blood, and the prayer of faith have not lost their power over the centuries." How does this quotation relate:

- To us—as individuals?
- To us—as a body of believers?
- To the specific needs of people in our local community?

"As a minister I firmly believe," Pastor Cymbala writes, "that I am not allowed to preach what is not in the Bible."

- How is this belief similar to or different from the belief of other pastors, as evidenced by their preaching?
- Do you believe this completely biblical focus should be an essential part of church life today? Why or why not?
- What can happen within a church when its pastor(s) disobeys 1 Corinthians 4:6 and goes "beyond what is written" in the Bible?

Pastor Cymbala likens the Bible—God's written, revealed body of truth—to a deep well that no human being can fathom. But instead of going *down* into this well, some of us have the tendency to "splash around in truth for a while" and then jump *out*side the well. What are some of the fads that Christians pursue rather than really probing the depths of the living waters inside God's "well"?

After mentioning that many Christians have become enamored with what he describes as "deliverance from dark powers," Pastor Cymbala goes on to say that some people in the church blame the devil instead of facing the sin in their lives and repenting of their own wrongdoing.

- What is it about the word *sin* that is so offensive to some people today?
- What is the result when people tend to focus on how they have been victimized rather than focusing on their personal responsibility and the transforming power of God that can enable them to work in his service regardless of their past?

Personal Reflection

What can you do this week to avail yourself of God's promises concerning your life? Your family? Your church?

Chapter Eight: The Lure of Marketing

After quoting Acts 4:29, "Enable your servants to speak your word with great boldness," Pastor Cymbala writes, "Boldness can only be impacted by the Holy Spirit." Contrast this point with the belief that we can learn this kind of boldness on our own.

Do you agree with Pastor Cymbala that in order to build the church Jesus intended, we must have a "bold, aggressive attitude in proclaiming God's Word"? Why or why not? Explain your answers.

What might happen within local churches if their leaders followed the following admonition? "We have no permission whatsoever to adjust the message of the gospel. Whether it seems popular or not, whether it is 'hip' to the times, we must faithfully and boldly proclaim that sin is real but Jesus forgives those who confess."

Do you agree or disagree with Pastor Cymbala that some Christians, even pastors, are afraid "to speak the truth about sin" in order to be nonconfrontational and appeal to a wider audience?

- If not, why not?
- If so, what effect is that fear having on our churches today? On our families? On our overall view of biblical standards?

Personal Reflection

Pastor Cymbala writes, "What has become of standing unashamed for the gospel of Christ? No one is smarter than God. When he says to do his work in his way, we can be assured that he will produce his results for his glory. We don't need to get 'creative' on him. God knows exactly what we need to do and expects us to trust and obey him in childlike simplicity."

- Are you standing unashamed for the gospel—in your home, at work, among friends?
- Are you willing to obey God and allow him to produce the results *he* desires in *his* way?
- Are you trusting and obeying him in childlike simplicity?

CHAPTER NINE: THE LURE OF DOCTRINE WITHOUT POWER

In which area(s) of your life do you especially need to depend on God's power to make an ongoing difference? Are you willing to call on God to revolutionize you in a supernatural way? How would you recognize God's supernatural work?

A Time to Share

If Jesus, who will one day judge each of us, asked us point-blank, "Are you being boldly faithful to my Word?" which changes might we each need to make in order to answer, "Yes"? Break up into small groups of three or four people and discuss areas in which you are *not* being boldly faithful to the

Bible—and the change(s) you will need to make in order to be boldly faithful.

"In too many churches today," Pastor Cymbala writes, "people don't see manifestations of God's power in answer to fervent praying. Instead, they hear arguments about theological issues that few people care about." What effect do you think this theological wrangling has on Christians attending those churches? On non-Christians who are observing "from the outside"?

Why do people—Christians and non-Christians alike—pay attention when they see and hear firsthand that God actually changes people and sets them free?

Just as Jesus touched lepers and died on the cross for all sinful, evil-hearted, unholy people, God calls us to reach out compassionately to people whose lives are in chaos, who are different, who are dirty, who are unlovely and need his love and forgiveness. But what are some of the reasons why we often hesitate to reach out to people like that?

Pastor Cymbala asks, "Where are the crowds of new converts? Where are the joyful baptisms? Where are the vibrant prayer meetings?" What is the value of thinking about these questions—and the changes we might need to make in our lives and in our churches?

Personal Reflection

Which person(s) in your sphere of influence desperately needs to be surprised by the power of the loving, almighty God? Will you pray for this person regularly? How might you reach out to this person(s) soon with the gospel of Jesus Christ?

Do you agree or disagree with this statement: "If we do not yearn and pray and expect God to stretch out his hand and do the supernatural, it will not happen." Why or why not?

Why is it important, as Pastor Cymbala emphasizes, that biblical teaching be combined with God's power?

Pastor Cymbala writes, "Does anyone really think that America today is lacking preachers, books, Bible translations, and neat doctrinal statements? What we really lack is the passion to call upon the Lord until he opens the heavens and shows himself powerful."

- Do you really believe it is necessary to have this kind of passion? Explain your answers.
- Do you really expect God to answer by opening heaven's gates and showing himself powerful? Why or why not?

Personal Reflection

Are you experiencing the living Christ in your life? If not, in what way(s) would you like your relationship with him to be different? Which step(s) are you willing to take this coming week to draw closer to him?

God, through Jeremiah, said, "You will seek me and find me when you seek me with all your heart" (Jeremiah 29:13). If you have a close friend with whom you can discuss virtually anything, discuss with this person an area in each of your lives in which you passionately need to ask and expect to see God work with power in your life *here and now*, to do what only he can do. (At work? In your home? In a key relationship?)

Pastor Cymbala writes, "We must not succumb to fear of the Holy Spirit."

- In what ways do you think Christians today are afraid of the Holy Spirit?
- What impact is that fear having on our churches? On our outreach to non-Christians? On our families? On our local communities?

Chapter Ten: Too Smart for Our Own Good?

What happens when some of us who have been Christians for a while lose sight of what God has done (and is still doing) in our lives and de-emphasize our need for him? What are we missing out on?

When we seek the Lord, as young Asa did so many years ago in the land of Judah, why is it important for us to "clean house" and deal honestly and fully with the sin in our lives?

A Time to Share

Pastor Cymbala writes, "Sin grieves the Holy Spirit and quenches his power among us. Without his blessing we miss out on what God has for us and wants us to be." What, then, are the reasons we so often rationalize our sin and refuse to completely "clean house" in confession and repentance?

If we truly applied the following verse, Hebrews 11:6, how might our lives—and the lives of people around us—change? "Anyone who comes to [God] must believe that he exists and that *he rewards those who earnestly seek him.*"

Personal Reflection

How serious are you about seeking God's blessing and giving him your first loyalty, which includes repenting of your sin and honoring him despite any social and cultural pressures you may be facing?

What causes Christians to stop feeling their need to seek the Lord, as the older Asa did when he cleverly (so he thought) used the Lord's money to pay off King Ben-Hadad of Aram? We obviously don't pay off kings, but what similar things do we do?

A Time to Share

Describe a time when you used "what worked," instead of seeking God's leading and power with a heart fully committed to him, to deal with a situation. Then discuss the consequences.

As Pastor Cymbala points out in the story of Asa, how we respond to rebuke and correction reveals the spiritual condition of our hearts. Why do many of us resist godly rebuke and correction, preferring to go our own way and justify our sinful actions? What happens as a result?

CHAPTER ELEVEN:
IN SEARCH OF ORDINARY HEROES

Pastor Cymbala points out that just as a group of courageous warriors assisted David in establishing his God-ordained rule in Israel so many years ago, mighty, deeply spiritual men and women who dare to take risks and fight valiantly in the power of the Holy Spirit will plant the gospel of Jesus Christ today in hostile cities. God, he writes, "meets us in the moment of battle." What kind of risks is God calling us to take on the front lines to turn back today's slide toward godlessness, prayerless churches, family breakups, and waning evangelistic fervor?

"God's plan for the local church," writes Pastor Cymbala, "has always centered in evangelism."

- Why is evangelism so important?
- If few people in your church are converted to Christ, what is it your church is trying to do?

When we, as spiritual men and women of prayer and faith, attempt to do something significant for God, the enemy is sure to resist us.

- What are some of the enemy's common tricks?
- What are the most important ways we can confront and overcome those tricks?

Personal Reflection

Do you believe God's promises to use you to truly make a difference for his kingdom? If not, why not? If so, which steps will you take to "get into the spiritual battle" and step out in faith to obey God? He wants to use you in a special way!

What may be keeping you from taking God's promises seriously and becoming a mighty warrior in the Lord? A personal or church situation that seems hopeless? The strategies of the enemy? What is keeping you from going boldly to the throne of grace and meeting the enemy at the very point of attack?

FRESH FAITH

PART 1

~

Something Is Missing

ONE

~

Stolen Property

I LIVE IN A CITY where things get stolen all the time. Along Flatbush Avenue, where our church is, car thefts are an everyday occurrence. So are muggings, purse snatchings, and apartment break-ins.

Once in a Sunday night sermon I made the mistake of asking our congregation to raise their hands if they had personally experienced some kind of rip-off. The place broke into laughter as 98 percent of the hands went up. What a silly question to pose to a crowd of New Yorkers!

My wife, Carol, and I live in the borough of Queens, east of LaGuardia Airport and Shea Stadium, where the Mets play. I came out to my car parked in front of our house one morning a few years ago and noticed it had been vandalized. As soon as I opened the door and got inside, I saw a huge, gaping hole in the center of the steering wheel where the air bag had been.

Crack cocaine addicts love air bags because they are a quick-sale item. Within minutes they can walk into a "chop shop"—an illicit garage that deals in used auto parts—and trade an air bag for up to $200 cash. It is just one of the ways that crack has devastated New York and other major cities in America. Heroin was one thing, snorting cocaine another— but crack has brought massive destruction.

214 ~ FRESH FAITH

I moaned to myself about the loss. When I called my insurance agent, he took it in stride. "Well, that's the Big Apple for you," he said. "Happens all the time." We filled out the claims paperwork and ordered the part from the dealer. I didn't ask what this would do to my rates next time around; I didn't really want to know.

A few months passed before I finally got around to taking the car in for the replacement. At last the damage was repaired.

And wouldn't you know—within three weeks I got ripped off again! Same parking place in front of my house, same window forced open. I'm almost sure it was the same thief.

This time I didn't even bother to file an insurance claim. I just paid the $800 for replacement out of my pocket rather than risk my rates going through the roof.

I even found a way to joke about it with someone: "You know, maybe I should leave coffee and cake for this guy on the front seat ... with a note that says, 'Hey, let's be friends! If I'd just supply you with other stuff to sell, at least you wouldn't have to break into my car every few months.'"

MORE THAN MERCHANDISE

FORTUNATELY, AIR BAGS CAN be replaced. As much as you hate the loss and inconvenience, you gradually go on with your life. A year later, you won't even remember that it happened.

But in the spiritual realm, a kind of stealing is going on in many lives that is much more serious. Satan is in the business of ripping off things far more important than an air bag. That is his nature. As Jesus said in John 10:10, "The thief comes only to *steal* and kill and destroy."

Satan obviously doesn't want car parts. Nor does he want your house; he doesn't live in a house. He doesn't need your vehicle, for he has other modes of transportation. He has no interest in your clothes; he's a spirit being. He doesn't care about your investments; what would money mean to him?

> **In the spiritual realm, a kind of stealing is going on in many lives. Satan is in the business of ripping us off.** ~

But he is very interested in stealing *spiritual treasures*—things that have value with God and are of eternal significance. Take, for example, our very purpose for living. Satan loves snatching men and women on the streets of my city and your city—people who have potential—and turning them into glassy-eyed wanderers through life, with no goal from day to day. They lie in bed at night staring at the ceiling, saying, "What's the point? Just to make money? Just to have kids? Why?"

People turn to drugs and alcohol because they don't have a clue as to why they're alive. Others turn to career achievement, or pleasure, or materialism ... something, anything to fill the void. But it doesn't work. God created them to worship and enjoy him forever, but this awareness has been stolen from their consciousness.

Notice the progression in John 10:10. Satan's first move is just petty larceny. Once he manages that, he can move on to actual killing, and from there to mass destruction. "Steal ... kill ... destroy." But it all starts with stealing.

What Happened to "First Love"?

EVEN AMONG THOSE WHO are Christians, the devil has a strategy of theft. For example, as a pastor I have seen over and over the tragic loss of our *"first love"* for Jesus. There was a time in our lives when we loved Jesus so much more than we do today. Our appetite for God's Word was voracious. Our love for God's house was enthusiastic. Our eagerness for spreading the gospel was so strong.... Now, how is it? Yes, we still love the Lord. We still come to church. But what happened to all that energy and passion?

That is the problem Jesus addressed with the Ephesian church in Revelation 2:2–5: "I know your deeds, your hard work and your perseverance.... Yet I hold this against you: You have forsaken your first love. Remember the height from which you have fallen! Repent and do the things you did at first. If you do not repent, I will come to you and remove your lampstand from its place."

Where does "first love" go? Our zeal and our intensity don't evaporate. Satan steals the hot embers of devotion and consecration. We get ripped off.

> **The Bible has no retirement plan. God can keep his people on fire for him, keep them sharp and intense.** ～

Someone might say, "Well, you have to understand that back when I met Christ, I was an energetic teenager. A lot has happened since then. You know, we all mellow out with time." Does anyone really believe that? The Bible says God's plan for us is that we be "transformed into his likeness with *ever-increasing* glory, which comes from the Lord, who is the Spirit" (2 Corinthians 3:18). There is no end to the power he wants to exhibit in our lives. The Bible has no retirement plan. God can keep his people on fire for him, can keep them sharp and intense. We need to be honest and admit what has really happened. There is no point in conning ourselves. We've been ripped off by the master thief.

FADED CALLING

OR HOW ABOUT THAT unique *calling* that rests on every Christian's life—the gifting to serve others in the name of the Lord? Ten years ago there was a stirring inside of you; he gave you a dream about what he wanted to do in your life. Maybe he wanted you to teach children. Maybe he wanted you to sing. Maybe he wanted you to be a prayer warrior, standing in the gap for other people in need. Maybe there was even a pull toward the mission field that was birthed by the Holy Spirit himself.

But then ... you got discouraged. Somebody let you down. Something went sour at your church. You tried once or twice, but somebody criticized you. Soon the dream was gone, and the calling wasn't so real. All the inspiration you had felt was missing.

Sometimes I meet pastors in this condition—a hollow shell of their former selves. All the energy is gone; they're just going through the ministerial motions now.

You would tend to imagine this happening mainly through the many discouragements that ministers face and their over-burdened schedules leading to burnout. Actually, those are only two of Satan's strategies for going after the shepherds who work among God's flock. He has many others as well.

Years ago I met a man who really seemed sincere as he labored tirelessly to build up a congregation of believers in a major city. God's blessing upon his preaching was evident. The church began to flourish.

A few years later, I happened to visit one of his services. Something had obviously changed. The pastor had somehow come to believe that *he* was special. The spotlight was now more on him than on Jesus Christ. The messenger had tragically become bigger than the message.

We chatted afterward, and he pointedly asked me what I sensed about the direction of his church. I encouraged him as best I could, but then added, "Remember, my friend— don't take yourself too seriously. This is about God's Spirit working in the lives of people to draw them nearer to Jesus. We're just called to serve them. Preach the Word faithfully, and then disappear into the background so God will get all the praise."

He didn't seem very excited about my last remarks.

His limited fame seemed to go quickly to his head, and soon the simple sincerity and childlike faith that had characterized his earlier efforts for God were replaced by a slick, affected flamboyance, which is very destructive to the cause of Christ. The man's effective preaching and spiritual fruit quickly disappeared.

Where do you think they all went? Something very precious was stolen along the way.

The devil is always trying to rob us of something God blessed us with. When he succeeds, the spiritual gifts seem to fade, and the material things occupy our attention twenty-four hours a day.

HOME BURGLARIES

CONSIDER THE SUBJECT of marriage. The latest surveys by researcher George Barna show that the divorce rate among churchgoers is just about equal with the population at large. If I were an atheist or an agnostic, I'd say, "Look—how come Jesus can't keep you two together? I thought you said he was so wonderful. . . ."

Why are Christian couples breaking up? Is it because they shouldn't have gotten married in the first place? Or because they came from dysfunctional homes and had bad role models? There is more to it than that. *The thief comes to steal....*

> **The divorce rate among churchgoers is just about equal with the population at large. If I were an atheist, I'd say, "How come Jesus can't keep you two together?"** ～

In fact, Satan fully intends to destroy my marriage to Carol, even though we have served side by side in the ministry for more than twenty-five years. These are the realities of spiritual warfare. Only the power of Christ can keep the two of us together as God has planned and can give us victory over Satan's destructive power. No honest minister of the gospel will deny the fact that the devil has made major assaults on his or her marriage. It's usually not talked about in public, but many tears are shed and prayers offered up to God as sincere servants of the Lord do battle against the demonic forces set on stealing their marriages, credibility, and effectiveness.

What about *our children* and *our grandchildren?* They were dedicated to God at an altar once upon a time. We stood before a minister and said with all sincerity, "O God, this baby belongs to you." But something has happened in the years since then. Now the young man or young woman is not living for God—there's no use pretending that they are.

Let's not close our eyes and make-believe otherwise. Before we can see God do what only he can do, we must spiritually diagnose exactly what is going on around us. Denying reality is not part of true Christian living.

MOST OF ALL: WHERE DID THE FAITH GO?

AT THE CORE OF ALL these losses I have mentioned is the silent theft of the most crucial element in our spiritual walk: our *faith*. What is faith? It is total dependence upon God that becomes supernatural in its working. People with faith develop a second kind of sight. They see more than just the circumstances; they see God, right beside them. Can they prove it? No. But by faith they know he's there nonetheless.

Without faith, says Hebrews 11:6, it is *impossible* to please God. Nothing else counts if faith is missing. There is no other foundation for Christian living, no matter the amount of self-effort or energy spent. Nothing else touches the Father's heart as much as when his children simply trust him wholeheartedly.

I meet people who at one time would pray over anything and everything! Even if they lost their glasses, they would pray to find them—and amazingly, the glasses would show up. Now the same people seem not to believe that God can do much of anything.

Oh, they will still give you the standard confession of faith: "Yes, I have faith in the God who answers prayer." But that vibrant trust and expectation are no more. They aren't saying, "Come on—let's go after this problem in the name of the Lord." They've been robbed.

There is an obscure story at the end of 1 Samuel that speaks to this matter in vivid detail. It is one of the low points on the roller coaster of David's life. The young conqueror of the giant Goliath is now on the run from King Saul. So many threats, so many close calls ... he actually goes to live among the Philistines for a year, for he has run out of places to hide in Israel.

David has his own little militia of six hundred men, plus wives and children. They set up at a place called Ziklag.

When the Philistines decide to go to war against Israel, it puts David in a real crunch. He's a fighter, of course, a warrior, so he lines up with King Achish. But the Philistine generals spot him and say to their king, "What does David think he's doing?"

"Why? What do you mean?"

"The famous son-in-law of King Saul, right? No way is he going on this campaign with us!"

Achish tries to defend David's loyalty but gets nowhere. The generals say, "Look, don't you know that song they sang all over Israel? 'Saul has slain his thousands, and David his tens of thousands'—and some of those tens of thousands were us! He is definitely not going into battle with us."

So David and his militia get sent back home.

When they come close to Ziklag, they start to see smoke on the horizon. They begin a fast trot—and soon discover something dreadful: Every wife, every son, every daughter, every cow and lamb is gone. Someone has made a secret raid, burning down the city and stealing everything.

These husbands and fathers are stunned by the desolation. They are heartbroken ... imagine them thinking of their wives and daughters being captured by some roving band of marauders. *My lovely wife is missing! What is happening to my fourteen-year-old daughter right now?* They can only imagine the unrestrained brutality and heartlessness that have surely occurred. They begin to cry so hard that they run out of tears. They are devastated.

David's family is gone, too. Everything is lost.

At such a moment of human sorrow, other emotions come into play. Anger and resentment boil up. When people cannot deal with the agony of the moment, they often turn on those in authority. They can't bear the pain, so they lash out. David's men begin saying, "What were we doing out there, anyway? Whose bright idea was it to go join the Philistine army? We should have been taking care of our families. Let's stone David for this!"

Then comes this wonderful phrase in 1 Samuel 30:6: "But David found strength in the LORD his God." As the bottom was falling out of his life, he must have gone to a quiet place to pray and gather himself before God.

No matter how low you get, no matter what collapses around you, no matter who rejects you or slanders you—God is able to encourage you. He will help you get through. He will strengthen you deep within your heart in a place no one else can reach.

Having gotten back his poise, his spiritual equilibrium, David goes to the priest for a consultation with God about what he should do. Whenever David was walking in grace, he never just shot from the hip; he first sought the Lord. This is the right thing to do for anyone who is uncertain about the next move.

"Should I chase those who marauded our town, and if I do, will I find them?" he asks. A very wise question. (Think of all the terrible consequences we would avoid if we did what David did here!)

God replies, "Yes, go after them—and you will find them."

So they take off. Along the way, riding across the desert, they come upon a half-conscious Egyptian slave. After they revive him with some cool water, the man admits some vital information. "I was with the Amalekites, and we raided the area. We burned down Ziklag—but then I got sick."

"Well, how would you like to help us now—in exchange for your life?!"

The man doesn't have to think too long about that one. He agrees to guide David and his army, so they set out again.

Soon they come over the brow of a ridge to see the Amalekites below, having a big party. Drunken debauchery is the order of the day.

And in the name of the Lord, David leads his men down the hill against them. For a full twenty-four hours—all night and all the next day—they hit the Amalekites hard.

COMING BACK IN A BIG WAY

THIS WAS THE DAY that David found out that God is more than a creator. He is more than a defender. He is more than a rock or a strong tower, as David calls him in some of the Psalms. God is more than a protector from King Saul when you're hiding.

David learned the powerful truth that *God recovers stolen property*. He has a way of getting back what's been ripped off. What the enemy steals, God alone is able to recover.

And here is the best part of all: David discovered that every wife, every son, every daughter was still alive! Amazing! Not even one lamb was gone.

Listen to how the Bible describes the scene. It says that the Egyptian slave

> ... led David down, and there they were, scattered over the countryside, eating, drinking and reveling because of the great amount of plunder they had taken from the land of the Philistines and from Judah. David fought them from dusk until the evening of the next day, and none of them got away, except four hundred young men who rode off on camels and fled. David recovered everything the Amalekites had taken, including his two wives. Nothing was missing: young or old, boy or girl, plunder or anything else they had taken. David brought everything back. He took all the

flocks and herds, and his men drove them ahead of the other livestock, saying, "This is David's plunder" (1 Samuel 30:16–20).

What a victory! In addition to all the recovered goods, David and his army captured an impressive amount of Amalekite goods, so that when they marched back to Ziklag, there was a *surplus*. Everyone was praising God. They were shouting, "Look what God gave us!" They came back with more than they had lost.

Why am I telling you this obscure Old Testament story? To get to this critical point: David and his men came to a moment when they chose to *get up and go after stolen property*.

The moment must come for you and me when we say, "Wait a minute—am I just going to keep sitting here feeling bad for myself? In the name of the Lord, my daughter, my son, my grandchild is going to be reclaimed. In the name of the Lord, I am *not* going to give up on my calling, my potential in life. Satan, you're going to give back that property! I come against you and resist you in the name of Jesus Christ my Lord."

Remember, we are not wrestling against flesh and blood. We are engaged in spiritual warfare. In your life and mine, here at the beginning of the twenty-first century, somebody has to step up and fight for stolen property with the weapons of faith and prayer. You have to say to the devil, "Enough! I'm going to be like David and go after the stolen goods." Get on your horse!

Our enemy Satan has no feelings of sympathy. If you don't resist, he'll rip you off every week, all year long. That's his diabolical work. But Jesus came that we might have life— abundant life. He can revive your marriage. He can bring fire back into your soul. Your spiritual calling can bloom once again.

You can recover the faith that the devil stole. I am not talking here about the mental assent you give to Bible truths you've heard over and over again. I'm talking about vibrant heart-faith and childlike trust in the risen, supernatural Christ—the kind of faith that changes the way you live, talk, and feel.

> **Here at the beginning of the twenty-first century, somebody has to step up and fight for stolen property with the weapons of faith and prayer.** ～

Satan wants to snatch this more than anything else, for he knows "the righteous will live by faith" (Romans 1:17). He knows that "without faith it is impossible to please God" (Hebrews 11: 6). He knows that real faith is our lifeline to God's grace and power. If he can sever the *faith connection*, he has gained a tremendous victory. He knows that without a living faith, prayer as a force in our lives will be extinguished. We will soon be just mechanically going through the outward forms of religion while experiencing nothing of God's power.

But God can revive fresh faith in our souls if we ask him. He will bring faith alive in us through his Word, as Romans 10:17 declares: "Faith comes by hearing, and hearing by the word of God" (NKJV). Nothing is impossible with God. In fact, you will see God recover more than you lost, just as David did. That is what the Bible promises when it says we can be "more than conquerors through him who loved us" (Romans 8:37). The only question is, Do you and I really believe that our God will recover our stolen property? Or do we think our situation is too far gone for him?

That is why I want to tell you the story of a woman named Amalia, who had one of the most amazing recoveries I have ever seen in my life. However badly you've been plundered and ransacked in your personal life, you probably won't be able to match her traumas. But her experience will show how the power of God can turn it all around.

TWO

~

Amalia's Story

THERE'S SOMEONE WHO CAME to church the last two weeks who really needs to talk to you," Pastor Carlo Boekstaaf, my longtime associate, said one Tuesday afternoon in my office. "If it's all right, I invited her for six o'clock this evening, before the prayer meeting starts. I know a little of her story, and it's incredible. But God has definitely begun to work in her life."

Having lived my whole life in New York City and having pastored for a number of years, I figured I was beyond surprise when it came to stories from the wild side. But I must admit that what I heard that evening took my breath away. A tough-looking but attractive young woman walked into my office. She seemed to send out a strange combination of signals; while she had obviously spent time on the "mean streets," there was also a vulnerability and deep sorrow that showed through the tight-fitting clothes and heavily made-up face.

"Hi, Amalia," I said softly, motioning toward a chair. "I'm Pastor Cymbala. They said you wanted to talk to me."

She nodded slightly and sat down, tugging at her hemline.

"Tell me about yourself, if you will. How I can help you?"

In a low, husky voice she began her amazing, utterly dismal story, and for the next hour, this is essentially what I heard....

I GREW UP IN THE Smith Projects on the Lower East Side.* I was the third of seven children packed into an apartment on the sixteenth floor. My father was a kitchen worker in one of the big hotels; he and my mother had both come from Puerto Rico.

The thing I remember most about our home was its fighting and arguing. We never stopped, it seemed. My father was an alcoholic and made our lives miserable. He had a wooden stick that he would swing like a crazy man at any of us who got in his way or irritated him. I never remember the family sitting down to eat a meal together. I felt very confused growing up; I mainly just tried to stay out of trouble.

My parents would argue a lot about money, since it seemed that my father never gave my mother enough to feed and clothe all us kids. Catholic Charities would help us out from time to time. Even though there wasn't enough money for the necessities, there was definitely money for alcohol. And that only made the fights worse, of course. When I would see him hitting her and pushing her around, I would just run to my room and seethe with anger.

I was about nine years old the first time I stood up to him. In the middle of the yelling, I said to him one night, "If you hurt my mother, I'm going to kill you!" How I would actually do that, I had no idea, of course; I was just upset at him.

I turned to my mother and continued, "Look—you go sleep in my bed to get away from him, and I'll sleep in yours." I thought I was helping the situation. She was really a sweet woman, and I wanted to protect her somehow.

But that was the biggest mistake of my life—because there in my parents' bedroom that night, my father began to

---

*The Smith Projects are among the infamous public-housing high-rises that dot New York; this one sits more or less between Chinatown, Little Italy, and Wall Street in lower Manhattan.

molest me. I couldn't understand what he was doing, or why. I didn't know what to say—after all, I was just a fourth-grader.

Somehow I made it through that night, but emotionally I was a wreck.

Soon the next household fight came along—now what was I going to do? I told myself I should try again to protect my mom; maybe it would be different this time.

It was not. An ugly pattern began to be set. The only words I could find were "No, Pop, I don't want to."

"Well, if you don't," he would say, "I'm gonna beat up your mom." So I was trapped; I felt I had to go along with his wishes.

Before long, it started looking as if he was actually *starting* arguments with my mom in order to get us to switch for the night. Or he would just openly call from his room, "Come in here, Amalia. I want you in here with me." In time, I realized to my horror that I was replacing my own mother in some sick kind of way.

"Don't you ever tell your mom about this!" he would order me. "If you say a word, I'm going to kill her." The whole point of my original idea had been to somehow protect my mother, so I kept my mouth shut.

With all of this going on at home, school was an ordeal for me. I couldn't concentrate. I would be sitting in class and, instead of listening to the teacher, I'd be thinking, *Oh, no—in just another two hours I have to go home again.* I was so confused and depressed. I didn't know what to do. I didn't have a chance to grow up normally, playing with dolls and being a happy little girl. I was numb inside.

One time I got to go to a girlfriend's house after school; her name was Jeanette. To my amazement, there was no fighting in this place. It was peaceful and loving, and the family members actually listened to each other and smiled. My heart just welled up within me. *Oh, I wish I could live in a home like this!*

It was so nice being there that I stayed longer than I should have. When I realized the time and stepped outside, my mother was waiting. "Where have you been?" she asked in a worried tone. "Your father is looking for you. He's really mad!"

The minute I set foot back inside our apartment, he grabbed me and pulled me into his room. I caught such a beating that when I came out again, I was covered with blood. My mother took one look at me and immediately got me into the bathtub, where she lovingly washed the blood from my arms, legs, face, and hair.

It came to the point that when I knew I was going to have to spend the night with my father, I would hide a screwdriver or a knife under the mattress, intending to kill him. *Yes, he's my father,* I would tell myself, *but this is absolutely wrong. He is so evil that he needs to die.*

> **"Yes, he's my father, I would tell myself, *but this is absolutely wrong. He is so evil that he needs to die."*—Amalia** ❧

When it actually came to using my weapon, though ... I could never muster up the courage. Night after night I would go ahead and submit to him. Of all the girls in the family, I guess I was the most shy and naturally compliant. I just couldn't make myself stand up to him.

This went on for years, until I was sixteen and was eagerly plotting—like my sisters and brothers—to get out of the house as soon as possible. For me, the escape route was a boy named Richard, who lived in the building across from us and was in my grade in school. We started hanging out together—much to my father's displeasure. The only way I knew to get Richard to accept me and love me was to give him my body. Wasn't that what all men wanted?

We soon found a minister to marry us and had a big Puerto Rican reception in the community center of our project. I don't recall that my father even attended; he was always hostile to any of my boyfriends, and certainly my new husband.

We couldn't afford a honeymoon; we just moved into a house a distant relative let us use. This was basically the end of schooling for me. Richard had a job at Metropolitan Hospital, and I figured he would take care of me from now on; I didn't really need to finish high school. Any dreams of what I myself might accomplish in life were left to fade away.

It was hard to have a normal sexual relationship with my teenage husband. Intimacy of any kind always got me thinking about my father again. Our marriage never really had a chance.

Meanwhile, Richard introduced me to drugs, starting with pot. At first I didn't like it, but he kept coaxing me along, and soon I realized it could make me forget all my problems at least for a while. Then came LSD and cocaine. I tried shooting up with some heroin, too—but I didn't like it, because it was a downer. I wanted anything I took to lift me up and make me happy.

The marriage lasted little more than a year. I found myself intrigued with other men, and some women as well. Richard and I split up, and he soon headed off to the army. Meanwhile, I got involved with one man after another, trying to stay high twenty-four hours a day. I got odd jobs as necessary—a shoe factory, a donut shop, whatever I could find with my limited education. But any man who would offer me some sweet talk and a place to stay could have me. And if he would provide drugs as well, so much the better.

I wore crazy outfits to catch attention on the street. I got a sales job at a pretty wild boutique called "Superfly" on Forty-Seventh and Broadway, which kept me up on all the latest fashion. Somehow I earned a reputation for dating boxers. One night I was in an underground disco when a world-famous boxing champion came in. His friend dared me to go ask him for a dance, and I did. By the end of the evening, he had invited me to his hotel.

I was with another guy that particular evening, so I turned the champ down. But a few days later, he showed up in my store, drawing a big crowd of fans on the street. He came around not so much to shop as to ask me out to dinner, and I accepted. That night, after we had been seated at our table in a fancy restaurant, he said, "Here's a pill for you. Take it—it'll make you feel good."

"What is it?" I asked.

"Just trust me. You'll like it," he said.

Whatever he hoped it would do to me—it had the opposite effect. Within minutes I was in the ladies' room throwing up! All through the meal I felt awful. Afterward he took me to his hotel room, but there definitely wasn't going to be any "action" that night—I was too sick to my stomach. I finally told him I really needed to just take a taxi home. I asked him for some cash; he was so disgusted with me that he refused. So I had to pay my own fare.

Another guy I dated in those days was actually a pimp, although I didn't realize it. When we were out, he would park his Cadillac along West Forty-Second Street and watch certain prostitutes, leaving me to wonder, *Why? Isn't he interested in me?* I didn't get it: Those were his girls! Only when he tried to put me into his business, too, did I wake up and stop seeing him.

I was now in my mid-twenties, and all this fast living just wasn't as great as I thought it would be, you know? I decided that maybe I should get a steady line of work. So I signed up to take a bartending course. Why, I don't know, because I hated all alcoholics.

When I finished the course and got my certificate, I had trouble finding a job. A lot of places in those days still weren't too open to the idea of women bartenders. When I applied at a place in Midtown called "Metropole," they said no but offered to hire me as a barmaid instead. With my low self-confidence, I said okay, I'd take the job.

Not until I reported for work did I realize what the tiny stage in the center of the bar was for. This was in fact a topless go-go bar. *Now what have I gotten myself into?* I said. But a job was a job—and I definitely needed one, so I went to work.

The men who would come there were friendly to me, and sometimes they'd say things like, "Hey, why don't you go up there, too?"

I would glance at the girls on stage . . . and soon I came to realize that that's where the real money was. Here I was, slaving away for $200 a week plus tips, while they got paid a regular salary plus all the twenty- and fifty-dollar bills that customers would tuck into their costumes when they danced. I was afraid . . . but after a while, as the encouragements kept coming, I got the bar owner to switch my job.

My first time on stage was nerve-wracking. In fact, I probably couldn't have done it if I hadn't gotten high to start with. But as minutes went by and the customers started cheering and throwing money my way, I saw the benefits of this line of work.

. . . And that's what I've been doing for the past four years. I'm not wild about it—but what else am I going to do? Sometimes I think to myself, *How did I ever get into all this? I'm degrading myself. This isn't what I really want to do.* I get depressed and just think there's nothing else. My father already destroyed everything I once dreamed of being. I don't care how far I go now ... but then again, I do care, you know?

My finances really took a hit a couple of years ago as the result of meeting this man named Gilbert at the Metropole. I was attracted to him. We started dating. And then one night, right in the middle of a dance, I passed out—collapsed right there on stage.

I figured I had had too many Black Russian drinks that night. But the real cause was, I was pregnant. I'd been pregnant before, several times, and had always just gotten abortions so I could keep working. But this time it was different. For some reason, I wanted to go ahead and see what having a baby would be like.

"I'd been pregnant before, several times, and had always just gotten abortions. But this time, for some reason, I wanted to see what having a baby would be like."—Amalia ～

Gilbert wasn't interested in sticking around for that, though, and promptly took off. I was devastated. I was left all alone—and unable to work due to the pregnancy. Eventually the electricity was cut off because I wasn't able to pay the bill. I really hit bottom. I decided it would probably be best if I just killed myself, either by slashing my wrists or else jumping off a bridge. I took a blade and started making a line on my wrist. I began to bleed. But I couldn't bring myself to cut deep enough to finish the job.

I had to humble myself and ask my mother if I could move back home. (My dad had left her by this time—the police had been called to restrain him so many times that he finally decided he'd better get out of New York City.) She took me in. I admit that I dumped a lot of anger on her. She asked me one day why I couldn't seem to finish a single sentence without using a four-letter word. We got into a big fight. Underneath, I think I was still mad at her for what happened years before.

In time, I gave birth to a healthy baby boy, whom I named Vinny. This was the most beautiful experience of my life. When I looked at him in my arms, I couldn't help feeling grateful to God.

Now I'm asking myself, how am I going to bring him up? What am I going to teach him? I don't know. . . .

In order to support him, I've had to go back to my old work. My mother takes care of the baby while I'm gone each day.

Once, after another argument with my mother, I went up on the roof of our building. Looking down eighteen stories toward the street below, I thought about the lousy job of mothering I was doing—coming home stoned at three in the morning and making my mother do all the real work. Maybe I should just jump. I began shaking and crying.

Somehow I pulled myself away, went downstairs, and went to sit in the quietness of the Catholic church my mother attends. I kept shaking and crying as I said, "God, why am I going through all this? How come you let my life get so out of control? It's all your fault."

Then my latest lover broke off our relationship, and I was devastated and even more confused. I got really serious about making a definite plan for suicide; I would go on one of the bridges and jump into the East River. I was scared to do it, but I was more scared to go on living.

My sister's husband, whose name is Mickey, has done plenty of partying with me in the past. But now he has become a Christian. So has a friend named Carmen. Suddenly she's not interested in getting high with me; now she keeps talking to me about Jesus.

So a couple of weeks ago, Mickey invited my mother and some of the rest of us to come with him here to your church. "All right, I'll go," I said.

We sat in the balcony. I probably wasn't dressed right for church, but—whatever. Mickey seemed so happy, sitting there with a big smile on his face. I couldn't figure out why.

When you got up there to preach and started to speak about God's love, I listened. I remember you saying something about "Jesus loves you no matter what you've done. He will forgive you and take you past whatever has been done to you in your life."

Pretty soon I was going, *How does he know what I'm going through? Did Mickey tell him about my life, or what?* I couldn't believe that God really understood my crazy life. All kinds of questions came to my mind.

Then, without warning, I started to cry. That's not me—I'm pretty tough. But I couldn't hold back the tears. It was ruining my makeup.

When you asked people to come to the front for prayer, I got up and went with the rest. A woman came along and laid her hand on my shoulder. That kind of spooked me—I'm not used to anything like that. But all she was doing was praying for me.

When I went home, I kept thinking about it all. I was still confused about some things. The next day, one of your pastors called to thank me for coming and to ask me how I was doing. At the end, he said, "Are you ready to trust Christ with your life?"

"Well, I don't think I'm ready for that," I answered. After all, I used to laugh at Christian television programs when I'd get high on LSD. But something was happening inside of me. I decided I should come back to your church and at least find out if I'd been "set up," if you all had some kind of plan to get to me.

So I came back this past Sunday. Your message was about the peace of God.

That same pastor caught me again and asked if I wanted to speak to you. I tried to act cool and said, "Well, why should I?" But inside, I knew I needed to.

> **I looked at this poor woman, so ravaged by sin and Satan, and my heart just broke. She turned to me as if to say, *What next? Am I hopeless?* ~**

If something doesn't change soon, then—Pastor, I'm really messed up. I'll be honest with you—I feel really dirty even being here in your office. I don't know if I should have told you all this, but . . . anyway . . . um, maybe I should stop talking now. . . .

~

THE TEARS HAD BEEN welling up in my eyes as Amalia told her story. A knot in my throat kept me from speaking. We sat there in the silence, both of us thinking deeply. It seemed to me that she had already lived three or four lives—all of them incredibly horrible.

I looked at this poor woman, so ravaged by sin and Satan, and my heart just broke. She turned to me as if to say,

What next? Am I hopeless? Do you want to just kick me out into the street, or what?

I glanced at the clock and realized the prayer meeting would soon be starting. Suddenly, I knew exactly what to do.

"Amalia," I said, "we're going to go into the prayer meeting now and ask God to do a miracle. Jesus Christ can cleanse you and make you into the woman he wants you to be. He brought you here so we could tell you the way out of the mess you're in.

"If you want Christ to save and change you, then come with me right now, and I'll have the whole church pray for you."

She kind of nodded, and we left my office. We walked down the center aisle of the church as people were already praying all around us. We sat down in the front pew.

Later, I took the microphone and announced that God had sent a special visitor to us that night. Soon Amalia was standing in front of the whole congregation. I told them none of her story—only that she had come to a crisis in her life and wanted to receive Christ as Savior. What a wonderful time we had as we prayed together and then worshiped "the Father of compassion and the God of all comfort" (2 Corinthians 1:3)!

Amalia told me later that when she went home that night to her mother, who was baby-sitting young Vinny, she exclaimed, "Mom, guess what I did tonight! I gave my heart to Jesus Christ, and he saved me! He cleansed me! I'm not the same anymore."

Her mother was speechless. Was this troubled daughter of hers finally going to straighten out?

"That night was the best sleep I'd ever had," Amalia reported, "because I felt clean. Jesus did it! No more nightmares, no more drugs, no more self-hatred, no more despair."

Pastor Boekstaaf and his wife, Ingrid, got Amalia into a Monday night discipleship group in their home. We began to see a transformation in her life. She began to look different. Her eyes brightened. Her wardrobe changed. She began to carry herself like a godly young woman instead of what sin had made her become. She found a job as a receptionist in a small law firm, then moved on to a Wall Street insurance company.

Eventually Amalia joined the Brooklyn Tabernacle Choir. A year or two later, when we held a big public concert at Radio City Music Hall, we asked her to share her testimony just before a song my wife, Carol, wrote entitled, "I'm Clean!" After her story, the choir began to sing:

> There is a blood, a cleansing blood that flows
> from Calvary,
> And in this blood, there's a saving power,
> For it washed me white and made me clean. . . .
> Oh, I stand today with my heart so clean;
> Through the blood that Jesus shed I'm truly free.

While the choir sang, we showed a series of slides on the big screen—one picture after another that Amalia had loaned us. The hardness and degradation kept building until finally the frame dissolved slowly into the beautiful woman she had now become, in a sequined white choir gown. It seemed that all six thousand people broke down in tears together.

A few years after her salvation, Amalia met a dental technician in our church, and they fell in love and were married. The Lord gave them a son together, a half brother to Vinny, and the family moved in 1987 to another state. There they continue today to walk with God, worshiping and serving in a church pastored by a good friend of mine.

I have told Amalia's story at some length here to make the point that no matter how thoroughly the devil messes up a life—no matter how early in childhood he starts, and how frightfully he corrupts the human soul—God can take back this stolen property.

If God could change Amalia, then what are you facing that is "too impossible" for him? If God responded to her cry for mercy and grace, what is stopping you from calling on the Lord right now? God invites you to do that, and there is no better time than today. Listen to his loving invitation: "Call upon me in the day of trouble; I *will* deliver you, and you will honor me" (Psalm 50:15).

> No matter how thoroughly the devil messes up a life—no matter how early in childhood he starts—God can take back this stolen property. ～

You can see Jesus Christ prove himself more powerful than the thief who steals. This very moment is crucial, even as you read these words. Face the reality of your spiritual situation, and go after anything God has shown you to be stolen property that Satan has cleverly taken from you. The zeal and love for Christ you once had *can* be recovered. The calling on your life to serve the Lord in a particular ministry can still be fulfilled.

It's not too late, either, for God to reach that son and daughter, no matter where they are or how they seem to be doing. The family that is falling apart right now is not too hard a case for Jesus Christ if you will just stand and begin to ask in faith that he restore what the thief has tried to steal. God will do it, and you will praise him in a new way.

THREE

~

The Question Nobody
Is Asking

Wʜᴇɴ ᴍᴏsᴛ ᴏꜰ ᴜs think about how we are doing spiritually, we think about surface things. We zero in on behavior
patterns, such as have we been gossiping, have we been staying true to our marriage, have we been reading our Bibles,
have we been tithing? We concentrate on outward works
while forgetting that they are simply the fruit of a deeper
spiritual factor.

In the organized church, too many pastors are interested
in attendance alone, which has nothing to do with a church's
health. What matters is not how many people are showing
up, but how active and vibrant their faith is in the God they
serve. You can easily pack a building without pleasing God,
because crowds do not equal spirituality.

When Paul sent Timothy to check up on the new Thessalonian church (where he had been able to spend only three
weeks before getting run out of town), you think he would
have asked first about the church's growth. Did they have a
building of their own yet? How many people were attending
on Sundays? Were the offerings enough to cover the bills?
And what about the individual people: Had they stopped
swearing, drinking, carousing? Going to see bad entertainment? Sleeping around?

Not at all! Instead, in 1 Thessalonians 3, the apostle Paul reveals that his primary concern is for the *faith level* of his precious converts. He wants to take a temperature reading of their spiritual health, and faith is what he is looking for. He doesn't just assume that because they are Christians, they are automatically walking in robust faith. Listen to his words and see how unfamiliar his approach is to our modern ears:

- "We sent Timothy . . . to strengthen and encourage you in *your faith*" (v. 2).
- "When I could stand it no longer, I sent to find out about *your faith*" (v. 5).
- "But Timothy has just now come to us from you and has brought good news about *your faith* and love" (v. 6).
- "Therefore, brothers, in all our distress and persecution we were encouraged about you because of *your faith*" (v. 7).
- "Night and day we pray most earnestly that we may see you again and supply what is lacking in *your faith*" (v. 10).

From top to bottom throughout this chapter, Paul is churned up about one simple word. In fact, this is more than a checkup, an inspection. He has sent Timothy to "strengthen and encourage" the people in their faith—in other words, to do what he could to make the report better.

Timothy has brought back a great summary, as quoted above. Nothing is said about the Thessalonian building, you notice. Nothing about the sound system or the lights or the carpet. Instead, a lot of attention to their faith. But even that isn't enough for Paul. In verse 10 he says he wants to make another trip there himself to "see you again and supply what is lacking in your faith." Faith. Faith. Faith. Faith.

Why this emphasis?

WHAT MOVES THE HEART OF GOD

WHAT PAUL KNEW, but what we seem to have forgotten, is that when people break down in their behavior, backslide into sinful living, or grow cold in the Lord, it is because their faith has broken down first. When someone's temper keeps flaring out of control, that is not the real problem; down underneath is a weakness of faith. So it is with all our departures from right living.

My ministry goal in the Brooklyn Tabernacle is not to fill the building. It is to preach the Word of God in such a way that people's faith in Christ is built up. God doesn't need the beautiful music of a church choir. If he wanted great music, he'd have the angels sing! They never miss a word or sing off-key. But what he is really after is a people who show a strong, personal faith in him.

> **God doesn't need the beautiful music of a church choir. If he wanted great music, he'd have the angels sing!** ~

What do you think it would take to amaze Jesus? After all, through him the world and all humanity were created in the first place. He has forever existed in heaven itself. While on earth, was there anything that impressed him to the point of exclaiming, "That's really something! Wow!" Never in any chapter of the four Gospels was Jesus astounded by anybody's righteousness. After all, he was entirely pure and holy himself. Never was he impressed with anyone's wisdom or education. Never did he say, "Boy, Matthew sure is smart, isn't he? I really picked out a financial genius there."

But he *was* amazed by one thing: people's faith.

When he told the Roman centurion he would go to his house to heal his servant, and the centurion said not to bother but just to speak the word of healing, Jesus "was amazed at him, and turning to the crowd following him, he said, 'I tell you, I have not found such *great faith* even in Israel'" (Luke 7:9). The Jewish listeners probably didn't appreciate being outclassed by this Roman, but that is the way it happened, regardless.

> **Never in the four Gospels was Jesus astounded by anybody's righteousness. Never was he impressed with anyone's education. But he *was* amazed by one thing: people's faith.** ∼

When another "foreigner," a Canaanite woman, came pleading on behalf of her demon-possessed daughter and wouldn't take no for an answer, Jesus exclaimed at last, "Woman, you have *great faith!* Your request is granted" (Matthew 15:28).

On the other hand, when he went back to his hometown of Nazareth, where he had grown up, "he could not do any miracles there, except lay his hands on a few sick people and heal them. And he was amazed at their *lack of faith*" (Mark 6:5–6). You can be sure that no sickness was too extreme, no demon too powerful for the Son of the living God. But on that particular day in Nazareth, his hands were tied by their unbelief. In fact, he laid down this statement as a first principle: "According to your faith will it be done to you" (Matthew 9:29).

We can't twist the story theologically by saying, "Well, maybe it wasn't God's will for him to heal those folks in

Nazareth." The text gives no indication of that. It clearly says the Son of God was limited that day.

Faith alone is the trigger that releases divine power. As Peter wrote, it is "through *faith* [that we] are shielded by God's power" (1 Peter 1:5). Our trying, struggling, or promising won't work—faith is what God is after. Faith is the key to our relationship with him.

MORE THAN TALK

I AM NOT JUST talking about our words. Faith is far more than talk. Sometimes we are not much better than those in Isaiah's time, of whom the Lord said, "These people come near to me with their mouth and honor me with their lips, but their hearts are far from me" (Isaiah 29:13).

> **In our time, the whole notion of faith has been derailed in some quarters into an emphasis on saying certain words, giving a "positive confession" of health, prosperity, or other blessings.** ∾

In our time, the whole notion of faith has been derailed in some quarters into an emphasis on saying certain words, giving a "positive confession," or announcing a superconfident description of health, prosperity, or other blessings. You know, a kind of spiritual mantra. A mental formula of "how the Bible will work for you" is front and center, while the question of a true heart-faith and communion with the living Christ is rarely emphasized.

This formula is not the spirit or message of the New Testament, and it leads to gross absurdities. It actually has

246 ~ FRESH FAITH

dampened the desire for real prayer meetings all across the land. People cannot call out to the Lord for answers to their problems because, according to their teaching, you shouldn't even say you have a problem. To admit that you're sick or in trouble is supposedly bad; you're using your mouth to say something negative, and that is not "living in faith."

If that is true, why did the apostle James declare, "Is any one of you in trouble? He should pray. . . . Is any one of you sick? He should call the elders of the church to pray over him and anoint him with oil in the name of the Lord" (James 5:13–14). How can we truly pray, or ask others to pray, unless we first admit we're facing some kind of real problem? Believers in the New Testament obviously did this.

A minister once told me that when people come to the altar in his church for individual prayer, he has trained them not to say, "I have a cold" or "I have diabetes" or whatever. Instead, they are to say, "I have *the symptoms of* a cold" or "I have *the symptoms of* diabetes." Otherwise, they would not be walking "in faith." (I guess when someone has stopped breathing for two weeks, they have only "the symptoms of death.")

To me, this is little more than a mind game. The faith God wants for us does not shrink from facing the reality of the problem head-on. When Abraham saw the years going by without a child coming into his home, he didn't say, "My wife and I seem to be having some of the symptoms of infertility." Instead, he was totally straightforward: "*Without weakening in his faith*, he faced the fact that his body was as good as dead— since he was about a hundred years old—and that Sarah's womb was also dead. Yet he did not waver through unbelief regarding the promise of God, but *was strengthened in his faith* and gave glory to God, being fully persuaded that God had power to do what he had promised" (Romans 4:19–21).

Isn't that a powerful Scripture? Realism about the problem was not anti-faith in the slightest. In fact, it made Abraham say, "O God, you are the only one who can change this situation. Come and help us, we pray!"

Paul and the other biblical writers were not promoting "fantasy faith" or "hyper-faith." Nothing in 1 Thessalonians 3 even seems to touch on how the Christians in that city talked or what kind of declarations they made. Paul was looking for something far deeper: true faith.

STRUGGLE ON AND ON?

BY CONTRAST, THERE ARE many others going to church today in America whose faith has gone dormant. They would never admit that, of course. They would claim to have faith in God and his Word. They stand in church on Sunday morning and recite the Apostles' Creed.

But if you watch carefully, you will see a hybrid Christianity. You will see people who think that the object of Christianity is to read the Bible every day, try to live a good life as best they can, and thus earn God's approval.

> **Whatever happened to the core truth of the Protestant Reformation, namely, that we do not earn our way with God but rather receive his grace by faith?** ~

Their key word in describing the Christian life is "struggle." They say things such as "I'm *struggling* to obey the Lord and do his will. I'm doing the best I can. We all *struggle*, you know." What this reveals is a Christianity focused on our ability rather than God's.

Whatever happened to the core truth of the Protestant Reformation, namely, that we do not earn our way with God but rather receive his grace by faith? Like the Galatians, we have walked away from something vital. No wonder the apostle Paul sent them a stern letter that said, "Are you so foolish? After beginning with the Spirit, are you now trying to attain your goal by human effort?" (Galatians 3:3).

True Christianity is, rather, to know Jesus and trust in him, to rely on him, to admit that all of our strength comes from him. That kind of faith is not only what pleases God, but is also the only channel through which the power of God flows into our lives so we *can* live victoriously for him. It is what Paul meant when he wrote, "I can do everything *through him [Christ] who gives me strength*" (Philippians 4:13).

My coauthor, Dean Merrill, was at a wedding recently in which the bride and groom's responses to the vows were not just the traditional "I do" but rather "I will, with the help of God." The minister who wrote that ceremony knew that human effort alone might not carry the young couple in today's world "until death do you part." He therefore called on them to implore the help of God in building their marriage.

> **When most people break down in their Christian life, they simply "try harder." Lots of luck! Try harder with what?** ~

This declaration was very much in keeping with what Solomon said at the dedication of the Temple: "May the LORD our God be with us as he was with our fathers; may he never leave us nor forsake us. *May he turn our hearts to him*, to walk in all his ways and to keep the commands, decrees and regulations he gave our fathers" (1 Kings 8:57–58). In that sentence Solomon showed great insight into the fact that God himself must turn our hearts toward him, or else we will stray.

When most people break down in their Christian life, they simply "try harder." Lots of luck! Try harder with what? I've looked inside of me—and stopped looking. There's nothing in there that's good or usable. On the other hand, if I turn the other way and begin "looking unto Jesus, the author and finisher of our faith" (Hebrews 12:2 KJV), I find everything I need.

It does no good to try to control people and get them to behave by giving them only laws and threats about hell. That won't cut it. They won't change. How do the righteous actually live? "By faith."

> **The greatest Christian is not the one who has *achieved* the most but rather the one who has *received* the most.** ∼

When I was growing up, I thought the greatest Christian must be the person who walks around with shoulders thrown back because of tremendous inner strength and power, quoting Scripture and letting everyone know he has arrived. I have since learned that the most mature believer is the one who is bent over, leaning most heavily on the Lord, and admitting his total inability to do anything without Christ. The greatest Christian is not the one who has *achieved* the most but rather the one who has *received* the most. God's grace, love, and mercy flow through him abundantly because he walks in total dependence.

I remember an afternoon many years ago when God made this truth come alive in my heart. While driving down a New Jersey boulevard, I was listening to an elderly minister from Great Britain whose books had blessed me as a young pastor. The radio station was broadcasting a tape of one of his last messages preached at a well-known Bible conference here in America.

The speaker related how, after many years of successful ministry as a teacher and expositor of God's Word, he was forced to stay home due to a lingering illness. This change from his usual busy schedule of speaking, traveling, and writing began to slowly bring on a sense of depression. He struggled to overcome it by fastening his attention on God's Word, but that was difficult due to his ill health.

"Suddenly," he related, "it seemed as if a sewer top had been lifted, and an ugly host of temptations, irritations, and evil thoughts rose up to besiege me." Here he was, a noted Bible teacher and author, fighting against things he had not encountered for many years. His voice broke slightly as he shared his horror at being tempted even to swear, something that had never surfaced in his entire life, even before he became a Christian.

"How can this be?" he cried to the Lord. "After all these years of Christian service and careful study of the Bible, why am I in such a desperate battle?"

As he sought the Lord, God made real to him that his human nature had never really changed. Oh, yes, "if anyone is in Christ, he is a new creation" (2 Corinthians 5:17)—but only because *Christ* is in him as the indwelling Savior and Helper.

I pulled over to the curb that afternoon and wept. One of my heroes in the faith had stunned me with his vulnerability. In the same way, I had to admit that Jim Cymbala the man had never changed—the "old man," the flesh, my sinful nature. Apart from God's grace and power, I too was hopeless.

The truth is that God never works with our "flesh," or old nature—that's how depraved it is. That is why we never stop needing the power of the Holy Spirit during our whole pilgrimage here on earth. We never reach a place where we can live victoriously apart from his daily grace in our lives. Only the Spirit can produce *his* fruit, in and through us, that makes us the people God wants us to be. And God has to show us regularly how needy we are.

The great apostle Paul himself had to learn that seeming contradiction of God's strength coming out of personal weakness. He writes in 2 Corinthians 12:9–10 that the Lord "said to me, 'My grace is sufficient for you, for my power is made perfect in weakness.' Therefore I will boast all the more gladly about my weaknesses, so that Christ's power may rest on me. That is why, for Christ's sake, I delight in weaknesses, in insults, in hardships, in persecutions, in difficulties. For when I am weak, then I am strong."

Paul is not just trying to be overly humble or self-deprecating here. He has found the secret that we were created to be receiving vessels only—not having any strength in ourselves but merely depending on God to fill us hourly with all we need. Paul also knew that God uses trouble and trials of all kinds to heighten that sensitivity so that by faith we can use divine resources.

Don't give up today because you feel weak and overwhelmed—that's the very place where divine power will uphold you if you only believe and call out to the Lord in total dependence. Childlike faith in God is not only what pleases him but is also the secret of our strength and power.

"Help, Lord!"

IF WE ONLY ATTACK the symptoms of unbelief—the various outbreaks of sin in our churches, for example—we will never get to the root cause. That is why legalistic preaching never produces true spirituality. It might seem to do so for the moment, but it cannot last. Christians become strong only by seeing and understanding the grace of God, which is received by faith.

> **If we only attack the symptoms of unbelief—**
> **the various outbreaks of sin—we will never**
> **get to the root cause. Legalistic preaching**
> **never produces true spirituality.** ～

Some years ago I was taking my granddaughter Susie on a walk when a couple of homeless men came walking toward us. Their scruffy appearance made her afraid. In her little mind, she thought she was about to be harmed. She was already holding my hand, but instantly I felt her push her body into mine as she grabbed onto my pant leg. "Papa!" she whispered. Of course, I put my arm around her and said that everything was going to be all right. The men passed us on the sidewalk without incident.

Inside, my heart was brimming. That instantaneous reflex of reaching out for my aid meant that she thought I could handle anything and everything. This was a more precious gift than any sweater she would ever give me for Christmas. She showed that she had a deep faith in me. I would come to her rescue. I would meet her urgent need. I would take care of her.

That is the very thing that delights the heart of God. When we run to him and throw ourselves upon him in believing prayer, he rejoices. He does not want me out on my own, trying to earn merit stars from him. He wants us, rather, to lean into him, walking with him as closely as possible. He is not so much interested in our *doing* as in our *receiving* from him. After all, what can we do or say or conquer without first receiving grace at God's throne to help us in our time of need (Hebrews 4:16)? And all that receiving happens through faith.

Possibly there is a need in your life today to stop all the struggling with your own strength. Let it go, and call out to God in simple faith. Remember that no one has ever been disappointed after putting trust in him. Not one person throughout all of human history has ever depended upon God and found that God let him down. Never! Not once!

Face the obvious fact that the problem or need is far too big for you to handle. Use the very fact of your inadequacy as a springboard to a new, wholehearted trust in God's unfailing promises.

> Therefore let everyone who is godly pray to you
>   while you may be found;
> surely when the mighty waters rise,
>   they will not reach him.
> You are my hiding place;
>   you will protect me from trouble
>   and surround me with songs of deliverance. *Selah*
>
> I will instruct you and teach you in the way you
>   should go;
>   I will counsel you and watch over you.
> Do not be like the horse or the mule,
>   which have no understanding
> but must be controlled by bit and bridle
>   or they will not come to you.
> Many are the woes of the wicked,
>   but the LORD's unfailing love
>   surrounds the man who trusts in him.
>
> Rejoice in the LORD and be glad, you righteous;
>   sing, all you who are upright in heart!
>   (Psalm 32:6–11)

PART 2

~

Getting Past
the Barricades

FOUR

~

Free from a
Hurtful Past

ALL THIS TALK ABOUT faith and God's promises is wonderful, but I've learned that it sometimes falls on deaf ears. Many
people carry scars from days gone by. Life has not been kind
to them. The idea that God might act powerfully on their
behalf strikes them right away as too good to be true. *Maybe
somebody else, but not me. Others can get answers to their prayers,
but not me. Nothing much can change my life now. Too much has
happened, too much has already gone wrong....*

Whenever I meet this kind of person, I always think
about a special secret in the life of Joseph. Even if the person
has heard his story before, I go through it again, telling how
Joseph grew up in what we would call a classic "dysfunctional
family." Most circumstances in his boyhood years were
beyond his control. After all, he was the eleventh son out of
twelve—far down the line.

Joseph's father, Jacob, favors him. For some reason,
something about Joseph strikes a tender cord inside of Jacob.
The boy has come along late in his life and is the firstborn
son of his beloved wife, Rachel.

All this attention turns out to be a curse for Joseph
instead of a blessing. The special coat he receives from his
father makes him a marked young man. The more Jacob does

for him, the more his older brothers hate him. (Siblings have a way of picking up on any little inequity; they notice it right away, and they resent it.)

When Joseph is seventeen years old, he tattles on some of his brothers about something they have done out in the field (see Genesis 37:2). This obviously does not improve the situation. Nobody likes a snitch, especially if he's the father's pet.

On top of all this, God begins to give Joseph dreams about the future. Joseph hasn't asked for this; it just happens. In his youthfulness, he makes the mistake of talking about his dreams—the sheaves of grain that all bow down to his sheaf, and the sun, moon, and stars that bow down to him. With this last one, even his father gets upset. "Get a grip, son!" says Jacob (I'm paraphrasing here). "What are you trying to say— that you're going to run the whole family? That your mother and I and all your brothers are going to bow down to you?"

"I don't know what it means, Dad. I'm just telling you what I saw."

Obviously, this family is not functioning smoothly. For all of us who had rough moments growing up, for all of us who have ever been hurt by a family member, we can understand. Joseph's brothers can see no good in him and never say even one kind word. All of this is taking a toll on Joseph's tender heart.

The Plot Thickens

Joseph is sent one day to see how his brothers are getting along with the sheep in the open fields. After a couple of stops, he finds them near Dothan. As he is coming toward them, they look up and see that colorful coat. "Here comes Daddy's boy," someone snarls. Anger boils up anew.

They are all alone on the wide plains. This is a perfect setting for revenge, and a plan takes shape in a matter of minutes. They will not just ignore him, curse him, or even hit him—this time, *they will kill him.*

Within seconds, they grab him and rip off the hated coat. Joseph, being in his late teens, no doubt puts up a vigorous fight. He struggles, but in vain; clearly outnumbered, he is mauled. Several of them intend to kill him immediately, but Reuben, the oldest, suggests shoving him into a cistern, a deep pit in the ground that retains water. Quickly he goes sliding down into the mud hole, his heart pounding with panic, feeling their hatred up close.

Joseph, a sensitive young man, could actually hear his own brothers talk about murdering him. Imagine the emotional trauma of crouching there, helpless, and listening to this from your own siblings. What a jolt to his young mind and heart!

Meanwhile, his brothers coldly sit down to have lunch (Genesis 37:25).

While they are eating, a trading caravan comes along. Older brother Judah suddenly gets a bright idea. "Look, guys, it will be less messy if, instead of killing him, we just sell him as a slave to these traders. That way we can make a little profit on the deal."

Imagine Joseph being pulled back up out of the pit by his brothers, his clothing a muddy mess, if not already torn off. See his eyes wide with shock as his brothers haggle with the traders: "Good-looking kid, don't you think? How much will you pay for him? Only twelve shekels? Ah, come on—he's worth more than that! Twenty-five at least."

Joseph is numb by now. His own brothers are selling him down the river. The bargaining continues. Finally, they settle on twenty shekels. "Sold!"

He watches the silver pieces being counted. Tears well up in his eyes. This can't really be happening, can it? He won't be going back home. Strangers grab him roughly, treat him like a piece of meat, and thrust him toward their caravan.

(It's a good thing Joseph didn't know what his brothers said when they returned home to Jacob: "Look, Dad!—we found Joseph's coat with all this blood on it. It looks like something terrible has happened." And when their father collapsed in tears of grief, they had the gall to pretend to mourn along with him. "God be with you, Dad. It's hard, we know! He was a wonderful brother…." What a charming group of young men.)

A FUTURE AFTER ALL?

BUT THE BIBLE SAYS in Genesis 39:2 that "the LORD was with Joseph." Somehow, standing there on the block in the Egyptian slave market, Joseph ends up getting purchased by Potiphar, a man of prestige and wealth.

An odd thing begins to happen as the weeks and months go by. His master notices that whatever Joseph touches seems to prosper. Potiphar realizes he can trust his young Hebrew slave and gradually gives him more responsibility. In time, he makes him the general manager of his household.

The only trouble is, Potiphar's wife is apparently having other thoughts about Joseph, who is a little too young and handsome for her to ignore. She begins to make a move on him. He turns her down, but she is not easily dissuaded. She keeps flirting with him, until the day comes when her husband is at work, and nobody else is around—just the two of them. Suddenly she reaches for him, grabbing his coat and insisting that he yield to her desires.

But Joseph does not want to disgrace either God or Potiphar, his master, by giving in to this woman. If he loses God's approval, he will lose everything valuable in life. He quickly wrestles his way out of his coat and runs for the exits.

(Funny how Joseph seems to keep having trouble with coats, isn't it?)

Potiphar's wife, humiliated, immediately begins to scream, "Rape! Rape!" The other servants come rushing in, and by that evening Potiphar has heard her whole twisted version of the story. The next day, Joseph's life comes crashing down for the second time. He is promptly arrested and ends up in the slammer.

What is he thinking now? *How could this happen? Why?!* Yet, even in prison, God is with Joseph. His talent and honesty rise like cream to the top. The warden begins to notice the same characteristics that had originally caught Potiphar's attention. Before long, Joseph is put in charge of his cell block. The place is not as plush as Potiphar's house, to be sure, but at least he has some room to maneuver.

Months go by. Joseph lies awake every night thinking about all that has happened to him. The disaster that day in the open field outside Dothan ... the caravan ride to Egypt ... the hopes that got dashed while working for Potiphar. Now he's a convict. His family has no idea where he is, and most of them don't care. There is no legal statute to appeal to, no court-appointed attorney. Where is God in all of this? How will those dreams ever come true?

Joseph lies awake every night thinking about all that has happened to him. Where is God in all of this? ~

One day a couple of new prisoners show up. Pharaoh has gotten irritated with his baker and his cupbearer, the fellow who had the lucky job of tasting all Pharaoh's wine ahead of time to be sure it wasn't poisoned. (What a great way to make a living!) On the same night both of these prisoners have dreams. The baker's has to do with bakery goods, and the cupbearer's has to do with wine. Both suspect that the dreams have significance, but they can't figure them out.

Joseph then steps in with interpretations from God— one of them a disastrous outcome, the other a happy one. And his predictions come true.

As the cupbearer is dancing out the door to freedom, Joseph says, "Please, friend ... remember me when you get out of this place, okay? I'm doing time for no crime at all. I really don't deserve to be here."

"Sure. Don't worry—you can count on me."

Joseph's heart skips a beat with anticipation. Maybe this will be his big break.

More Darkness

But unbelievably, the cupbearer somehow "forgets." And for two more needless years, Joseph rots in his cell.

And we think we have problems? People have forgotten to appreciate us? How would you like to help somebody and have that person promptly forget that you even exist?

After two years, God steps in to overrule human frailty. This time, a vivid dream comes to Pharaoh himself. In fact, it is a "double feature." First he sees seven fats cows coming out of the Nile followed by seven skinny cows, which swallow the fat ones. Then he sees approximately the same thing again, only with heads of grain.

He calls for Egypt's best magicians and occultists—a specialty in Egyptian culture—and asks for the interpretation of what he has dreamed. They are completely baffled.

Off in one corner, the cupbearer is muttering to himself, "Dreams ... dreams ... oh, now I remember! Pharaoh!

There's a young Hebrew in prison I totally forgot about. He's amazing at dream interpretation."

And that is how Joseph ends up before the imperial throne, saying, "I cannot do it, . . . but God will give Pharaoh the answer he desires" (Genesis 41:16). Joseph proceeds to unfold the divine crop forecast for the next fourteen years. The first seven will be years of blessing and plenty, followed by seven years of famine and shortage. Joseph proposes that with good advance planning, Pharaoh can not only prevent mass starvation but also turn his country into the food supplier for the whole region.

That very day Joseph becomes the second-most powerful man in all of Egypt. Pharaoh installs him immediately with authority to prepare the land for the coming famine.

The court officials are stunned to see this thirty-year-old Hebrew, who has come out of nowhere, being given a royal ring of authority, a gold chain around his neck, a government-issued chariot, and a linen robe. (He finally gets a coat *back*, a very expensive one this time!) Within a matter of hours, people on the street are required to kneel down as his chariot roars past.

The bumper crops begin to come as Joseph predicted, and he is very busy managing the abundance. The whole commodities business of the Middle East looks his way. Senior managers wait outside his office; staff members send him monthly reports. The granaries steadily swell with food for the future.

REVENGE AT LAST?

WHAT WOULD YOU have done with all this power? What would you do if you were Joseph now?

I'll tell you what I might have done. I might have said, "Chariot driver, I have a couple of stops I need to make.

Drive me over to Mrs. Potiphar's house, if you will. I have an old score I need to settle. That woman got me sent to the slammer for a big chunk of my life. It's payback time at last!"

Then I would have headed back to the palace and said to Pharaoh, "Excuse me, but I need to take a week off, if you don't mind. I'm leaving with a couple of army squadrons on a run up to Canaan. I've been waiting to visit my brothers up there for a long, long time." Oooh, how sweet it would have been—vengeance at last!

But not Joseph.

The Bible records that "before the years of famine came, two sons were born to Joseph by Asenath daughter of Potiphera, priest of On. Joseph named his firstborn *Manasseh* and said, 'It is because God has made me *forget* all my trouble and all my father's household'" (Genesis 41:50–51).

> **When Joseph held the first little baby boy in his arms, he said, "I will name this boy Manasseh, because *God has made me forget* all the evil that has been done to me."** ~

When Joseph held the first little baby boy in his arms, he named him Manasseh, which sounds like the Hebrew word for "forget." Names in those days were not chosen just for their pleasing sound; they always had a meaning.

Joseph could have named his son "Crops" or "Gold" or "Success." He did not. Instead, he focused on the really great thing God had done in his life. As Joseph stood there holding the infant and thinking of all that had happened, he singled out the best of God's blessings as he said, "I will name this boy Manasseh, because *God has made me forget* all the evil that has been done to me."

He didn't say he had learned to forget. He didn't say he had enrolled in a seven-step course or gone to a psychiatrist for help. Instead he said, "God *made me forget.*" God can still touch us supernaturally where no therapist can reach.

Neither was Joseph referring to amnesia. The facts were not erased from his memory. But God took the sting out, so there was no bitterness. The temptation of a mean spirit was conquered. God cleansed Joseph's mind of all the residue that would have naturally festered there from the mistreatment he had suffered. What happiness would his position and wealth have brought if he had been an embittered and angry man?

One of the subtle ways Satan hinders us today is by playing unpleasant tape recordings in our minds over and over and over. People lie in bed at night watching old videos on the inner screen of their hearts. They ride in the car looking out the window but seeing nothing; instead, they daydream about the time someone hurt them, took advantage of them, made them suffer. Hurtful words said by others are heard again and again. Horrible, ugly scenes are repeated hour after hour, day after day, year after year.

> **God can make you forget. He does not obliterate the events, but he can deliver you from the paralysis of the past.** ∼

Possibly you are haunted by painful chapters from your past. Some hellish things might have happened to you. Maybe many of them were beyond your control. Whatever the case may be, I want you to know beyond a doubt that God can make you forget. He does not obliterate the events, but he can deliver you from the paralysis of the past.

Earlier I told you about Amalia—but there is more to her story. I remember how, in the early months of her walk with the Lord, I would come onto the platform each Sunday and look up to see her in the same balcony seat. My heart would rejoice as I would notice her with hands raised, praising the Lord and then listening carefully to God's Word.

Every Monday night she was in a home discipleship group. The change in her was dramatic.

Then one Sunday, some months later . . . she wasn't there. I was concerned. Silently I prayed, *O God, watch over Amalia!*

The next Sunday, she was back. I saw her in the lobby. "Hi, Pastor Cymbala," she said with a big smile on her face.

"Hello, Amalia. I missed you last Sunday. Is everything okay?"

"Yes, I was away. You know, you preached something about the love of God and forgiveness—so I took the bus upstate to where my father lives."

Her father? I was stunned to hear him even mentioned.

"Yeah—I had to. He lives with his sister up there now, just sitting in a little trailer out in the countryside drinking beer day after day. I forced myself to go see him after all these years."

"How did it go? What did you say?" I asked. It was the last place I expected her to visit.

"I was very nervous. Finally, after the evening meal, I said, 'Pop, I need to talk to you about something. I want you to be serious. You know, I've been remembering the things that happened back when I was a girl. Those years were really hard, and I have to admit that I hated you—'

"'Oh, don't worry about that,' he butted in. 'That was a long time ago; we don't need to talk about that now.'"

Amalia felt the anger well up inside of her again, but she held her composure. She continued, "Yes, we do, Pop. It really hurt me, and I wanted to kill you so many times. . . . But I came up here this weekend because I want to tell you that I'm a Christian now. I gave my heart to the Lord, and he changed my life.

"You used to be in all of my nightmares. I used to think about you every day. But now, God has made me forget. . . . Pop, what you did was wrong. But I don't hate you anymore. I forgive you! God can change your life and forgive you, too, Pop. I love you! . . ."

The man squirmed in his chair at these words from his grown daughter. He quickly found a way to slide off the topic and lighten up the atmosphere. He never did apologize; it proved to be a one-way conversation, which was a great disappointment to Amalia. The rest of the short visit passed without the hoped-for breakthrough or reconciliation.

But Amalia returned home with a peace in her soul for having done what she knew was right. And the seed of God's Word had been planted.

TIME TO FORGET

THE ONLY REASON AMALIA could do what she did is that God is the God of Manasseh, the God who can make us forget.

If you are paralyzed by your past, if Satan is destroying your gifts and your calling by his incessant replaying of old tapes, you're actually being hit by a double whammy. The original damage in the past is one thing—but now you're letting yourself be hurt and sidetracked again by the memory of what happened.

Think of all the people in the church today who go around with an "edge"—some kind of inner anger or constant irritability. Think of others who seem permanently depressed in spirit because something happened, somewhere, sometime. The ugly memories are like chains around them. We should not be ignorant of Satan's devices, and these ugly memories are one of the main weapons in his arsenal.

God wants to remind you today that the same God who has dealt with every sin and wrong deed you've ever done has the ability to make you forget the negative and hurtful things in your life. The grace of God can overcome their power to haunt you.

> **God's people have found that the most precious fruit often grows in the midst of overwhelming difficulties. Faith grows best on cloudy days.** ᵔ

When a second son came along for Joseph, he chose another significant name. "The second son he named Ephraim and said, 'It is because God has made me *fruitful in the land of my suffering*'" (Genesis 41:52). God taught Joseph that if you put your life in his hands, the worst damage can be turned to good. You can be spiritually fruitful even in the hardest place. In fact, God's people have found that the most precious fruit often grows in the midst of overwhelming difficulties. Faith grows best on cloudy days. Never forget that name of *Ephraim*—"fruitful *in* the land of my suffering."

Every one of us has had painful experiences in life. If you're alive and breathing, somebody sometime has hurt you! In a city such as mine, nasty behavior is everywhere. But you don't have to live in New York City to be hurt. The pain can come from your own family, your in-laws, or other people you genuinely care for.

If you live in that hurt, if those tapes play over and over, you will be paralyzed by them. Every time the Holy Spirit nudges you to step out in faith and do something God wants you to do, this strange bondage to the past will hold you back from God's best for your life.

Do you believe God can set you free, or are you going to keep being a victim of your past? God is the God of Manasseh. He can make you forget. Approach his throne of grace boldly and ask him for that grace to help you right where you need it.

FIVE

~

Can I Trust God
to Lead Me?

IT MAY NOT SEEM obvious at first glance, but the way we make decisions in life tells a lot about the kind of faith we have in Jesus Christ. The very process of decision making often reveals our "faith temperature." What does the Bible teach us about this crucial subject?

Some decisions, of course, are about *moral* issues. For example, shall I steal supplies from my employer? We don't need to pray about this one—just read the Bible. There's no need to say, "Lord, is it okay to have this rotten attitude toward my teenager?" The Book already tells us.

Lying is wrong; you don't have to ask God for special insight into the matter. The same thing is true about hating, about prejudice, about marrying a non-Christian. Young women in love will sometimes say to their pastors, "Oh, he's not a believer now, but the Lord showed me he'll come around after the wedding." That cannot be a word from God, for it violates his truth revealed in Scripture. If something is contrary to the Bible, it's wrong. Don't waste your time by praying about it. God gave us a very long "letter" with all kinds of moral instructions. What we need to do is simply read the letter!

Every moral decision, every supposed manifestation of the Spirit, every sermon by a preacher no matter how clever

or charismatic—each is to be judged by God's Word. That is
what shapes our theology and practice, rather than religious
tradition or secular philosophy.

THE FORGOTTEN STANDARD

I AM REPEATEDLY AMAZED as I travel across the country and
meet Christians who do not use the Bible as their guide and
goal in pursuing spiritual things. Instead, people merely follow the particular spiritual culture into which they were born,
never carefully comparing it to the biblical model. In fact,
many devote themselves to perpetuating their way of doing
things as if they had found it in Scripture itself. Their faith is
stale because they are relying on something other than the
living God who reveals himself to us through the Bible.

To give an analogy: I was born in a Brooklyn hospital to
a Polish mother and a Ukrainian father. I did not ask to have
Eastern European parents; I did not ask to be white. That
was simply the accident of my birth. To make a big thing
about my color or ethnic background is senseless; it just happened to be the way I providentially came into this world.
When people get all puffed up about these things, it is really
an extension of their own ego. If they had been born a different color or raised in a different country, they would be
boasting about that instead.

The same is true about the circumstances of our spiritual
birth. The church or denomination where we started out just
happened to be where we found ourselves at the time of
receiving God's salvation. And as in our natural birth, our initial surroundings gave far-reaching shape to our understanding of things. Our first church atmosphere, with its pastors
and teachers, automatically set the definitions for many key
words such as *prayer, worship, church, evangelism, God's power,*

faith, even *Christian* itself. We didn't first learn those concepts so much from the Scripture as from what we saw around us at church. We unconsciously absorbed a Presbyterian or Baptist or Nazarene or Pentecostal understanding of those important words.

Today those impressions still leap to the forefront of our minds every time we hear the words—whether they are what God intended or not. Thus, instead of coming to the Scriptures like a child, saying, "God, teach me," we go looking for ammunition to back up what we've already embraced. Too often our main goal is to perpetuate the traditions handed down from our elders. We're not really that open to change and growth.

The little church where my parents took me as a boy had some very good qualities to it—but it was also an all-white, mostly Eastern European group in the middle of Bedford-Stuyvesant, one of the best-known black neighborhoods in America! And the church members clearly wanted the church to stay the way it was. They did not seem at all interested in welcoming people who were "different."

> **When we stand before God, we will not be asked, "Were you a good evangelical?" or "Were you a good charismatic?" What will really matter is whether we honestly let God's Word shape our spiritual thinking.** ～

Even though I learned many truths from the Bible there, should I now spend my life trying to replicate that tradition just because it's the place where I started out learning about Jesus? When I stand before God, I will not be asked, "Were you a good evangelical?" or "Were you a good charismatic?" As a matter of fact, God doesn't recognize our divisions. His calling is for us to be Christlike rather than a good member of some man-made denomination.

What will really matter is whether we honestly search God's Word and let it shape our spiritual thinking and values. This is one of the great battles in the Christian life: to approach the Bible without presuppositions, letting it shape us instead of vice versa.

I love what the great John Wesley, catalyst of the Methodist awakening, said in the 1700s: "Would to God that all party names, and unscriptural phrases and forms which have divided the Christian world, were forgot.... I should rejoice ... if the very name [Methodist] might never be mentioned more, but be buried in eternal oblivion."[1] A century later, the equally great Charles Spurgeon, prince of Baptist preachers, said from the pulpit, "I say of the Baptist name, let it perish, but let Christ's name last for ever. I look forward with pleasure to the day when there will not be a Baptist living."[2]

This kind of talk may burst a few bubbles, but here is the truth: Neither your personal background nor mine is the norm! What the Bible teaches is what we should pursue. Whenever any of us encounter something new or different, we should not ask, "Am I used to that when I go to church?" but rather "Do I find this in the Bible?"

WHAT ABOUT THE GRAY AREAS?

SOME DECISIONS IN LIFE are not about moral issues per se, but they simply need *sanctified reasoning*.

For example, the Bible doesn't explicitly say that you should show up for work on time every day. But if you understand God's principles of sowing and reaping, you will be punctual. Also, you are to do your work as if serving the Lord himself.

The Bible doesn't tell you how to respond to your spouse in every situation. But if your husband or wife is upset and discouraged, it's wise for you to be comforting and supportive.

Now, with this foundation, what about the third kind of decision making—those important situations in which we don't have a right-or-wrong element and no Bible passage directly applies? There are many forks in the road where we have to make a choice. What are we to do if we want God's will in everything?

Many people today are making these kinds of decisions without a passing thought of seeking God. They think that as long as they don't lie, kill, steal, or commit adultery, they are in the will of God. They proceed to make other important life decisions based on common sense—or sometimes even less than that. Just "I felt like it!" "My friends are doing it." "My world calls this 'success.'"

When we leave God out of these decisions, we are not really walking in faith. Instead of tapping into God's great resources of wisdom, we rely on mere human ideas.

Isn't it silly to think that the God who gave his own Son for us doesn't also care about the details of our lives?

A faith-filled believer will pray earnestly until he finds God's will for things such as

- Changing jobs
- Dealing with a difficult child
- Choosing a school for your children
- Moving. When you get a job offer in another state, is it just a matter of making more money? Seeing a glossy brochure with lots of green grass? Climbing the ladder of your profession or trade?
- Which believer to marry. (Hint: You're probably not going to find his or her name in the Bible!)

- Buying a home. God has a plan for our lives as detailed as for any person in Scripture. He wants to protect us from being in the wrong place at the wrong time.
- Joining a ministry in the church, such as the choir, the youth ministry, or Christian education.

The all-knowing Creator of the universe *wants* to show us the way in these matters. He has a plan for where we belong and where we don't belong. Therefore we need to seek his direction.

AN INQUIRING HEART—FOR GOD

ONE OF THE BEST Bible examples of a godly person seeking to do God's will is David when he faced a major question at Keilah. The little-known story appears in 1 Samuel 23, during the time David was on the run from King Saul. David had enough trouble of his own trying to protect his modest band of men from the Israelite army—but then word came that this particular town was being threatened by the Philistines.

He began by asking God, "Shall I go and attack these Philistines?" (v. 2). Notice that he didn't assume that just because he had once been anointed by God's prophet, he could win at any time in any place. He knew how important it was to be led by the Lord in every new situation. Not every opportunity for battle meant that he must engage in it.

This is true for us today. Not every Christian cause, not every plea for money—no matter how well intentioned— automatically means that we should respond.

David also knew that if God did lead him into a situation, God's provision would follow. Wherever God leads us, there is an umbrella of protection and supply that stays over our heads. Under that umbrella are the divine resources of wisdom, grace, finance, and all the other things we need to do what God has asked.

That does not mean there won't be problems and difficulties. But wherever the Lord leads, he must then by necessity help us.

However, the umbrella goes only where God leads us to go. If we choose to turn left when God wants us to go right, we cannot expect God to support the plans we made on our own.

Christians today are demonstrating this truth all the time. They are trying to make the umbrella follow them as they make unilateral decisions in life, and it doesn't work. Just because you have declared yourself to be a Christian doesn't mean that God is obligated to supply your needs as you do your own thing.

> **If we choose to turn left when God wants us to go right, we cannot expect God to support the plans we made on our own.** ∽

The Brooklyn Tabernacle Choir has recorded a song based on Psalm 119:133 that says, "Order my steps in Your Word, dear Lord; lead me, guide me every day.... / Humbly I ask Thee, teach me Your will; while You are working, help me be still.... / Order my steps in Your Word." A minister of music in one church recently told my wife that while the song was a blessing to him personally, his senior pastor had asked him not to use it because "when you have the word of faith, you don't need to ask God to order your steps." In other words, you are so spiritually macho that you can do whatever you choose, and God must go along with you!

This is not in line with the Bible. You cannot tell God what to do and where to go. That is pure spiritual arrogance. How easily we forget that we are not the center of the universe; God is. We must never lose track of the fact that "the world and its desires pass away, but the man *who does the will of God* lives forever" (1 John 2:17).

David was "a man after God's own heart" (see 1 Samuel 13:14; Acts 13:22) because he humbly asked God's direction for his daily life. He knew that if he didn't have the umbrella of God's supply, he had no business tangling with the Philistines outside Keilah. He asked for God's plan, and in this case God said yes—go ahead.

Even then, David came back a second time: "God, my men are not very thrilled about this idea. They say we have enough worries of our own with King Saul chasing us—*so why am I now wanting to take on the Philistines? Should I really do this? Have I truly heard from you?*"

The answer again was yes. "Go down to Keilah, for I am going to give the Philistines into your hand" (1 Samuel 23:4).

This incident reminds us that one of the first rules of spiritual guidance is to assume that we could be wrong. David was humble enough to say to himself, "Possibly I misheard God. I'd better check again." He didn't pretend that he was in constant twenty-four-hour communication with God and above all chance of making a mistake.

> **One of the first rules of spiritual guidance is to assume that we could be wrong.** ∾

I remember reading some years ago about a powerful television evangelist who was asked by a reporter from one of the national newsmagazines, "What if you felt God told you to do something, and your whole board of trustees said no?" The preacher quickly boasted, "I'd fire the whole board." It sounded like bold faith, but what he was really saying is that he could never be wrong. Before too long, that man's ministry came crashing down in scandal.

It is not a sign of weakness to look for confirmation. It is often a good idea, in fact, to get a prayer partner, or call a pastor, who can validate your sense of God's will as you inquire of the Lord.

When I first heard about a four-thousand-seat theater in downtown Brooklyn that was for sale and might possibly solve our church's space problems, I got excited. Even though the building was in terrible shape and would require millions of dollars for restoration, I could see the potential for this to become the new Brooklyn Tabernacle.

Very quickly, however, I said to my associate pastors, "You go see it for yourselves and then pray. Unless all six of you feel that God is leading us this way, we won't even present it to the congregation." Would God hide such an important matter from my fellow leaders and reveal it only to me? I don't think so. I also brought other ministers whom I respect, such as David Wilkerson, to see the building. I wanted confirmation that God was leading us this way.

In time, we felt an agreement in our spirits that this step was right. Although the price tag was huge, we moved ahead in faith and confidence.

The story of Keilah shows us that David was firmly convinced in his heart and mind of what he wrote in Psalm 25:9. "He guides the humble in what is right and teaches them his way." In another place, David wrote, "For this God is our God for ever and ever; he will be our guide even to the end" (Psalm 48:14). David triumphed over the Philistines and delivered Keilah, and all of this happened because he inquired of the Lord. David lived by faith, not by sight.

MORE DECISIONS

BUT THEN KING SAUL, who was living in the worst kind of spiritual illusion, heard that David was suddenly vulnerable to capture because he had come inside a walled city instead of staying out in rugged terrain. That put a big smile on Saul's face. He was now so deceived in his heart that he even gave the Lord credit for these events! "God has handed him over to me," he said (1 Samuel 23:7).

God had obviously done no such thing. People who are not prayerful and who do not yield to God's will can come to all sorts of wrong conclusions. God was protecting David from Saul, and Saul didn't even have a clue! He immediately called up his army to go capture his nemesis. But David was still inquiring of the Lord. "God, I've heard that Saul is coming, but I'm not sure. Is he really coming?"

Answer: *Yes.*

The next inquiry was "Will these people here in Keilah protect me, since I just saved their necks? Or will they throw me over the wall to Saul?"

Answer: *They'll turn you over.*

So David gathered up his men, and they quickly left town.

Isn't it wonderful that God can even show us who our real friends are and who should not be trusted? He can warn us about what other people are doing behind our backs.

Thus Saul failed to catch David. In other words, success is not by might or power or computers or IQ, but by God's Spirit (Zechariah 4:6). King Saul had better weapons and a far bigger army. But David had the leading of the Holy Spirit. He was in touch with the King of kings.

DOES GOD STILL LEAD?

IN TODAY'S CHURCH, we have a serious shortage of faith in a living, speaking God. Pastors and laity alike do not seem to believe that God really leads and directs. Research by George Barna shows that fewer than 10 percent of churchgoing Christians make important life decisions based on God's Word and seeking his will! In other words, more than 90 percent decide on the basis of their own intelligence, peer opinion, whim, or fancy. They marry people and move to new cities without so much as a ten-minute prayer. Yet every Sunday they sit in church pews singing songs like "Where he leads me, I will follow."

> **Too many church leaders, having been turned off by fanaticism in certain quarters, have stopped believing in an active Holy Spirit at all. The baby has been thrown out with the bathwater.** ❧

Too many church leaders, having been turned off by overblown claims and fanaticism in certain quarters, have stopped believing in an active Holy Spirit at all. The baby has been thrown out with the bathwater. Mention of the Holy Spirit's leading people is scoffed at. If someone says the same thing that Paul said in Acts 16—namely, that the Spirit wanted him to go to one town rather than another—that person is viewed as eccentric. We are strong in presenting our doctrinal positions as correct, but weak in stressing the daily need of being led by God's Spirit.

I want to affirm that God is not dead; he really does communicate today. He's interested in every part of your life, your home, your finances, every kind of decision—and more than just the moral issues. His eye is always on you. He wants to lead you. But you have to believe that he will indeed speak to you when you wait before him in believing prayer, with a yielded heart to do his will.

I fear that unbiblical excesses done supposedly under the inspiration of the Holy Spirit have frightened people off who should really know better. Pastors today operate church services that are so regimented, there is no place for any spontaneous leading of the Holy Spirit. Events are programmed right down to the minute. Song selections are cast in stone for days in advance. There is no allowance for God to lead anyone in another direction—certainly not during the meeting itself. We aim, rather, at being "smooth" and "slick." What we value most are great organization and "having our act together."

As I've said more than once, if God led the Israelites through forty years in the desert, surely he can lead me through a Sunday service. But God has had to teach me over and over about my own need for sensitivity in this matter.

> **If God led the Israelites through forty years in the desert, surely he can lead me through a Sunday service.** ~

Two summers ago in a Sunday afternoon service, our choir was about to sing. As Carol walked past me toward the podium, I asked what songs she had chosen, knowing that she often changes her mind at the last minute as she senses God's direction in a particular meeting. She named two songs. I then took a seat on the front pew in order to better enjoy the choir's ministry.

The first song was about God's great redeeming love, featuring a solo by Calvin Hunt, a young man who has recorded with our choir and now travels in full-time ministry for the Lord. I closed my eyes and let the words sink in.

Somewhere along about the second verse, I sensed the Holy Spirit saying to me, *Go and preach the gospel—right now. Go up and tell them of God's love.*

At first I thought I was maybe just getting a little emotional about an inspirational song. Or maybe Satan was tempting me into some kind of weird behavior.

Then I thought, *My goodness, we haven't even taken the offering yet! This isn't the time to preach and give an invitation; that comes at the end of a meeting, not this early.* (As if God doesn't know what needs to be done in his own church!)

But the impression would not go away. In another thirty seconds I felt that if I did not respond, I would be grieving the Holy Spirit. I silently prayed, *God, I don't want to fail you by not doing your will. I'm going up there at the end of this song. Somehow stop me if I'm wrong.* I felt I had to obey, but I was still nervous about interrupting the meeting.

As the final chord was resolving, I quickly moved up the steps and onto the platform. Carol glanced at me with a quizzical look on her face. I took the microphone from the soloist and said, "Before you go, Calvin, tell the people briefly what God has done in your life."

He went into his story of terrible addiction to crack cocaine and how God had set him free.* Oddly enough, he didn't stumble for words. It was as if he had been prepared for the moment. He gave a powerful statement of the Lord's redemptive power.

---

*For a fuller account of Calvin Hunt's testimony, see chapter 9.

When he finished, I spoke for about ten minutes about the gospel and proceeded to give an invitation. The organist played softly; the choir stayed quietly in place through all this, just waiting to see what would happen next. From all over the auditorium, dozens of people began coming forward to the altar. The sound of weeping could be heard as people were moved upon by the Spirit and now turned to Christ. We prayed with them all, and it was a blessed time of spiritual harvest. Conviction seemed deep and real as the Holy Spirit blessed the simple gospel message.

Eventually I told them to return to their seats, saying, "Well, we haven't taken the offering yet. Let's do that as the choir sings another song." The meeting continued on to its conclusion.

Sometime that following week, the phone rang in our church offices and was answered by Susan, my daughter, who at that time was working in the music department. A man's voice said, "I would like to get the sheet music for such-and-such a song. You sing it in your church, and I want to pass it along to my church here in Texas."

"Well," Susan replied, "I'm very sorry, but we don't have written music for most of the songs we sing. We just do them by memory. Only if we record a song does the publisher then create a written score to sell."

The man was clearly disappointed. "I just heard you all sing it this past Sunday when I was there, and I really want to get that song somehow."

Susan tried to think of something else to say. "Well, I'll mention it to my mother, and maybe she'll decide to put the song on the choir's next album," she said.

There was silence on the line. "Did you say 'your mother'?" the man asked. "Excuse me, but who are you?"

"Susan Pettrey—I'm one of Pastor and Carol Cymbala's married daughters. I work here at the church."

At that, the man began to get a little emotional. "Would you please tell your dad something for me?"

"Yes."

"My family and I were just on a visit to New York for the weekend. We have a nineteen-year-old son who has totally hardened to the things of the Lord. We brought him up to be a Christian, but he has drifted away in the opposite direction. We've been so concerned about him.

"On this trip, we invited him to come with us. I promised him we would take some time to enjoy the city together, but our real plan was to bring him on Sunday to your church in hopes that God would somehow reach him.

"We enjoyed seeing the city all day Saturday. On Sunday, as we took a cab to your church for the afternoon service, I checked our airline tickets once again and realized I'd made a terrible mistake. We wouldn't be able to stay for the whole thing—or else we'd miss our flight home.

"I was kicking myself for not planning better. My son probably wasn't going to hear the message, which was the point of the whole visit.

"But then early in the service—out of nowhere—your dad walked up onto the platform and started to share the gospel. Suddenly my son was standing up with the others and heading for the altar! He just broke down before the Lord, calling out to God for forgiveness. When he came back to the seat, he was a different person.

"We had to leave a few minutes after that for the airport. . . . Just tell your dad that, all the way back to Texas, we could hardly take our eyes off our son in the next seat. This has been the most incredible transformation that you could ever imagine. My wife and I are overjoyed for the great thing God has done."

God changed the whole meeting that afternoon just for the sake of one nineteen-year-old. He knew the need in his life and the timing of flights and knew that something out of the ordinary schedule should occur. God knows things we have no way of knowing. When we don't inquire of the Lord and ask in faith for guidance, we totally miss what he wants to accomplish.

LET GOD GUIDE

WHAT ABOUT THE SITUATIONS you are facing right now? Are there forks in the road that call for a decision to turn one way or the other? Remember that many seemingly unimportant decisions have consequences far beyond what we could ever imagine. Just think how limited we humans are in really knowing the right thing to do. We "see through a glass, darkly" today (1 Corinthians 13:12 KJV), not understanding so many complexities, so many other things hidden from our view. We know nothing of what tomorrow will bring; we're only guessing about the future and what it will hold. Yet these decisions face us again and again.

But our God knows all things and has all power. Even "the king's heart is in the hand of the LORD" (Proverbs 21:1). God knows exactly the plans he has for you, "plans to prosper you and not to harm you, plans to give you a hope and a future" (Jeremiah 29:11). And his desire as a Father is to share these blessed plans with you.

For that to happen will mean yielding to his will for our lives—that's for sure. Then we will be able to hear his voice and sense his direction. It will also mean learning to wait and listen in his presence. But what blessings will be ours as we join the happy company of those who "will neither hunger nor thirst, nor will the desert heat or the sun beat upon them. He who has compassion on them will guide them and lead them beside springs of water" (Isaiah 49:10).

SIX

〜

The High Cost
of Cleverness

TRUSTING GOD COMPLETELY to lead and guide us sounds good in a book such as this, but let's be honest: It can also be a bit unnerving. Our friends may look sideways at us and think (or sometimes say) that we are going overboard with all this "spiritual" stuff. Seeking direction from God goes against the modern mind's reliance on self. Our culture teaches us to take charge of our lives and call our own shots.

In sharp contrast to the open, inquiring heart of David, the Bible tells about another king less than a hundred years later who had every chance to be as great as David—until he decided to do what seemed smart and clever to his own mind instead of what God had said. David, as you will recall, was followed by his son Solomon, who drifted from God. God had warned Solomon not to take a large number of wives, especially foreign women who would draw him away from the worship of the true God. The mixture with their gods proved to be fatal, because Solomon ended up building temples for his wives' gods right in Jerusalem, the place God had chosen for his presence to dwell.

Near the end of his life, Solomon took notice of a young man with some leadership ability named Jeroboam and, in fact, promoted him in the civil service. One day Jeroboam was innocently walking in a field when a prophet came to him out of the blue, took off his outer garment—and ripped it into twelve pieces! How strange! Giving ten pieces to Jeroboam, the prophet said that God would soon judge Solomon for what he had done and would tear the nation apart—and amazingly, Jeroboam would wind up being king of ten of the twelve tribes. This was followed by some unusual promises from the Lord:

> As for you, I will take you, and you will rule over all that your heart desires; you will be king over Israel. If you do whatever I command you and walk in my ways and do what is right in my eyes by keeping my statutes and commands, as David my servant did, I will be with you. *I will build you a dynasty as enduring as the one I built for David and will give Israel to you* (1 Kings 11:37–38).

Jeroboam must have stood there with his mouth hanging wide open. Why him? He had no claim to anything royal. But out of nowhere, he was selected as God's sovereign choice. Talk about a tremendous "break" at the beginning of your career!

Consider the greatness of these promises to this young man. They are as grand as what the mighty David had received: Control of a nation ... an ongoing dynasty ... the promise of God's abiding presence. Jeroboam, we would say, was set for life.

A STINGING REBUKE

NOW FAST-FORWARD the videotape many years to 1 Kings 14. Jeroboam has indeed risen to the throne of the Northern Kingdom (the ten tribes), just as Ahijah the prophet said that day in the field. But by now, Jeroboam has totally drifted away from God. In this chapter we see the powerful king and his wife with a family crisis: Their little boy has fallen seriously ill, and the worried parents are fearing for his life.

Jeroboam says to his wife, "You know, maybe that old prophet could help. He surely was in touch with God the time he prophesied over me. Why don't you go find him and ask him to pray for our son?"

But Jeroboam knows that his lifestyle has been far from godly. His reputation with Ahijah is at its low point. If his wife shows up to visit, the prophet is likely to scold her or give a bad word of some kind. So he tells her to wear a disguise.

Actually, this wasn't necessary, because by this time, Ahijah is so old that he has gone blind. He can't see whether Mrs. Jeroboam looks like a queen or a scrubwoman. On the other hand, Ahijah is still in close communion with God—and you can't disguise yourself from him. You can act like an Academy Award winner, but God will see through the whole thing in an instant. The minute the woman knocks at the prophet's front door, Ahijah calls out, "Hello, Mrs. Jeroboam-dressed-like-somebody-else—come on in!"

Perhaps she nervously chuckled or tried to make small talk with the old prophet. If she did, it didn't last long. Very quickly the conversation got serious. The woman sat there stunned as Ahijah launched into a shocking prophecy:

> I have been sent to you with bad news. Go, tell Jeroboam that this is what the LORD, the God of Israel, says: "I raised you up from among the people and made you a leader over my people Israel. I tore the kingdom away from the house of David and gave it to you, but you have not been like my servant David, who kept my commands and followed me with all his heart, doing only what was right in my eyes. You have done more evil than all who lived before you. You have made for

yourself other gods, idols made of metal; you have provoked me to anger and thrust me behind your back...."

As for you, go back home. When you set foot in
your city, the boy will die. All Israel will mourn for him
and bury him. He is the only one belonging to Jeroboam who will be buried, because he is the only one
in the house of Jeroboam in whom the LORD, the God
of Israel, has found anything good.

The LORD will raise up for himself a king over
Israel who will cut off the family of Jeroboam. This is
the day! What? Yes, even now. And the LORD will
strike Israel, so that it will be like a reed swaying in the
water. He will uproot Israel from this good land that
he gave to their forefathers and scatter them beyond
the River, because they provoked the LORD to anger
by making Asherah poles. And he will give Israel up
because of the sins Jeroboam has committed and has
caused Israel to commit (1 Kings 14:6–9, 12–16).

What a stinging rebuke! By the time the old man finished, Mrs. Jeroboam must have been sobbing. Within hours
she was going to lose her son, and soon afterward her husband's kingship would be history. In fact, the whole nation
would collapse.

We read this kind of story, and we can't help wondering:
How in the world did this happen! What do you have to do
to go from being chosen by God as the next king ... to the
same prophet now telling you that you're cooked meat—
headed for the garbage pail of history, with no hope of sal-
vaging your kingdom or even your life?

God was saying, *Jeroboam, it's all over. You have provoked
my anger. You are now rejected as king. In fact, I'm going to pun-
ish your whole nation for what you got them to go along with.*

My goodness, what did this man do!

The Perils of Getting "Smart"

The answer lies in just about eight little verses back in 1 Kings 12, between the first and last meetings with Ahijah. Jeroboam was king, and one day he got to thinking about his strategic position. Yes, he was firmly on the throne—but because of the divided kingdom, God's temple was not in his territory. It was down south in Jerusalem, the capital of the Southern Kingdom. Every holy day (two or three times a year) when his people went to worship, they would have to go down to his rival's turf. God had made himself clear that Israelites could not worship and sacrifice their animals just anywhere and everywhere; they had to go to his one chosen location in Jerusalem. Hmmm . . .

The Bible says:

> Jeroboam thought to himself, "The kingdom will now likely revert to the house of David. If these people go up to offer sacrifices at the temple of the LORD in Jerusalem, they will again give their allegiance to their lord, Rehoboam king of Judah. They will kill me and return to King Rehoboam."
>
> After seeking advice, the king made two golden calves. He said to the people, "It is too much for you to go up to Jerusalem. Here are your gods, O Israel, who brought you up out of Egypt." One he set up in Bethel, and the other in Dan. And this thing became a sin; the people went even as far as Dan to worship the one there (1 Kings 12:26–30).

What poignant tragedy lurks in those four words *Jeroboam thought to himself* (v. 26). His whole downfall began with an attempt at cleverness. He started to strategize. Instead of simply trusting the promises God had given him, he tried to "help things out." Otherwise, it seemed, his power would suffer. That's how this tragedy began: Jeroboam thought to himself and forgot about God and his word of promise.

It is horrible when we use human cleverness instead of faith in God. The old gospel song said it well when it advised us just to "trust and obey, for there's no other way to be happy in Jesus."

What Jeroboam ended up doing here was starting his own religion—an insidious mixture of the true and the false. The following verses tell how he "appointed priests from all sorts of people, even though they were not Levites. He instituted a festival on the fifteenth day of the eighth month, like the festival held in Judah" (vv. 31–32). You didn't have to be called by God to be a leader in the Jeroboam religion; you only had to pay money, and you were installed.

God had clearly said in the Second Commandment never to make anything physical as a representation of himself, but Jeroboam now set up two golden calves to anchor the people's devotion. God, in fact, is spirit, and those who want to worship him "must worship in spirit and in truth," as Jesus said (John 4:24). Anything material would never do justice to the greatness of the invisible God, and even if you make something out of pure gold, it can still be wrong to God. He is not impressed with physical appearance or glitter; instead, he looks at the heart. I once heard Anne Graham Lotz say that gold must not mean much to God, for he uses it as paving material in heaven! The saints will walk all over it throughout eternity.

God put this story of Jeroboam in the Bible as a flashing red light to us. It fairly shouts that when unbelief gets into a leader, or anyone else for that matter, it leads to the first bad decision, which leads to the second, which leads to the third, until the momentum builds out of control. God had said to this man out in the field, "If you do whatever I command you and walk in my ways and do what is right in my eyes . . . , I will be with you." But Jeroboam opted to make up his own game plan, and at the end God thundered against him with words so devastating that they make us shudder to read them.

What Jeroboam did—when you think about it—made excellent logic. Any king would want to carefully monitor the movement of his people, right? Trusting God to build the kingdom as he had promised probably seemed too simple. Jeroboam decided to improvise to secure his position of leadership. In fact, unbelief often clothes itself in "being smart." We use cleverness to cover the tracks of our lack of faith. But who can be wiser than God?

> **Unbelief often clothes itself in "being smart." We use cleverness to cover the tracks of our lack of faith.** ~

As a pastor I sometimes see men in the congregation who are working two or three jobs in order to get ahead financially. They are going to expand their business, make money for a rainy day, or buy a rental property here or a little side business there, and their assets will grow even faster. Yes, it means missing church on Sunday and missing time with their kids, but they use the old saying "Mama didn't raise no fool, you know." In a little while, they tell me, their schedule will lighten up so they can give more attention to the Word and prayer, their service for the Lord, their marriage, their child-raising responsibility . . . soon, but not yet. At the moment, they have to virtually kill themselves for the almighty dollar. These men are sure they can improve on

God's formula: "Seek first [God's] kingdom and his righteousness, and all these things will be given to you as well" (Matthew 6:33).

Jeroboam must have felt *so* smart putting those idolatrous calves in Dan and Bethel—two towns in *his* territory. He told his people he was saving them that long, arduous trip down to Jerusalem. But his new religion was no salvation. It was a dangerous perversion of the true worship of God.

> **In the church today, we are still busy inventing new forms of religion as Jeroboam did. The new models are just as logical and "user-friendly."** ∾

In the church today, we are still busy inventing new forms of religion as Jeroboam did. The new models are just as logical and "user-friendly." We must make it *easier on the people*, we say. After all, we need to make church convenient for the busy, modern lifestyle. No one can be expected to sacrifice precious time and energy for the Savior. Subtly, our comfort level becomes the center of the action rather than God. If a weeknight prayer meeting isn't to your particular liking . . .well, hey, God's everywhere, you know! Stay home and do your own thing.

In fact, why even have a prayer meeting? That was only for those old Bible days anyway.

At the heart of "Jeroboam religion" is doing *anything* to keep the crowd. Even as Jeroboam's tragic plan altered God's plan for his people, we have church-growth consultants who know how to slickly play the numbers game. They are experts on what will "work." But sadly, they are blind to the fact that only God "works."

No attendance numbers can hide the fact that our new kind of Christianity is foreign to the Bible and grievous to the Holy Spirit. All over America, churchgoers chafe at a Sunday morning service that runs an hour and ten minutes, but have no problem with three-hour football games on television. Where do we find such a mentality in the New Testament?

I am convinced that in many places today, Jeroboam religion has become so institutionalized that even many in leadership have no clue as to what a true, Spirit-filled church would look like.

TALKING TO OURSELVES

UNBELIEF TALKS TO ITSELF instead of talking to God. How much better it would have been if Jeroboam had analyzed his fears and then taken them to the Lord. If only he had prayed, "O God, I didn't ask to be king, but I know you put me here. The way it looks to me, I could lose everything if my people keep trekking down to Jerusalem. But you said you would be with me and establish my dynasty. So tell me what to do." Jeroboam didn't do this. Instead he talked to himself.

> **If you are headed in the wrong direction, you can always find a few cronies who will pat you on the back and agree with you.** ∾

When we talk to ourselves, we're not talking to anyone very smart, because our outlook is very limited. But if we talk to God, we're talking to someone who knows everything. He knows what he promised in the beginning, and he knows exactly how to fulfill those promises no matter the circumstances.

Jeroboam also turned to some advisers (1 Kings 12:28), who reinforced his disobedience. If you are headed in the wrong direction, you can always find a few cronies who will pat you on the back and agree with you. What Jeroboam needed was a godly prayer partner who would have stopped him cold by saying, "Wait a minute—didn't God give you a promise in the beginning? How can doing wrong bring about something good?"

This is not a story about embezzlement, or meeting a woman in a motel, or smoking some illegal drug. This is a story about simply drifting away from God and his Word. *Yes, I'm aware of what God said—but in the present situation, I really feel the need to do such-and-such.* Instead of focusing on the faithfulness of God, we focus on what the circumstances seem to dictate.

But faith enables us to see God on top of all our problems. If we see only the problems, we get depressed and start making wrong decisions. When we have faith, we see God bigger than any mountain, and we know he is going to take care of us.

> **When you're walking in unbelief, you get out of bed saying, "Oh, no! Is this the day I'm going to lose it all?" The glass is always half-empty.** ～

If *God* is for you, it doesn't matter how many demons in hell try to oppose you. If *God* is for you, it doesn't matter what your opponents whisper in the ears of people. Unbelief has a devious way of envisioning negative things. When you're walking in faith, you get out of bed in the morning saying, "Surely goodness and love will follow me all the days of my life, and I will dwell in the house of the LORD forever" (Psalm 23:6). But when you're walking in unbelief, you get out of bed saying, "Oh, no! Is this the day I'm going to lose it all?" The glass is always half-empty.

Those who walk in faith are still realists. They often admit that they don't know how everything is going to work out; but they insist that their God will supply nonetheless.

LISTENING TO THE VOICE OF FAITH

JEROBOAM'S WORRIES EVENTUALLY led to fatalism. Over time he went from imagining the loss of the people's loyalty all the way to fear that "they will kill me" (1 Kings 12:27)! Unbelief loves to paint the bleakest picture it can. It loves to get us mumbling to ourselves, *I'm not going to make it. I just know this is going to turn out terrible. The future is bound to crash on me.*

Let me tell you that God, who began a good work in you, is not about to stop now. After sending his Son to die for your sins, after saving you at such incredible cost, why would he let you fail now?

Let us declare war this very moment on the cleverness that is really a mask for unbelief. Bring your problem to God, as a little child would, in total confidence that he alone can fix whatever is broken. Open your Bible and let the Holy Spirit plant in you the seeds of a fresh faith that will blossom as you wait on the Lord. Don't give up asking, seeking, and knocking—no matter what pressure you feel to "do something."

How can our heavenly Father do anything but respond to our persistent prayer of faith? Jesus said, "Will not God bring about justice for his chosen ones, who cry out to him day and night? Will he keep putting them off? I tell you, he will see that they get justice, and quickly. However, when the Son of Man comes, will he find faith on the earth?" (Luke 18:7–8).

SEVEN

~

Faith Runs on
a Different Clock

REMEMBER THE FATHER from Texas who brought his wayward son to church and was worried about catching a flight?
He got an eye-opening lesson that God's timetable is not
always the same as ours. The man thought his prayers had
gone for naught because of an airline schedule, while God
had everything under control to achieve his purposes regardless of how things seemed to be unfolding.

Many of our struggles with faith have to do with timing.
We believe, at least in theory, that God will keep his promises—
but when? If the answer does not come as soon as we expect,
fear begins to assault us, and then soon we are tempted to
"throw away [our] confidence," ignoring the fact that "it will
be richly rewarded" (Hebrews 10:35). How many times have
you prayed for a son's or daughter's salvation? Are you still
praying? Do you really believe God is listening?

It would be a good idea if we all just admitted that we
need to learn about God's way of doing things. One of the
best illustrations of divine pacing in the Bible is the story of
Zechariah and Elizabeth, which is laid out in elaborate detail.
In fact, the Gospel of Luke has almost as much to say about
these two senior citizens as it has about Mary and Joseph.
Why didn't Luke write as Mark did in his Gospel and just cut

to the chase: "God sent a forerunner, John the Baptist, to tell people to repent and get ready for the great Messiah"—and that would have been enough?

> **Many of our struggles about faith have to do with timing. We believe, at least in theory, that God will keep his promises—but when?** ∽

No, God wanted to teach some special lessons through the details of this story.

Zechariah was an elderly priest who had no children. Folks in town naturally assumed he and his wife would never have a family. Not only was Elizabeth barren, but she was now too old to give birth.

Zechariah was simply going about his work in the temple one day when an angel appeared and startled him with a message from God. "Do not be afraid, Zechariah; your prayer has been heard. Your wife Elizabeth will bear you a son, and you are to give him the name John. He will be a joy and delight to you, and many will rejoice because of his birth" (Luke 1:13–14). The boy, in fact, would turn out to be John the Baptist.

GOD MAKES SOME VERY ODD CHOICES

RIGHT AWAY THIS STORY shows us that God's way of doing things is very different from ours. Even the way he chooses to order events holds specific lessons for us.

If you were God in heaven looking down on the earth, and you could choose any set of parents across the land of Israel to raise this important messenger, whom would you pick? No doubt you or I would select a healthy young woman about twenty-three or twenty-four years old, at the height of her childbearing years, with plenty of energy to get up in the middle of the night with this baby and do all the things a mother must do. We would look for a husband perhaps twenty-four or twenty-five, physically strong, and well established in his career. We would also want this couple to have money and a good education, so the child would have a stimulating environment. They should live in a safe neighborhood in an upscale suburb, with the best schools and all kinds of cultural enrichment nearby.

The couple should also be planning on having one or maybe two more children after this first one, so the boy would not grow up alone. After all, peer companionship is important. Remember, this baby has a divine mission in life.

But what does God do? He casts his eye all across the land of Israel and finds a woman who can't have a baby! While all her friends in the little desert town seem to have gotten pregnant, she has remained childless. Then God waits and waits until she is past childbearing years, so that even if she *could* have conceived a child, it is now too late. She is doubly disqualified as a special mother for this special child.

And the God of heaven says, "That's the one! As the boy grows up, from the time he is nursed to the time he grows into manhood, his mother will be able to tell him over and over the story of his birth, the miracle of his aged parents— all of it reinforcing in his tender mind that 'nothing is impossible with God' (Luke 1:37)."

Many times in life, God waits while a situation goes from bad to worse. He appears to let it slip over the edge, so that you and I say, "There's *no way* now for this ever to work out." But that is the point when the omnipotent God intervenes in our hopelessness and says, "Oh, really? Watch this...!"

More than worrying about John the Baptist's schooling or music lessons or anything else, God wanted him to grow up in a godly atmosphere of praise and worship. At least once a day that old, devoted couple must have looked at that little boy and said, or at least thought, "Our God is an awesome God! Blessed be his name!"

So many times when we get into emergencies and the situation seems totally hopeless—it's actually a setup. God wants to do something great. He wants to demonstrate his power, so that his name will be praised in a new and greater way. The next generation will hear all about it. After all, their spiritual nurture is far more important than mere material things. Did you know that parents can feed their children three nutritious meals a day and put the latest $120 sneakers on their feet—and still deprive them spiritually? To withhold from children the knowledge of the wonderful and loving God who created them is the worst kind of parenting. They cannot truly live without Jesus, regardless of the top-drawer education they might receive.

> **So many times when we get into emergencies and the situation seems totally hopeless— it's actually a set-up. God wants to do something great.** ∼

Even beyond our own families, God wants to publish everywhere through our lives the testimony of his mighty power and salvation. Beyond our head knowledge of Bible verses, he wants to demonstrate tangibly that he has never changed. Let's not forget the next time we face the "impossible" that our God is *still* an awesome God.

God Is Drawn to Prayer

Notice also how much of this story is centered around prayer and worship.

Zechariah, the old priest, trudged from his home to Jerusalem to serve his rotation in the temple. His assignment that day, Luke 1:9 says, was to "burn incense"—an act of worship. The placing of spices on the fire on the altar resulted in a sweet scent arising to God. Meanwhile, at that specific hour in the temple courtyard, a large crowd of people "were praying outside" (Luke 1:10). They were all opening their hearts to God as best they knew, reaching out and communing with him—the highest activity that any human being can aspire to.

That was the moment when the angel appeared.

God could have shown up at any time, but over and over in the Bible, he revealed himself when people began to pray.

- Peter went up on a rooftop to pray (Acts 10). There God gave him a vision about reaching out to other ethnic groups with the gospel.
- The early church gathered after some persecution to pray. Suddenly, "the place where they were meeting was shaken. And they were all filled with the Holy Spirit" (Acts 4:31).
- The twelve disciples never asked Jesus to teach them to preach. But they did say, "Lord, teach us to pray" (Luke 11:1). They saw something about his communion with the Father that was so outstanding that they couldn't help saying, "Help us to pray like *that*."

The minute the angel showed up, Zechariah panicked. The first words out of the angel's mouth were "Do not be afraid, Zechariah; your prayer has been heard" (Luke 1:13).

306 ~ Fresh Faith

What prayer? Obviously, his many prayers over the years for Elizabeth to have a child.

By this stage in life, Zechariah had probably stopped thinking that fatherhood was even possible for him. *But it didn't matter*; his many years of praying in faith were still on record! When prayer comes from a sincere heart, it rises into God's presence *and stays there*. The more prayers you add, the more they collect in heaven. They don't evaporate like a gas. They remain before God. Remember how another angel said to Cornelius, the Roman centurion, "Your prayers and gifts to the poor have come up as a memorial offering before God" (Acts 10:4). Those prayers didn't just float away. They added up, until the day when God sent a special messenger to this man.

When we seek God for answers, we must persevere in prayer, letting it build up day after day until the force of it becomes a mighty tide pushing over all obstacles. No wonder God says his house is supposed to be known as a house of prayer—not merely a house of preaching or of singing, but especially of prayer. How else will we receive great answers from God unless we persevere in prayer?

> **How must God feel every Sunday when, all over the nation, so many people gather in churches but do so little actual praying?** ~

How must God feel every Sunday when, all over the nation, so many people gather in churches but do so little actual praying? Congregations make time in the weekly schedule for everything from basketball leagues to weight-loss classes, but they can't seem to find a slot for a prayer meeting. The Lord waits to bless his people with his abundant supply, but we don't take the time to open the channel. What a terrible epitaph: "You do not have, because you do not ask God" (James 4:2).

God is drawn to prayer. He delights in communion with us. Prayer releases his blessing into our lives.

GOD DOES NOT APPRECIATE SECOND-GUESSING

WHEN ZECHARIAH RAISES his objection (Luke 1:18), he betrays the fact that he apparently hasn't been praying for a child recently. In his mind, he pictures Elizabeth back home in the small town. She is certainly no spring chicken.

His question—"How can I be sure of this?"—is logical, I suppose. You might think that Gabriel would reply, "Well, old man, let me tell you: God is going to help you. He will empower you and your wife, and everything will work out fine."

No. The angel has already declared, on God's behalf, what is going to happen—so there's nothing left to discuss. Facts have been stated: Elizabeth *will* have a son, you must give him the name John, he will be great in the sight of the Lord, etc., etc. Case closed.

But Zechariah questions God's ability—and suddenly there is a strong reaction. The angel announces that the old man will lose his speech for nine months! If Gabriel had been from Brooklyn, he might have said, "Yo! What's your problem? I'm Gabriel, the angel God sent to tell you this good news. If you don't want to believe it, then you won't speak at all till you see the baby!"

When God sends his divine promise, he is very grieved and saddened if his people do not believe him. It breaks his father-heart to hear his own children say, "Well, maybe … I hope so … but how could that be, really, now? … Yes, God has said he will bring back my daughter—but, you know, she's so hard. . . ."

Is it not enough that God declared he would do something? He doesn't have to explain any of his methods in advance. "Nothing is impossible," remember?

> **God gets fairly irritated—and rightly so— with Christians who refuse to believe, who question his veracity, who start backpedaling after he has said he's going to do something.** ~

Zechariah's mouth is zipped shut. This response gives potent meaning to the oft-quoted words of Hebrews 11:6: "Without faith it is impossible to please God." God gets fairly irritated—and rightly so—with Christians who refuse to believe, who question his veracity, who start backpedaling after he has said he's going to do something. The Lord wants to shout, "Will you please just *trust me!* Is anything too hard for God?"

One time Jesus said to a woman whose brother had died and who thought it was therefore too late for Jesus to help, "Did I not tell you that if you believed, you would see the glory of God?" (John 11:40). Jesus then proceeded to the cemetery and called Lazarus right up out of his grave.

The great battle of our spiritual lives is "Will you believe?" It is *not* "Will you try harder?" or "Can you make yourself worthy?" It is squarely a matter of believing that God will do what only he can do. That is what God honors. He treasures those who respond and open their hearts to him. He's looking for faith so strong that it will anchor on his

Word and wait for him, the One who makes everything beautiful in its time.

INNOCENCE AT RISK

I SHALL NEVER FORGET the Sunday night we finally persuaded shy, soft-spoken Wendy Alvear to stand in front of our congregation and tell fifteen hundred people her story. She started off hesitantly, telling about her growing-up years in Williamsburg, the Brooklyn neighborhood right at the east end of the Williamsburg Bridge that comes across from lower Manhattan. The people on those streets were a curious but harmonious mixture of Hasidic Jews and Puerto Rican immigrants like her parents. Even the drug addicts, she remembers, were nice to the children on the sidewalk.

> **The great battle of our spiritual lives is "Will you believe?" It is *not* "Will you try harder?" or "Can you make yourself worthy?"** ~

Growing up the second of four children in the family, Wendy characterized herself as "a romantic," dreaming of the day she would get married to a handsome husband and raise a houseful of children of her own. She loved kids and was an enthusiastic baby-sitter. Her sunny disposition was only partly suppressed by the strict-minded Spanish church she attended with her mother and siblings three or four nights a week. There she learned about Jesus and soon welcomed him into her life—even though they said he had a long list of rules that she had to obey. Wendy's father was not a Christian, but he didn't seem to mind the rest of his family going to church.

One of the rules in that church was that women and girls always wore skirts. When Wendy's ninth-grade class at school went on a field trip to an amusement park, she felt uneasy. A friend said, "I'll bring some pants from home for you to borrow, okay?" And Wendy gladly took her up on it.

"The only trouble was, the trip ran late," Wendy recalls, "and we didn't get back to school at the appointed time. When we finally arrived, my mother was there waiting to pick me up. I was trapped! I could do nothing but get off the bus and face the music."

That was the point when the attractive young adolescent asked to stop going to church. Her father, of course, supported her request. While alone in her room, however, she did feel the need to offer an apology to God: "I'm sorry about this— but I'll go back to church when I get married. I promise."

By her senior year, Wendy's life was taken up with dance clubs, smoking, and drinking—but "no hard drugs," she affirmed to God. Her first real boyfriend, who went by the Hispanic nickname of Papo, was battling to overcome heroin. "I thought I could help him," she admits with a slight smile. "I would plead with him not to do drugs. So as a compromise, we'd drink wine together instead." Papo may have in fact consumed less heroin as a result, but his dark-haired girlfriend became a steady drinker.

One night in McCarren Park, the two of them and a large group of friends were hanging out after midnight, the boys playing basketball and the girls just talking nearby. All had had plenty to drink. Wendy relaxed on a park bench and, in time, fell asleep, while the others gradually drifted away, leaving her alone.

She awoke with a start when she felt the rough hands of a man moving over her body. Her eyes flew open. Papo and the group were nowhere to be seen—just this stranger, intent on having his way with her.

"In my panic, I tried to think what to do. Suddenly an idea came to me. I said to him, 'Okay, okay—this is cool! But you know what? I have to use the ladies room first. . . . I live just a couple of blocks away. Let's go there!' "

Amazingly, the gullible fellow agreed. In fact, the distance was more like fifteen blocks! "Here he was, walking me all the way to my building, where I cheerfully said, 'I'll run upstairs and be right back!' Thank God, he wasn't too swift." Once in her parents' apartment behind locked doors, of course, Wendy promptly went to bed.

The next morning, she soberly said to herself, "Wow!— I was really in danger last night, wasn't I? How come Papo left me there on the park bench, anyway?" The process of finding a nice young man to marry was turning out to be harder than it looked.

Mr. Right at Last?

THE NEXT BOYFRIEND was better, at least in some ways: He was drug-free and had a job as a shoe salesman. His name was John. Wendy had known him from the beginning of high school, and her family found him to be respectful and polite. There was the complication that he, being four or five years older than Wendy, had already been through a short and turbulent marriage, resulting in a daughter for whom he was now responsible. But the future looked promising.

"I was overjoyed," says Wendy. "Here was the man of my dreams. I had a solid job with New York Life Insurance Company, and he was doing well, too. When we got engaged on Valentine's Day, it was the highlight of my life."

They began planning for a summer wedding. But then, for some inexplicable reason, John's mood began to change. He became less gracious toward Wendy, and then abrupt and demanding. Were the bad memories of his past marriage starting to stir the waters? Wendy couldn't tell. He wanted physical intimacy, and when she declined until the wedding, he grew upset.

Within three months Wendy learned that John was seeking favors elsewhere. She promptly broke the engagement.

"Now I was really lonely," she says. "And I wasn't close enough to God to ask for his help. I sank into more drinking. And it seemed that whenever I would drink, I would become angry and aggressive—which caused me to ruin some parties and alienate my friends. I gradually withdrew into depression, just coming home from work each day and hiding in my room until the next morning."

This unhappy lifestyle continued until Wendy was twenty-five. Her father became suddenly ill and passed away. Shortly before, he had become a Christian, and the two of them had enjoyed some warm conversations. His death was a heavy blow to Wendy.

Two weeks after her father's burial, Wendy was finally ready to listen to the Lord. *Wendy, it's time to come home*, he seemed to say to her—and she responded. A great relief swept over her spirit as the heavenly Father she had long spurned welcomed her back into his arms.

By the next Sunday she was at the Brooklyn Tabernacle. The old legalism was missing—she even saw some women there in pants!—but instead, the love and grace of God pervaded the atmosphere. Wendy started to grow in the Lord, build Christian friendships, join the singles group, and sing in the choir.

Years went by. Wendy was a blessing to us all. Inside, of course, her desire to be married was as strong as ever. She was saying to herself, *Okay, God—where is he?* And God seemed not to give an answer to that heartfelt question. Meanwhile, she watched one friend after another get married in the church.

Wendy's thirtieth birthday came and went . . . then her thirty-fifth. By now she was worrying that maybe God's plan for her life did not include marriage or motherhood. That possibility saddened her greatly. We didn't see quite as many smiles on her face.

One Saturday, alone in her home, she set aside a time to seek the Lord. A couple of her sisters were going through deep waters, and she wanted to intercede for them. But even more, she wanted to talk to God about her singleness. She began to complain. The prayer time "turned into a full-blown pity party," she admits.

In response, the Lord seemed to say to her, "Wendy, you are hurting because you've taken your eyes off of me and put them on the situation. You have forgotten that I am the source of all happiness. Circumstances don't matter. Keep your eyes on me."

A dark cloud lifted as she said in response, "All right, Lord—I will place my desire for a husband 'on the altar,' so to speak. I will give it to you. Go ahead and burn it up like a sacrifice. Consume it! I will stop whining about this."

Peace came back into her soul, and Wendy went on with her life. The only change was that, after seventeen years at New York Life, she quit that job and accepted an invitation to join the Brooklyn Tabernacle staff. What an even greater blessing she became.

SURELY NOT . . .

ABOUT A YEAR LATER, a man came seeking help from Pastor Michael Durso at Christ Tabernacle, Queens, one of our daughter churches. During an appointment in the pastor's office, he gave his life to Christ. His name was John Alvear—the same John who had been in Wendy's life years before.

Soon John showed up at the Brooklyn Tabernacle, looking for Wendy. A couple of choir members passed the word along to her, which triggered sudden apprehension. She thought, "John wants to come back into my life? Oh, no! I can't handle this. It must be a snare from the Enemy!' People told me he had gotten saved and was serving the Lord now, but still—"

Wendy avoided John for a good while, only agreeing at last to go out with him as part of a large group of friends. John's attitude had indeed changed; he had become a new creation in Christ. He and Wendy began dating, and a warm affection blossomed.

Wendy was still concerned about getting involved with "a babe in Christ," as she puts it. After all, she had now been walking with the Lord as an adult for more than a decade, and John was only four months old in his Christian life. She urged him to talk to Pastor Dan Iampaglia, one of the Brooklyn Tabernacle associates at the time.

John and Dan had lunch together. The next day in the office, Wendy wanted to know how it had gone.

"He seems very nice, very sincere," said Pastor Iampaglia. "I believe his walk with the Lord is genuine."

Even that was not enough. Next, Wendy wanted to talk to me. I told her, "Don't be afraid of what God is doing in your life. John is a very special man."

Wendy still worried about whether she could really be finding God's choice for her life after all this time. Then one day, John called her at work. They began to talk about their relationship. With utmost sincerity, John said, "I am just trying to follow God's plan for me—that's the most important thing in my life. In fact, I never stopped loving you. But I want God's will so badly—even if it doesn't include you." At that, his voice broke as the tears came. Wendy began to cry as well.

And that is how, at the age of thirty-seven, Wendy finally became a bride. Their wedding was an explosion of joy. What a special couple they became in the life of our church!

Wendy feared that she had waited too long to ever become a mother. But by the next year, little Jeniece Rebecca was welcomed into their home. Then, at the age of thiry-nine, Wendy gave birth to John Eric. They were recently able to purchase their own home in the borough of Staten Island, across the harbor from Brooklyn.

As Wendy closed her remarks to the church that night, she said, "Whatever you do, keep seeking God's will for your life. He will do it! Don't settle for anything less. Wait for God—he knows how to give you the best."

LET GOD DO IT HIMSELF

THE HARDEST PART of faith is often simply to wait. And the trouble is, if we don't, then we start to fix the problem ourselves—and that makes it worse. We complicate the situation to the point where it takes God much longer to fix it than if we had quietly waited for his working in the first place.

The timing of God is often a mystery to us, and even sometimes a frustration. But we must not give up. We must not try to arrange our own solutions. Instead, we must keep on believing and waiting for God. We will not be alone as we patiently wait for his answer in his time. We will be joining the great host of saints down through the ages whose faith was tested and purified by waiting for God.

This is what David meant when he testified, "I waited patiently for the LORD" (Psalm 40:1). Instead of taking

matters into his own hands, or despairing of God's help at all,
David learned to wait for God to work out his plan in his
time. But after a while, God proved faithful as always, for
David continued his story by adding, "He turned to me and
heard my cry. He lifted me out of the slimy pit, out of the
mud and mire; he set my feet on a rock and gave me a firm
place to stand" (vv. 1–2). What happened was all-glorious,
but it came only after a time of waiting in faith.

**The timing of God is often a mystery to us,
and even sometimes a frustration. But we
must not give up. We must not try to
arrange our own solutions. ~**

Don't give up today, and don't give in to the voices of
unbelief and impatience. Remember these words from a
beautiful song I have enjoyed so much over the years:

Keep believing in what you know is true;
Keep believing—you know the Lord will
   see you through.
When troubles rise in your life, and you don't
   know what to do,
You'll be fine if you just keep believing.[1]

EIGHT

~

Overcoming Discouragement

WHEN SOMEONE SAYS something outlandish here in New York City, one of the common put-downs is "Get real!" or "Be real!"—in other words, please return to Planet Earth with the rest of us and talk some sense. No matter where you live, I'm sure you've heard the same kind of criticism—that someone is being "unrealistic." That person is not like the rest of us intelligent folks who live happily with both feet firmly planted in the real world.

Let me tell you about a time when a group of very smart folks showed great *realism* based on obvious facts—and the results were disastrous. Moses had brought the Hebrew people out of Egypt in response to God's promise that he would give them a wonderful land. After receiving the Ten Commandments and other instructions from God, Moses sent twelve spies to check out the real estate of Canaan. God had already said he would give it to the Hebrews; in fact, he had begun making that promise several hundred years before, to Abraham.

Moses sent the twelve simply to gather information, not to form opinions. All he assigned them to do was to "see what the land is like and whether the people who live there are strong or weak, few or many. What kind of land do they live

318   FRESH FAITH

in? Is it good or bad? What kind of towns do they live in? Are they unwalled or fortified? How is the soil? Is it fertile or poor? Are there trees on it or not?" (Numbers 13:18–20). Sounds like a fifth-grade geography teacher giving her class a research assignment in the encyclopedia.

Nobody asked the spies to draw conclusions. Nobody asked them to gauge the prospects for military success. God had already guaranteed that.

When they returned from their field trip, however, ten of the spies went far beyond their assignment. They reported the data accurately—and then immediately got "realistic" by adding, "We can't attack those people; they are stronger than we are.... The land we explored devours those living in it. All the people we saw there are of great size.... We seemed like grasshoppers in our own eyes, and we looked the same to them" (vv. 31–33). This report went against all God had promised, and thus their common-sense realism affected the destiny of a whole generation of Israelites. The people began to panic and murmur against God.

Who could have predicted that these men would cause a historic turning point? Who could have known that this report and the discouragement it triggered would provoke God to the point of saying, "All right—that's it! You will *not* go into Canaan now after all; you will spend another thirty-eight years wandering in this desert instead. In fact, nearly all of you here today will never get to the Promised Land at all. You're going to grow old and die out here on these sands."

What is so amazing is that these people had already seen God do many supernatural things. They had seen the ten remarkable plagues of Egypt. They had walked out into the Red Sea by faith, believing that the miraculous restraint on the water would hold firm until they got across. They had seen God shake a mountain with thunderous force. They had watched Moses bring down the divine law, written by the finger of God on a stone.

But now they chose to believe a human report rather than God's promise. The Bible calls the ten spies' summary "a bad report" (Numbers 13:32). The King James Version is even stronger: "an evil report." What was so wicked about it? After all, its facts were accurate. The Israelites were realistically no match for the fierce tribes of Canaan. But this report of the spies was full of unbelief and spawned deep discouragement among God's people. God was provoked by their distrust.

> **Do we believe what our feelings and circumstances tell us, or do we believe what God has promised to do?** ∾

Thousands of years later, little has changed for God's people: Do we believe what our feelings and circumstances tell us, or do we believe what God has promised to do?

CONQUERING "THE BIG D"

THIS STORY TEACHES us several things:

It's not starting the race that counts; it's finishing. These people, by giving in to discouragement, never saw the fulfillment of God's promise in their lives. Today we sometimes fool ourselves with a theology that mumbles, "Well, God will take care of everything somehow. It doesn't matter what we do; the Lord is sovereign, you know." Not exactly!

The truth is that without faith, it is impossible to please God. We receive things—even the things God has promised us—only if we have faith. As Jesus said to two blind men, "According to your faith will it be done to you" (Matthew

9:29). This means that my life or yours has only as much of God as our faith permits. The promises of God are appropriated only by faith. God is looking for a people who will believe him and take him at his word no matter what the circumstances say or what other people are telling us.

Joshua and Caleb, the "minority" spies, were two such people who took God at his word. "We should go up and take possession of the land," they said, "for we can certainly do it" (Numbers 13:30). Yet they had seen the same enemies the other spies had seen. This is why God gave that wonderful compliment in Numbers 14:24, saying, "My servant Caleb has a different spirit and follows me wholeheartedly." As a result of this willingness to side with God's promise, Caleb and Joshua got to enter the land. The other ten spies, however—and a million or two other people—died along the way.

Pressures are exerted all through life to make us want to lie down and quit. The most spiritual person in the world is tempted to get discouraged. I remember seeing a television interview with Billy Graham and his delightfully honest wife, Ruth. The host, David Frost, said something like, "So you two pray together and read the Bible together on a regular basis. But tell me the truth, Mrs. Graham: In all these years of living with Billy, have you never had problems or disagreements? Have you never even once contemplated divorce?"

"Not once," she fired back. "Murder, a few times—but not divorce!"

Obviously, there are challenges to overcome even in the Billy Graham home. You and I have our share of difficulties, but the most important thing is to finish our lives still trusting God, as the evangelist and his wife are doing.

In fact, the greatest battle on earth has not been fought on the Normandy beaches or on Iwo Jima or in the Persian Gulf. Rather, it has raged inside your heart and mine: the battle to believe. The just not only must begin by faith but continue to live by it as well (Romans 1:17). Faith is as essential to everyday living as it is to initial salvation.

As Athanasius, the early church father, said, "I can do nothing without the help of God, and that from moment to moment; for when, so long as we are on the earth, is there a single instant in which we can say we are safe from temptation or secure from sin?"[1] Only God's grace can keep us, and that grace is activated by faith.

Caleb walked in this attitude of faith his whole life. The book of Joshua shows him as an old man, long after the spying trip, making a rousing speech to his equally elderly partner Joshua, who is now in charge of the nation:

> I was forty years old when Moses the servant of the LORD sent me from Kadesh Barnea to explore the land. And I brought him back a report according to my convictions, but my brothers who went up with me made the hearts of the people melt with fear. I, however, followed the LORD my God wholeheartedly....
>
> Now then, just as the Lord promised, he has kept me alive for forty-five years since the time he said this to Moses, while Israel moved about in the desert. So here I am today, eighty-five years old! I am still as strong today as the day Moses sent me out; I'm just as vigorous to go out to battle now as I was then. Now give me this hill country that the LORD promised me that day. You yourself heard then that the Anakites were there and their cities were large and fortified, but, the LORD helping me, I will drive them out just as he said (Joshua 14:7–8, 10–12).

Caleb never retired! He just kept going, and faith kept him young and strong in heart. To the end, he wanted to fight the Lord's enemies no matter how entrenched they seemed. He knew that God could do anything, and he wanted to be a part of God's action as long as he could. Discouragement never seemed to sap his spiritual vigor.

Now we see the importance of the verse in Hebrews that says, "Let us not give up meeting together, as some are in the habit of doing, but let us *encourage one another*—and all the more as you see the Day approaching" (10:25). Going to church and having Christian fellowship should never leave us discouraged—there's enough of that everywhere around us. Even if God searches our hearts very directly concerning sin, we should still leave the building encouraged, because once the Spirit reveals our disobedience, he will bring cleansing and strength to our hearts. He will cause us to see his promises and his love in a new, clear light.

One of the primary names for the Holy Spirit is "the Comforter." And one of the primary names for the devil, who likes to impersonate the Holy Spirit, is "the Accuser." The Comforter encourages us and builds us up. The Accuser is in the business of tearing us down.

> **One of the primary names for the Holy Spirit is "the Comforter." And one of the primary names for the devil, who likes to impersonate the Holy Spirit, is "the Accuser."** ～

Wives who are negative and discouraging can sometimes cause more damage in their homes than any drug addiction. Husbands who talk down to their families and go against the promises of God are walking on dangerous ground. They are following in the footsteps of the ten spies! They are once again repeating, "Yes, but . . ." and "It sounds good, but we can't. . . ."

Americans are waging a mighty war against "the Big C"—cancer. The people and the government are investing huge sums to fight this horrible disease that invades millions of people. If only in the spiritual realm we would give equal effort to strike down "the Big D"—discouragement. It kills not the body, but the soul. Its dreadful toll on the people of God is greater than anyone could calculate.

> **The only hospital that can treat "the Big D"—discouragement—is the hospital of the Word of God, which is managed by the Holy Spirit. ∼**

I have often sat in my office, trying to counsel couples who know that they are in trouble. They are entirely accurate as to the surface facts of their situation. But they are also so negative and pessimistic that you want to scream. There is no faith or expectancy for what God has promised to do for his people.

Try to count all the times in the Bible that God says to us, "Be encouraged," or "Fear not," or "Be not afraid." The battle is always not about giving in to what we see around us, but about holding onto God's promises.

The only hospital that can treat "the Big D" is the hospital of the Word of God, which is managed by the Holy Spirit. Only there can our spirits be lifted.

Loose Talk

THE ENEMY USES ordinary people to discourage us. Who caused all the trouble that day in the desert? Not some demon with a pitchfork. Just people talking. People who were part of the

324 ~ FRESH FAITH

Israelite community, not pagan strangers. People everyone knew and even respected. People chosen by Moses himself.

It is very important for us to watch whom we talk to. Some voices are *not* good for us. Some folks need to be avoided. Those who are negative and don't really believe God will have an effect on your spirit. God has to give you wisdom on how to change the subject or even extract yourself from the situation without offending.

LOOSE EMOTIONS

DISCOURAGEMENT IS AT the heart of other reactions. Numbers 14:1 says, "That night all the people of the community raised their voices and wept aloud." The camp broke down into one massive pity party. While tears before God are usually valued highly in the pages of Scripture, this was a crying produced by unbelief and fear.

I have heard certain people pray with emotion, but their lack of faith made it sound more like the Israelites that day in their tents. They were not really pouring out their souls to God in faith, but rather venting their fear and frustration.

> **Let's stop blaming our unbelief on the pastor we once had, on our childhood, on circumstances, or on anything else. There is no excuse for not believing in the Lord.** ~

The Israelites' tears soon led to blasphemy. They accused God of bringing them out of Egypt only to die! (v. 3). Think of the blasphemy of that—and yet it all started with simply doubting whether the Lord would do what he promised. Now they had sunk to saying terrible things about the God of Israel.

Then (v. 4) they talked about getting rid of Moses. Discouragement led from emotionalism and blasphemy to rebellion. Things were coming apart at every seam. "It's the leader's fault," they said. How many churches have crumbled because people lost their focus on God's power and, before you could snap your fingers, they were wanting to dump the pastor?

Let's stop blaming our unbelief on the pastor we once had, on our childhood, on circumstances, or on anything else. There is no excuse for us not to believe in the Lord. Christ is still challenging us as he did Peter on the lake one night. Even though Peter was walking on the water, "when he saw the wind, he was afraid and, beginning to sink, cried out, 'Lord, save me!' Immediately Jesus reached out his hand and caught him. 'You of little faith,' he said, 'why did you doubt?'" (Matthew 14:30–31).

Faith for the Long Haul

Now we finally see why the Bible so many times holds up the great value of *endurance*. That virtue is not often mentioned in our day. We lean more toward spectacular things like great preaching and dynamic spiritual gifts. But the persistent faith that holds onto God, enduring all the various situations of life no matter how difficult—*that* is something we need to ask God for more and more.

Vincent and Daphne Rodriguez are the kind of steady, salt-of-the-earth people whom every pastor loves to have in a congregation. They live in Queens; he has been a reliable letter carrier for the Postal Service his whole life, while she has been a dedicated homemaker for their three children.

While he was volunteering at a children's camp in the Catskill Mountains one summer, Vincent's heart was touched by the boys and girls he met who didn't have fathers. He and Daphne talked about the children's obvious needs for love and care. In time, the Rodriguezes, then in their early forties, applied to the Salvation Army to become foster parents.

They had hardly finished their training when, a few days before Christmas 1988, the phone rang at one o'clock in the morning. A pitiful baby girl in Beth-Israel Hospital—born more than a month prematurely and addicted through her mother to crack cocaine, heroin, and morphine—needed a home. She had finally gotten up to five pounds in weight and could now be released to foster care. Her mother was a young addict who was clearly unfit to care for her, living most of the time in the streets as a prostitute. Would Vincent and Daphne take the baby?

"We didn't know anything about addiction in infants," says Daphne, like her husband a quiet person. "We had assumed we'd probably be getting a healthy child who was perhaps just from a poor economic environment. Without knowing what we were walking into, we said yes."

By ten o'clock the next evening, two social workers were on their doorstep with a bundle in blankets. For the next twenty-four hours, the Rodriguez family did little else but hover in a circle around the child and admire her! When she cried, which was often, they would pass her from one set of arms to the next. "We felt so sorry for her," says Vincent. "She was our surprise gift for Christmas, and we were happy that God had brought her our way."

But the girl didn't quite look like a normal baby, for the stress of drug withdrawal seemed etched upon her tiny face. At the church, she was dedicated to the Lord in a Sunday afternoon service when she was two months old—and weighed six pounds. I broke down as I held her up to the Lord, and the congregation adopted her as their own.

In the Rodriguez home, life was settling into the realities of taking care of a very disturbed newborn. She twitched and jerked and cried out constantly in the pain of withdrawal. Daphne had prepared herself for middle-of-the-night feedings, of course, but she was hardly expecting to be up every two hours, preparing more milk to calm the baby's frazzled nervous system. She would pace the floor, holding the baby tight to give a feeling of security. As the weeks wore on, this was turning into more of an ordeal than Daphne had bargained for. And yet they felt that God had led them to take this child.

"I kept telling myself that God had his hand on her, because he had allowed her to live, even though she was only two-and-a-half pounds at birth," Daphne says. "She hadn't even been given a name. So we chose one ourselves; at our teenage daughter's suggestion, we picked out a beautiful Bible name, Hannah."

Daphne figured out that if she put her teenagers in charge of the baby each afternoon when they came home from school, she could get at least a nap in order to fortify herself for the next night ahead. Otherwise, an hour of sleep at a time was the best she could hope for. Even Vincent's sleep was disrupted.

"But even in the times I was exhausted or didn't feel well myself, I kept going," Daphne remembers. "I tried to soothe her with Christian music through the day. One particular recording—'I Exalt Thee' by Phil Driscoll—seemed to calm her shaking in the bassinet. We played it every day, and the crying would stop."

When I would see them in church and ask how it was going, Daphne would just sort of shrug as she said, "Pastor, it's really hard! She needs me all night long, it seems; I can't get any sleep." I felt concerned for them, and more than once I asked the congregation to continue to bring the Rodriguezes' situation to God at the throne of grace.

In time, Hannah's health improved. She gained weight. At the end of the first year, she finally began sleeping through the night. Her crawling and walking came later than usual, but that was to be expected. So was her hyperactivity.

With a steady diet of love and prayer, Hannah developed into a toddler. Looking ahead toward the school years, however, Daphne saw trouble. Would this child be able to sit still and learn? She had Hannah tested for attention deficit disorder, and that led to placement in a special education program from age three-and-a-half to five. The program had the additional benefit of giving the tired mother a much-needed break from the daily vigil.

When Hannah reached five years of age, Vincent and Daphne formally adopted her. The ink was hardly dry on the adoption decree, making them permanently responsible for Hannah, when a whole new problem erupted. Hannah developed a cold that she couldn't seem to shake; her face became very dry and blotchy. The condition hung on until finally Daphne took her to the doctor and requested a full physical examination. Two days later, a nurse called: "You need to come back for a consultation."

"Why?" Daphne asked. "What's wrong?"

"Well, something is showing here that doesn't look right. The enzymes in her liver are way too high. We need to run these tests again."

Soon the truth came out: The little girl, having already fought off addiction to hard drugs from her birth mother, was also afflicted with hepatitis C—a serious disease that saps energy, sometimes turns the eyes and skin yellow, and wastes away the liver over time.

"Oh, God—how can this be?" Daphne cried. "After all we've been through with Hannah already—why wasn't this discovered back when she was born?"

So many questions, so few answers. Discouragement swept over the besieged family. When they told me the bad news, I realized that a new battle of faith for Hannah had begun for all of us at the church.

We enlisted the efforts of the Brooklyn Tabernacle Prayer Band (a group that intercedes around the clock, seven days a week), the members of the choir, and everyone else we could. We agreed together that God had created this child and had brought her through all the terrors of drug withdrawal, and we now stood united in faith against this latest threat. "God must be planning to use her for something great," we said.

In time, with the help of the Salvation Army, the Rodriguezes secured the help of a chief specialist at Schneider Children's Hospital, part of the Long Island Jewish medical complex, who took on Hannah's case. He put her on a regimen of medication to fight the disease. Vincent even steeled himself to give his daughter injections, which were required three times a week for the next eighteen months. Hannah's condition stabilized.

Throughout the primary grades, Hannah struggled to keep up with her learning. Daphne was a frequent face in the school hallways, working with the teachers to find solutions for her little girl. Performance gradually improved. They never gave up, no matter what new obstacle appeared. They just refused to stop fighting for Hannah.

Today Hannah's hepatitis C is in remission, and her medications have been dropped. She is a beautiful girl with a lovely round face and a shy smile. "We are just trusting in the Lord that he is healing her completely," Vincent says.

"What a testimony she will be able to give in years to come. I sometimes tell my daughter, 'Someday you will get to stand on the highest building in the city and tell everybody!' She always smiles when I say that, and I do, too. The miracle is on its way."

STAY THE COURSE

THE APOSTLE PAUL KNEW that this kind of spiritual endurance was vital for his own spiritual children. He told them that he never stopped praying for them to be "strengthened with all power according to his glorious might so that you may have great endurance and patience, and joyfully giving thanks to the Father" (Colossians 1:11). He brought them tenderly to God in prayer, that they might be able to keep on keeping on, no matter what attacks were made upon their faith.

Many sensational gifts and talents don't mean much over the long haul. The longer I live, the more I treasure people who just keep walking with God. They aren't up or down, left or right; they're always steady on the course, praising God and believing his Word.

> **Many sensational gifts and talents don't mean much over the long haul. The longer I live, the more I treasure people who just keep walking with God. ～**

Just as our bodies need strength in order to keep functioning, our spirits need endurance. When our faith becomes weakened through discouragement, we have trouble standing on God's promises. We struggle to say no to temptation.

It's easy to give in to the devil. "The Big D" threatens to snuff out our spiritual life. But with God, we can have the power to resist discouragement. He can give us the spirit of Caleb and Joshua that triumphs despite the difficulties facing us.

Notice that Paul *prays* for endurance. This was not something he could transmit by verbal teaching to the Colossian believers. This wonderful strength had to come directly from God at the throne of grace.

And it will *keep* coming as we *keep* asking and trusting in our God.

NINE

~

Grace That
Is Greater

MANY TIMES AT the end of our services, I meet people at the altar who are so ashamed that they often will not even look me in the eye. Their shoulders are slumped; their gaze is on the carpet. I sense no faith in them to ask Christ for mercy. Praise and worship seem impossible. They are living under the heavy burden of their own failure, with no hope that their life can be retrieved. They now feel too unworthy to expect any blessings from a holy and righteous God.

I am not just talking about people with the stereotypical inner-city problems of drugs, prostitution, or whatever. These are average-looking people who have simply given in to a besetting sin so often that they are convinced they will never rise above it.

Often, as the congregation is worshiping in the background with a song such as "Grace, grace, God's grace— grace that will pardon and cleanse within," I notice that the person before me isn't singing along. It is because the person isn't sure that the song could really be true for him or her. Sometimes I will gently try to lift the person's chin or perhaps the hands in upward openness to God.

How I love to remind these people of someone in the Bible whose life story is often forgotten. You might not think of him as a failure, because his name, in fact, shows up in very good company. One place is on the very first page of the New Testament, where the opening lines say,

> A record of the genealogy of Jesus Christ the son of David, the son of Abraham:
>
> Abraham was the father of Isaac,
> > Isaac the father of Jacob,
> > Jacob the father of *Judah* and his brothers,
> > *Judah* the father of Perez and Zerah, whose mother was Tamar (Matthew 1:1–3).

How nice and orderly. This passage sets down a clear track from Abraham, the father of the Jewish nation, to Jesus, so that everyone in the first century would know that this Messiah was honest-to-goodness Jewish. Along the way, that track runs straight through Judah and his family.

Then, on one of the last pages of the New Testament, the apostle John writes,

> I saw in the right hand of him who sat on the throne a scroll with writing on both sides and sealed with seven seals. And I saw a mighty angel proclaiming in a loud voice, "Who is worthy to break the seals and open the scroll?" But no one in heaven or on earth or under the earth could open the scroll or even look inside it. I wept and wept because no one was found who was worthy to open the scroll or look inside. Then one of the elders said to me, "Do not weep! See, the Lion of the tribe of *Judah*, the Root of David, has triumphed. He is able to open the scroll and its seven seals" (Revelation 5:1–5).

How wonderful that while many others were disqualified, someone who came from the tribe of Judah met the standard to open the mysteries of God. That someone, of course, was Jesus Christ.

This Judah must have been quite a godly man, right? Of all of Jacob's twelve sons, only he is mentioned in the genealogy of Christ. The other eleven were passed over by God. At the climax of history in heaven, it is Judah's offspring who is hailed as worthy when all others fail the test. When we get to heaven someday, we will no doubt continue to hear Judah's name often.

But what do you really know about this man Judah?

A SORDID TALE

JUDAH GETS A WHOLE chapter of the Bible to himself—Genesis 38—and that is the best place to get acquainted with him. If you have the stomach for it, that is. (You might not want to read this chapter aloud to your children in family devotions.)

The story begins with Judah drifting away from the rest of the family and marrying a Canaanite woman (vv. 1–2). That was his first mistake. His uncle, Esau, had already been down that road, getting into a mess by marrying outside of those who served the one true God (see Genesis 26:34–35). As a result, Judah's grandparents had gone to great lengths to make sure their other son, Jacob, didn't make the same error. They told him in no uncertain terms to avoid Canaanite women (Genesis 28:1) and sent him on a long trip to find the right kind of wife.

But Judah disregarded their counsel entirely. He married "the daughter of a Canaanite man named Shua" (Genesis 38:2). The children born to them apparently grew up getting mixed messages about the true God versus Canaan's idols. The bad results showed up quickly in the first son, who turned out to be so wicked that the Lord put him to death in early adulthood (v. 7).

That left behind a young widow named Tamar. Judah asked his second son to marry her, as was the social requirement in those days. But the son selfishly refused. Because of this, God brought destruction on him also.

Judah now procrastinated about giving his third son, Shelah, to Tamar. The years went by, and Tamar kept waiting. She was getting past her prime, and she was lonely. Finally, she heard about a trip her father-in-law, Judah, was going to take. It was sheep-shearing time, which was payday for those in the sheep business. Money flowed and people partied. To Tamar, this seemed like the perfect opportunity to carry out a terrible plan. She covered her face with some kind of shawl and posed along the road as a prostitute.

The Bible records that Judah, "not realizing that she was his daughter-in-law, . . . went over to her by the roadside and said, 'Come now, let me sleep with you'" (v. 16). Judah paid for her services, but it resulted in Tamar's becoming pregnant with twins. Judah went home none the wiser.

When the news came out that Tamar was having a baby, Judah threw a righteous fit. How dare his daughter-in-law cause disgrace on the family! "Bring her out and have her burned to death!" he stormed (v. 24).

As she was being dragged out into the public square, she calmly identified her sexual partner by holding up the personal property Judah had left with her as a down payment for her services. Judah was humiliated before all and had to admit, "She is more righteous than I" (v. 26).

DISQUALIFIED?

YOU JUST WANT TO shield your eyes from this kind of ugliness, don't you? It sounds like something in the *National Enquirer*. If you or I have an ancestor in our families who did something like this, we don't talk about it. We probably leave his picture out of the family album. We don't bring up his name to our children—and hope they never ask. People who so mess up their lives—and others' lives—are best left unmentioned.

Why would God put this seamy story in the Bible? It doesn't seem fit for print. Or, if God had to include the story, why didn't he then say to us, "The stern lesson of this is that the lineage of my holy Son will be Abraham—Isaac—Jacob—*Benjamin*," or one of the other sons? After all, hadn't Judah thoroughly disqualified himself?

Left to our own devices, any of us can self-destruct within an hour, just as Judah did. "There is no one righteous, not even one" (Romans 3:10). "We all, like sheep, have gone astray, each of us has turned to his own way" (Isaiah 53:6). "I know that nothing good lives in me, that is, in my sinful nature"(Romans 7:18). Thus, there is no need for self-righteous snickering as we read Judah's story.

> **We all can be self-righteous and pompous.**
> **If every moment of our past were put on the**
> **big screen at church, who of us would seem**
> **so wonderful?** ～

God has given clear testimony about our moral standing with him. But unfortunately, we are very good at condemning others for the very things we also do. "So-and-so in the church is selfish . . . so-and-so is racist . . . so-and-so is a hypocrite." But somehow, the mirror doesn't work for us.

Like Judah when he was told about his daughter-in-law's pregnancy, we can all be self-righteous and pompous. Not only are we weak, but we are judgmental on top of it! Wouldn't it be better to stop giving opinions about everyone else and do a better job of humbly looking after our own hearts? If every moment of our past were put on the big screen at church, who of us would seem so wonderful?

My main concern today is that we have lost sight of the reason God included Judah's ugly story in the Bible. We are drifting away from the New Testament's message of God's amazing grace to change and redeem soiled people; instead, we are moralizing and expressing self-righteous disdain over the horrible lives others are living around us. Instead of exalting Jesus, who came as a spiritual physician for the sick and unlovely, we are busy rehearsing all the commandments of God, as if that alone would change a single soul. We are giving people only the law, when what they crave is the love and grace of God.

We have forgotten that God specializes in cases such as Judah. We should return to preaching boldly what Paul wrote to the Corinthians—not stopping two-thirds of the way through the paragraph, but continuing on to the glorious end:

> Do you not know that the wicked will not inherit the kingdom of God? Do not be deceived: Neither the sexually immoral nor idolaters nor adulterers nor male prostitutes nor homosexual offenders nor thieves nor the greedy nor drunkards nor slanderers nor swindlers will inherit the kingdom of God. *And that is what some of you were. But you were washed, you were sanctified, you were justified in the name of the Lord Jesus Christ and by the Spirit of our God* (1 Corinthians 6:9–11).

The early Christian church had its own share of "Judahs," but "where sin increased, grace increased all the more" (Romans 5:20).

GRACE BEYOND REASON

THE DEVIL'S SPECIALTY is to swarm in on people and hiss, "You did it! You really messed up! If people only knew. . . . You're not what you seem to be. Do you think you're going to get away with this?" And the devil's victims hardly feel like living. They feel unworthy to go to church. They avoid their Bibles. They see no hope of change.

Satan wants to hide the fact that the mercy of God is for *everyone* who has messed up. As high as the heavens are above the earth, so are God's ways higher than ours (Isaiah 55:9). He delights in mercy. James writes, "Mercy triumphs over judgment" (2:13). God's specialty is forgiving and putting away people's sins from his sight. He delights in taking failures such as Judah and weaving them into the ancestry of his own Son, Jesus Christ.

What is even more remarkable is this: The genealogy of Jesus in Matthew 1:3 continues through Judah and then goes *not* to his legitimate son, Shelah—but to Perez, Tamar's boy, the child of incest. How incredible! It is as if God were saying, "Forever I want my people to know that I not only forgive mess-ups, but I can take them and touch them and heal them—and put them in the line that leads to Christ." What Satan means for evil, God is able to change and work out for good (Genesis 50:20).

To this very day, God delights in hearing Judah's name echo through the heavenly halls. He takes sinners like you and me and makes us right. He takes dirt and pollution and transforms them into holiness. He takes the crooked thing and makes it straight. He takes the tangles of our lives and weaves something new, so that we emerge singing Hallelujah. We love God, not because we've been so good, but because *he* is so good, and his mercy endures forever.

The Lion of the tribe of Judah is about deliverance, not condemnation. He takes our mistakes and wanderings and redeems them for his glory. Greater than his glory as Creator and Sustainer of the universe is the glory of his grace to losers like you and me. No record is so stained, no case so hopeless that he cannot reach down and bring salvation to that person.

> **God takes sinners like you and me and makes us right. He takes dirt and pollution and transforms them into holiness. He takes the crooked thing and makes it straight.** ～

One of the outstanding gospel singers in America today is a trophy of that kind of divine mercy. When audiences listen to Calvin Hunt's soaring tenor voice, they can hardly imagine that at one time he virtually destroyed his body with crack cocaine—and ravaged the lives of his wife and two stepchildren as well. His story is more than just self-destruction through drugs; it spreads its pain to the single mom he had rescued in the aftermath of her abusive first marriage, and to her innocent daughter and son.

Calvin met the trim, attractive Miriam and her two preschoolers when he was just twenty years old. Miriam lived in the apartment two floors below his mother, and she and Calvin warmed to each other right away. Little Monique and Freddy liked the handsome young construction worker with the hard hat who made them laugh. Calvin was also something of a weekend musician, playing guitar and singing in nightclubs.

Miriam's divorce was not yet final, and Calvin had to comfort her more than once after she had been beaten up by her estranged husband. On one occasion, when the man knocked her out cold, Calvin took Miriam to the emergency room. Their relationship flourished over the next year and then even survived a one-year army stint by Calvin that took him away from New York City.

"When I came back home," Calvin admits, "the easiest thing for me to do was just to move in with her. I went back to working road construction, and we had enough money to party through the weekends." The couple eventually added snorting cocaine to their fairly heavy drinking as they and their friends sought new thrills. Then they added marijuana to the mix, sometimes even sprinkling the joints with cocaine before rolling them in order to experience both drugs at once.

The live-in arrangement continued with little change, until five years later when Miriam told Calvin they ought to get married. And so in 1984, they wed.

SOMETHING NEW

ONE NIGHT THE BEST man from their wedding invited them to a party at his home that featured something new: "freebasing" cocaine, or heating it and smoking it through a glass bottle. Calvin was intrigued; he asked his friend for a hit. But the new drug didn't seem to have much effect, Calvin thought. Miriam gave it a try as well, with minimal results.

Or so they thought. Not until they left the friend's apartment at 7:30 the next morning, having been awake all night and having spent Calvin's entire $720 paycheck for the week, did they realize they had discovered something powerfully attractive—and deadly. They had now joined the world of crack cocaine.

"I remember us going back home, and I just felt horrible the whole weekend," Calvin says. "By the time I went to work on Monday, I was lecturing myself about being more responsible. I had a family to support, and I needed to get back in control.

"Would you believe that by the next Friday night when I cashed my check, I called Miriam and told her to get the kids ready for bed early, because I'd be bringing home 'the stuff'? I showed up with all the new paraphernalia, ready for action. I prepared the crack over the kitchen stove just as I'd seen my friend do it the week before, and again the two of us were up all night. By the time the sun came up Saturday morning, we had gone through another whole paycheck."

This pattern endured for eight months. Meanwhile, household bills went unpaid, the children lacked warm winter clothing, and the rent fell behind. Miriam's brothers, who were Christians, urged her to stop destroying herself, but neither she nor Calvin would listen.

> **If Calvin had any spare cash in his pocket, it went for crack. If he didn't have cash, he would manufacture some by stealing the battery or tires from a parked car to resell. ～**

Calvin's obsession with drugs grew ever stronger, and not just on the weekends. If he had any spare cash in his pocket, it went for crack. If he didn't have cash, he would manufacture some by stealing the tires or the battery from a parked car to resell. Some nights he didn't come home at all.

Obviously, Calvin's job performance suffered. One day his boss pulled Calvin aside for a talk. There were tears in the man's eyes as he said quietly, "You've been one of my most valued employees. I don't know what's happening, and I don't want to know—but whatever it is, you better get it fixed, because you're about to lose your job."

The truth was, Calvin had a new superboss in his life: crack. "I began losing a lot of weight," Calvin says. "I'd be gone three, four, even five days at a time—spending my life in crack dens. Yes, I had a home and a wife and two children—but when I was doing crack, home was the last place I wanted to be.

"The people I did drugs with were actually a pretty scary bunch—violent and heartless. But as long as I was high, I didn't even notice that."

BETRAYED

MIRIAM GREW INCREASINGLY CONCERNED. What was happening to the man she loved, her one-time knight in shining armor? Hadn't she already been through enough chaos with her first husband—and now this? One night she looked at her two children sleeping innocently in bed while Calvin and his friends were in the kitchen getting high. Moral principles once learned long ago seemed to rise up to warn her of where this was all heading. She promptly threw all the guys out—including Calvin.

Miriam began to see that she was being terribly betrayed by a man for the second time in her life. The first one had beaten her physically; the second one was hurting her and her children even more painfully with his addiction. Like Judah of old, he was wreaking tremendous damage on his family through his unbridled thrill-seeking.

"I pleaded with him to stop," says Miriam. "I said, 'Calvin, this is going to kill us! It's going to destroy our marriage.' The arguments got so bad that sometimes I had to have him escorted out of the house. My son began studying ways to add more locks to the apartment so Calvin couldn't get back in."

At the very time Calvin was deserting the family, Miriam put her faith in Christ. Her spiritual life deepened, and her prayer life increased. She found a church and would openly ask for the prayers of others to bring her husband back from the brink. She refused to contemplate the other options: separation, divorce, or his untimely death. She simply believed that God would somehow rescue their family.

She even began to tell Calvin, "God is going to set you free—I just know it!" Of course, that made him furious. He also got irked at the Brooklyn Tabernacle Choir music she had begun to play. She loved it and would respond in worship, sometimes even weeping for joy as she praised the Lord. Calvin would snap back, "If that stuff makes you cry, why don't you turn it off?" He would sometimes fling the cassette out the window, but his wife would quickly replace it.

One day young Monique found a flyer announcing a Friday night showing of the film *A Cry for Freedom*, being sponsored in a high school auditorium by Christ Tabernacle in Queens. The twelve-year-old insisted that Dad go with them to see it. He brushed her off.

Suddenly something rose up within the girl. She said, "Daddy, remember all the neat things we used to do together? We don't do anything anymore. You know what— it's all about you and that drug, whatever it is! Your problem is, you're hooked, and you won't admit it!"

Calvin flared back. "You shut up! Keep talking like that, and I'll give you a whipping!"

"Go ahead, Daddy!" the brave girl responded. "You can beat me and stomp on me if you want—but when you're finished, you'll still be hooked on that stuff." At that, she ran out of the kitchen.

Calvin picked up the flyer from the table. He looked at the sketch of a man inside the bottle that is used for smoking crack, his hands pressed against the glass with a desperate look on his face. Calvin's heart melted enough that he reluctantly agreed to attend the showing.

At the last minute, Calvin tried to back out, but without success. The film's story line turned out to be a shockingly close replica of the Hunts themselves: a husband addicted to crack, and his formerly addicted wife now praying for his deliverance. When the pastor gave an invitation at the end, Calvin was the first one kneeling at the altar. "I didn't actually ask Jesus to come into my heart," he says, "but I was just so guilt-ridden that I had to at least pray and admit the pain I was causing everyone. I started to cry. Miriam and the kids came alongside, and we all cried together."

The next Sunday, the family returned to church, and while Miriam and the children were overjoyed, Calvin still was not willing to get serious about the Lord. *God can't do anything for me*, he told himself. *What am I doing here?* By the next weekend, he was on the run again.

BEARING DOWN

NOW THE CHURCH BODY began to pray harder for Calvin Hunt's salvation. Calvin learned to time his visits back to the apartment during the hours when he knew everyone would be at church. He would sneak in to get a fresh supply of clean clothes and then quickly leave.

"I knew that Calvin was in a prison," says Miriam. "Being an ex-addict myself—I had done heroin before I ever met him—I knew the unbelievable power of this kind of substance. That's why I prayed so hard, crying out to God to set him free, and got all my friends to pray with me. Every mealtime prayer

346 ~ FRESH FAITH

with my kids, every bedtime prayer included, 'O God, please set Daddy free!'"

Another three years went by. Calvin got worse instead of better. At one point he was actually sleeping in a large doghouse in someone's backyard rather than going home to his own bed. He was seriously dehydrated, his cheeks sunken, giving him the wasted look so common among addicts. With no money, Miriam and the children had to apply for food stamps and Medicaid.

Finally, one night—the same night as Christ Tabernacle's weekly prayer meeting—Calvin headed once again for the family apartment after his wife and children had left. In the quietness he found some food in the refrigerator, then took a shower and put on clean clothes. There was still time for a short nap, so he decided to lie down.

But for some reason, he couldn't sleep. Soon he heard a noise. From a closet came the soft sound of someone weeping! He sat up. Maybe Miriam and the children were home after all.

He looked in the children's rooms, under the beds, inside the various closets. No one! But the sobbing continued. He stood in the living room and said out loud, "I know you guys are in here—come on out!" Nobody appeared.

Calvin thought of lying down once again, but something inside him seemed to say, *If you go to sleep tonight, you'll never wake up again.* He panicked. ~

Now Calvin was spooked. He thought of lying down once again, but something inside him seemed to say, *If you go to sleep tonight, you'll never wake up again.* He panicked. Running out the door, he dashed three blocks to the train station to go see if his wife and children were really at the prayer meeting or not.

He burst into the church and stood at the back of the center aisle, scanning the crowd. Suddenly the same sounds of crying struck his ears—only much louder than back in the apartment. The whole congregation was in earnest prayer, calling out *his* name to God in faith! Calvin was thunderstruck as he slowly moved down the aisle, gazing at the people's upraised hands and their eyes tightly shut in prayer, tears running down their faces. "O God, wherever Calvin Hunt is, bring him to this building!" they pleaded. "Don't let this family go through this horror another day. Lord, you are able! Set him free from his bondage once and for all!"

Soon Calvin found himself at the front, directly before the pulpit. The pastor in charge opened his eyes, took one glance—and then gazed upward toward heaven as he said into the microphone, "Thank you, Lord! Thank you, Jesus! Here he is!"

With that, the congregation went absolutely crazy. They had been calling upon the Lord to bring Calvin to himself, and it was happening right before their very eyes.

Falling to his knees, Calvin burst into uncontrollable sobs. Miriam and the children came from their pew to huddle around him as he prayed, "O God, I've become everything I said I'd never be. I don't want to die this way. Please come into my life and set me free. Oh, Jesus, I need you so much!"

That summer night in 1988 was the turning point for Calvin Hunt. Says Miriam, "It was almost as if he had walked slowly down the center aisle of the church as in a wedding, to be married to Christ. Jesus was patiently waiting for him at the altar. No wonder we all burst into tears!"

348 ~ Fresh Faith

On a New Kind of Road

THE OLD LIFE and old patterns put up some resistance for Calvin, to be sure, but the pastors of Christ Tabernacle spoke very straight to him about getting into a Christian residential program in Pennsylvania called Youth Challenge. He agreed to go.

Six months later, Calvin returned to New York City, strong in his faith and ready to live for God. He managed to get his old road construction job back. My wife and I saw him several nights with his crew out working on the Brooklyn-Queens Expressway as we were driving home after church. He was so happy in the Lord! Soon he began turning his singing talent to godly purposes.

Once in a restaurant, Calvin got up to go to the men's room, and there in a stall was someone smoking crack! All of the old desires began to tug at him, but he quickly prayed. *God, I need you to help me right now!* He steadied himself. When the man appeared, Calvin looked him in the eye and said, "Let me tell you something from experience: That stuff is going to destroy your life."

"Whatcha talkin' 'bout, man?"

"I'm serious. It will destroy you—but Jesus can help you overcome it."

The next thing Calvin did was head straight for a telephone to call Miriam and report his victory at overcoming temptation. They rejoiced together in the new strength God had given.

Today Calvin Hunt no longer wields a jackhammer on the highways of New York City. He has recorded two gospel albums and travels full-time, telling audiences nationwide about the road to God's power in their lives. He is also a featured soloist with our choir—the group he once despised—

and a member of the sixteen-voice Brooklyn Tabernacle Singers. Wherever he goes, people's hearts are lifted in praise for God's victory in his life.

Instead of destroying his family, Calvin is now its godly leader—including two new children that the Lord has graciously given to him and Miriam. Doctors had led them to believe that they had both so abused their bodies that conception was unlikely. Then came a daughter named Mia and, a couple of years later, a son named Calvin Jr. From the sin and hopelessness that seemed ready to swallow Calvin and Miriam, God has raised up another monument to the saving power of Jesus Christ, the Lion of the tribe of Judah.

> **May God deliver us from self-righteous judging and make us, instead, merciful carriers of Christ's salvation and freedom everywhere we go.** ～

Let us spread the message far and wide: Jesus Christ is mighty to save! No matter how ruined the life, his blood can erase the darkest stain, and his Spirit can breathe new life into fallen men and women. He is the God of Judah—the man who was a moral failure, a hypocrite, and a disgrace to God and his family. But through Judah we see more clearly the depth of the Lord's love and the incredible richness of his mercy.

May God deliver us from self-righteous judging and make us, instead, merciful carriers of Christ's salvation and freedom everywhere we go. Jesus "came into the world to save sinners," the apostle Paul wrote, even considering himself to be "the worst" of the lot (1 Timothy 1:15). But rejoice in why he was so candid about his condition, for it applies to us also: "For that very reason I was shown mercy so that in me, the worst of sinners, Christ Jesus might display his unlimited patience as an example for those who would believe on him and receive eternal life. Now to the King eternal, immortal, invisible, the only God, be honor and glory for ever and ever. Amen" (vv. 16–17).

PART 3

~

Following the
Divine Channel

TEN

~

Father of
the Faithful

HAVE YOU EVER READ in Scripture about "Father David"?
Or "Father Moses"?

What about "Father Daniel"?

These were all mighty men of God, to be sure. They
rank among the greatest warriors, kings, prophets, and leaders of sacred history. But none of them achieved the special
honor bestowed upon "the father of all who believe, ... the
father of [those] who also walk in the footsteps of faith, ...
our father in the sight of God, in whom he believed, ... the
father of many nations" (Romans 4:11–12, 17–18). His name
is Abraham.

We know that Jesus once disputed using the title *father*
in reference to any mortal human (see Matthew 23:9). Yet,
when the apostle Paul came to write the fourth chapter of
Romans, it sounds almost as if he couldn't help himself. *Abra-*
ham ... oh, my ... he's the very symbol of living by faith ... I have
to set him preeminent above all others ... he's the spiritual father
of all who believe God's promises.

This Abraham was obviously the great example when it
comes to faith. How did he ever develop such towering trust
in God?

He Lived by Promises, Not Commands

On that epic day when God first spoke to Abram (as he was then known), God said,

> Leave your country, your people and your father's household and go to the land I will show you.

> I will make you into a great nation
>   and I will bless you;
> I will make your name great,
>   and you will be a blessing.
> I will bless those who bless you,
>   and whoever curses you I will curse;
> and all peoples on earth
>   will be blessed through you (Genesis 12:1–3).

God directed Abram to do only one thing—"Leave"—and in return, God would do eight wonderful things for him. That number alone speaks of the graciousness and goodness of God.

But it did require Abram to leave his country, his people, and his relatives—in other words, his comfort zone. He had to give up the land he knew best, the culture he had grown up in, the familiar sights and sounds. People who walk by faith often hear God's voice telling them, "You need to leave now. It's time to move on to something new."

Sometimes that word has to do with geography, as in Abram's case. We are currently experiencing this at the Brooklyn Tabernacle as we get ready to leave our present building, where we have been since 1979, and head for the larger downtown theater where we believe God is sending us. We have bought this massive shell, built in 1914, even though as I'm writing this we still do not know how we will raise the millions needed for renovation. We are having to walk by faith.

At other times, God directs his people to leave certain work situations, sever pleasant relationships, or make other difficult changes. When you walk by faith, God never lets you settle into some plateau. Just when you reach a certain place spiritually and decide to pitch your tent and relax for the rest of your life, God says, "Leave." This was the story of Abram. In fact, he was never allowed to settle down permanently as long as he lived.

> **When you walk by faith, God never lets you settle into some plateau.** ∿

But we don't have to be afraid. God in the same breath can begin to inundate us with promises, as he did Abram. See the great things the Lord vowed to do:

1. "... the land I will show you." In other words, God will point out the destination.
2. "I will make you into a great nation."
3. "I will bless you."
4. "I will make your name great."
5. "You will be a blessing."
6. "I will bless those who bless you."
7. "Whoever curses you I will curse."
8. "All peoples on earth will be blessed through you."

Thus, Abram's family caravan left town in a mode of *living off the promises of God.* That was their source, and it must be ours as well. We cannot live off the commands of God, but rather the promises. The commands of God reveal his holy character to us, but they hold no accompanying power. Instead, the grace of God flows through the channel of his promises. God must first do for us what he promised, and only then will we be able to walk in obedience to his commands. Remember, he is our Source—everything must start from him.

It is true that God's moral commands teach us where we fall short. That is necessary—but it doesn't bring a solution to our human dilemma. Only the promises bring us hope, if we respond in faith, as Abram did. That is what sustained him throughout his life. By the time Abram arrived in Canaan, God was already adding more promises to the original group. He said, "To your offspring I will give this land" (v. 7). His abundance kept flowing.

But the great majority of us are command-oriented. Every day we wake up conscious of God's moral law and try to do right so he will approve of us at the end of the day. Yet this is a great struggle. We would do far better to wake up thinking about God's wonderful promises—what he has said he will do for us today. Then his power working in us will tenderly direct us in the way of obedience and right living.

> **God's moral commands teach us where we fall short. That is necessary—but only the *promises* bring us hope, if we respond in faith.** ∾

The tender love of God toward us, as revealed in his gracious promises, is the only thing that draws us to a closer walk with the Lord. Righteous commands alone, and the judgment always linked to them, can easily frighten us away. Martin Luther was originally repelled by the holy God he saw as only making demands and sentencing people to judgment. Then he saw the truth "the righteous will live by faith" (Romans 1:17). This spoke of grace and mercy to all who simply believe God. Out of this came the whole Protestant Reformation, which turned the world upside down.

Abram felt so close to God that "he built an altar to the LORD and called on the name of the LORD" (Genesis 12:8) there between the towns of Bethel and Ai. Abram's heart reached out to God in worship. This God had been so good to him, so generous, so affirming. Abram had not earned any promise or blessing by previous conduct; it was all because of grace. He could not help lifting up his heart and hands to God in adoration.

HE HAD NO MASTER PLAN

THE BOOK OF HEBREWS tells us that "by faith Abraham ... obeyed and went, even though he did not know where he was going" (11:8). He had no map, no AAA brochure, no lineup of motel reservations along the way. His caravan simply headed west toward the Mediterranean, and that was that. God had said he would show him where to stop sometime in the future when he got to wherever he was going.

You and I would struggle with this, wouldn't we? Not only in our vacation travel, but in guiding our careers and our churches, we simply have to have a comprehensive plan. I hear pastors say all the time, "Let's see, regarding this or that outreach—will it pay? Is it going to be cost-effective? How can I be sure it will work? Will everyone be pleased?" We do very few things by faith.

Abram didn't have a clue. If you had met up with his caravan at some oasis, the conversation might have gone like this:

"Mr. Abram, where are you going?"

"I don't know."

"Well, how will you know when you get there?"

358 ~ Fresh Faith

"I don't know that, either. God only said he would show me."

"You have quite an entourage here. When you do arrive, who will supply all the food you'll need? After all, if you're going to survive in a new place, how are you going to eat"?

"I don't know. He just said he would take care of me."

"You don't seem to have a security force. Who is going to protect you from the Jebusites, the Hittites, the Amorites, and all the rest of the warring tribes?"

Abram would just shake his head and wander away.

Faith is happy to step out not knowing where it's going so long as it knows Who is going along. As long as God's strong hand was holding Abram's, everything was going to work out just fine. The caravan moved ahead in faith.

> **Faith is happy to step out not knowing where it's going so long as it knows Who is going along.** ∼

We like to control the map of our life and know everything well in advance. But faith is content just knowing that God's promise cannot fail. This, in fact, is the excitement of walking with God. When we read the book of Acts, we never quite know what's going to happen with the next turn of the page. The Spirit is in control, and that is enough. Paul had no formula as to how he would evangelize; he was simply going by faith. God unveiled the route as he went along.

I was invited to speak at a huge conference of pastors where the entire meeting was plotted out, minute by minute. The man who called me graciously explained, "First there will be an opening song, and then one of our denominational leaders will speak for fourteen minutes on a doctrinal topic. Then will come some additional music, and then we'd like you to speak for twenty minutes. Following your remarks, a choir will present some of your wife's music, and then finally a third speaker will speak for twenty minutes. Then will come the benediction."

This was to occur on a Monday. I thought about the physical drain of leading four services in our own church on Sunday and then right away taking a long plane flight to this conference. Did God want all this travel and expense for such an occasion?

When I hesitated, the man said, "Oh, your book *Fresh Wind, Fresh Fire* has been a great blessing in so many of our churches. We really want you to come."

"Well," I said, "I guess what comes to my mind is this: How many points can an audience remember at one sitting? I mean, you've lined up three speakers, each making important statements. . . . People cannot feel deeply about more than a couple of truths at a time. I think I know the type of speaker you're looking for, but I don't think I'm the man. I'm not really sure that's the best way to minister to thousands of pastors anyway."

"What do you mean?" he replied.

"Well, since you mentioned my book, I have an idea. Why don't you think about scratching some of the program and having a prayer meeting instead? We pastors all need more of God. The general spiritual condition of churches all across America right now is not exactly fervent and prayerful. Divorces are plentiful; young people are falling away; pastors are resigning at record rates—maybe the best thing you could do in your conference is to allocate a block of time just to pray. Why not ask God to open up the heavens and come down? He's the one we really need."

This man graciously replied, "But we don't do those things at our conference."

I said, "I'm not familiar with the traditions of your particular group, but I do see in my Bible where some great promises are given to those who call on the Lord and wait for his blessing."

I finished the call by declining the invitation as politely as I could.

A week later, the phone rang again. "We've decided to adjust the service," the man said. "Why don't you come and bring your wife as well as some others, and you can have plenty of time. You can end the service any way you want."

I felt the Lord opening an important night of ministry. We agreed to make the trip. What a sight it was at the end of that meeting to see thousands of ministers reaching out to the Lord, many of them on their knees, and quite a few with copious tears. "Oh, God, we need you in our churches!" they prayed. "Come and light your fire among us." We were all in the same boat. I wasn't speaking down to them as some outside expert from New York City. I needed to pray the same prayer they were praying. What hope is there for the Brooklyn Tabernacle if we don't pray for God to come by his Spirit and do things we could never do?

The promise at the beginning of the book of Acts is "You will receive power when the Holy Spirit comes upon you" (1:8). No wonder Jesus told the disciples to "wait for the gift my Father promised" (1:4)—just as Abram and his wife Sarai had to wait with expectation for what God had promised them. Having faith in the promise is the key and the only hope for anybody's church, whatever the affiliation.

The great search in too many church circles is not for leaders with the faith of Abram who are willing to trust God wherever he leads, but rather for leaders who are sharp and clever at organizing. We forget that the Christian church was founded in a prayer meeting. It was led in its earliest and most successful years by simple men full of faith and the Holy Spirit. They concentrated not on "the secret of church growth," but on the secret of receiving the power God has promised. Because of their faith, the Lord gave them both power and growth.

We forget that the Christian church was founded in a prayer meeting. ~

Paul was humble enough to admit to the church at Corinth, "When I came to you, brothers, I did not come with eloquence or superior wisdom as I proclaimed to you the testimony about God.... My message and my preaching were not with wise and persuasive words, but with a demonstration of the Spirit's power, *so that your faith might not rest on men's wisdom, but on God's power*" (1 Corinthians 2:1, 4–5). This approach to ministry and igniting faith in God's people is rare today.

In fact, God has a wonderful plan for all his people. But he doesn't have to tell us much about it if he chooses not to. All he asks is that we take his hand and walk along in faith. He will show us soon enough what should be done.

HE FAILED DRAMATICALLY, BUT REBOUNDED

THE CHALLENGE, as we said earlier, is not just to start out in faith, but to continue to walk in faith. The Bible describes the next painful chapter in Abram's life. Although he had started out so wonderfully, he actually failed God by heading down to Egypt because of a famine. He felt the economic pinch, and he reacted. No Scripture shows him receiving any direction from God about this; he just pulled up stakes and moved.

Whenever we stop living by faith, we start unilaterally doing what we think is smart or what circumstances dictate. We soon find ourselves in a weakened position. We get into trouble quickly.

As they neared the Egyptian border, Abram took one look at his beautiful wife and said, "Sarai, I see some problems down the road. Pharaoh and his men will desire you, and they're going to eliminate me in order to have you. So we'd better lie and say you're my sister instead of my wife."

The little scheme only half-worked. Abram avoided losing his life, but poor Sarai was led away to join the royal harem. What an outrageous and low-life thing to do to your own wife! You can be sure the women in the harem didn't get to just sit around there in the palace having Bible studies. Abram saved his own neck, but risked Sarai's virtue and future.

God was watching this whole mess develop and decided to intervene with judgment.

Now, if anyone deserved punishment, it seems it would have been Abram! He was the rascal here. But instead, "the LORD inflicted serious diseases on Pharaoh and his household" (Genesis 12:17), which quickly led Pharaoh to summon Abram.

Pharaoh's wrath exploded in Abram's face: "What is your problem? Why didn't you tell me this was your wife? Take her and get out of my country—now!"

Imagine this great man of faith getting rebuked by a pagan king—justifiably! What a remarkable lesson that in the life of faith, we can wander from the promises and fail so miserably. Nobody yet has walked the perfect faith life. But the important thing is to get back up and back on track. Abram—

"the father of all who believe"—was not quite down for the count.

He and Sarai scurried back again to the land where they belonged, "to the place between Bethel and Ai where his tent had been earlier and where he had first built an altar. There Abram called on the name of the LORD" (Genesis 13:3–4). It seems he could not rest until he got back to the altar where he had once worshiped God—back to the place where he had stood so faithfully on the promises made to him.

> **Whenever we fail God, it is vital to return quickly to an altar of consecration and faith. God is waiting for us there.** ∽

Whenever we fail God, it is vital to return quickly to that altar of consecration and faith. God is waiting for us there, like the prodigal's father waiting for his son to return. He looks forward to getting us back on track. The greatness of Abram was not in his moral perfection, but in his getting back to God and believing again.

HE DIDN'T PRESS FOR HIS PRIVILEGES

SOON A QUARREL AROSE between Abram and his nephew Lot, because their cattle and sheep were crowding each other. God had blessed them both (even Abram, after selling his wife down the river!) to the point that a joint livestock operation was no longer practical.

> So Abram said to Lot, "Let's not have any quarreling between you and me, or between your herdsmen and mine, for we are brothers. Is not the whole land before

you? Let's part company. If you go to the left, I'll go to the right; if you go to the right, I'll go to the left" (Genesis 13:8–9).

Lot promptly chose the fertile plain—the best the human eye could see—leaving Abram to try to graze his sheep on the rocky mountainside.

But Abram did not protest. He could have "pulled rank"—after all, he was the senior man here, and the younger fellow had no right to take advantage of him. Instead, Abram showed that when you have faith in God, you know God will take care of you no matter what someone else chooses. Faith lets other people do their thing without getting anxious and worried. It leaves its case in God's hands.

Too many times we worry about who is forgetting us, who is not giving us credit, who is reaping benefits at our expense. We lose touch with the fact that when God "brings one down, he exalts another" (Psalm 75:7). Both in the secular environment and in church work, we are anxious about things that are better left in God's hands. Worry always nips at the heels of faith and tries to drag it down.

> **Faith lets other people do their thing without getting anxious and worried. It leaves its case in God's hands.** ～

Faith deals with the invisible things of God. It refuses to be ruled by the physical senses. Faith is able to say, "You can do what you like, because I know God is going to take care of me. He has promised to bless me wherever he leads me." Remember that even when every demon in hell stands against us, the God of Abraham remains faithful to all his promises. Jesus Christ can do anything but fail his own people who trust in him.

Why not start afresh today to follow in the footsteps of "Father Abraham"? Begin carefully and prayerfully to search the Scriptures, asking the Holy Spirit to make God's promises come alive to the point where you can live off them, even as Abraham did.

Don't be afraid when you don't know exactly how God will lead and supply for you. Rather, just hold firmly to his hand and walk in faith. There is no need to worry about what the other person might be doing. It really doesn't matter, because God has promised to uphold and defend you.

Finally, if you are someone who has "gone down to Egypt"—walked away from your initial trust and consecration to God—then return right now with all your heart to the Lord. Go back to that altar you once made as a place of worship and surrender to God. He has promised to receive everyone who comes to him through Jesus Christ our Lord. Don't hesitate because of how far away you have strayed or what you did while you were there. Although you cannot see him, the Father watches for you even now, waiting with compassion and love for your return home to him.

ELEVEN

~

God's Deeper Work

W<small>E HAVE SEEN</small> that walking by faith is what brings us into the realm of the supernatural power of God. The Spirit works in us to accomplish things that are impossible to the human understanding. God is indeed omnipotent. He has all power.

Many times, our expectation of that power is slightly misdirected. We are primarily looking for God to show his power in creation, in healing bodies, in supplying employment for his people, in bringing a new baby into the world—and these are all wonderful things. But the Bible declares that the greatest things he does are *internal*, not external. Ephesians 3:20 speaks of God "who is able to do immeasurably more than all we ask or imagine" (we like that part), "according to his power that is at work *within* us."

Only the internal things will go with us into the next world. We won't be dragging along our bodies, our cars, our houses, or our lands. The great church leader Andrew Murray once said, "Your heart is your world, and your world is your heart," and this is the main place where God works in our lives.

What good is it if God heals you and keeps you alive for an extra twenty years if you walk in disobedience for those twenty years? What good is any external blessing without God's peace and joy in your heart? What's the point of receiving a promotion and making a lot of money if your big, fancy house is not a true home, but rather a boxing ring of fussing and fighting?

I have been bothered ever since I was a child by Christian testimonies that neglect the internal to focus only on outside things. "Praise God for the $100 check that came in the mail." "Praise God for sparing me from a traffic accident." While these are definitely blessings, far greater are the things God waits to do within us.

> **Our problems are not merely due to our environment; they are deeply personal. Fixing up the environment doesn't often repair the person.** ～

God knows that our problems are not merely due to our environment; they are deeply personal. Fixing up the environment doesn't often repair the person. Some people, in fact, grow stronger in the midst of adversity; others have an easy life and still self-destruct.

SOILED ON THE INSIDE

NO ONE IN THE BIBLE wrote more honestly and eloquently about what God does inside us than David. And perhaps his most difficult piece of writing was Psalm 51.

Like all of us, David was a sinner. He gave in to pressure and temptation more than once. One spring in particular, he stayed home instead of going out with his army, and he got himself into major trouble.

And that is a warning of something I have noticed over the years: It can be dangerous not to go where God sends you, or not to do what he has called you to do. This is true for everyone, not just pastors and missionaries. I have seen choir members sing faithfully and with great effect for a while ... and then say, "I'm kind of tired; I think I'll go on leave now. Later on, I'll get involved in another ministry of the church." Carol and I have often observed that, if they don't go to the next place of service God planned for them, they eventually drift from the things of God altogether. Satan seizes that moment to reach in and distract them.

People who just hang around churches and "loiter" without getting active in the service God has called them to are in a very treacherous position. There is no difference of reward for preaching the gospel, as I have been called to do, or for serving faithfully as an usher or Christian education worker. If any of us pull back from our calling, we place ourselves at risk.

King David had too much time on his hands, and one night he couldn't sleep. Nighttime brings its own dangers. If you don't sleep well, my advice is that you had better start praising God *quickly*. Otherwise, worry, anxiety, and impure thoughts can easily creep in.

So during the night, David went out on his veranda and saw Bathsheba bathing. The woman was beautiful. He desired her—and being king, he could have anything and anyone he wanted. Everyone knows what happened next.

When Bathsheba's pregnancy became known, this "man of God" acted disgracefully. That's what sin can do to us. David called Bathsheba's husband, Uriah the Hittite, back from the battlefront in order to cover his tracks. It didn't work. So David got the man soused with liquor in a despicable attempt to sway his judgment. Even that failed. Finally, he sent Uriah back to his regiment carrying a letter to General Joab—a letter that was Uriah's own death warrant. David ordered what we New Yorkers call a "hit." He committed murder through other people's hands.

Everything was covered, David thought.

How he ever lived with himself for months and months is hard to understand. The man who had written such wonderful psalms went for most of a year with a wall between himself and God. Then God sent a prophet to confront him.

> **David ordered what we New Yorkers call a "hit." He committed murder through other people's hands.** ~

Only then did David admit his guilt. Finally we hear him come clean in Psalm 51: "Have mercy on me, O God.... Wash away all my iniquity and cleanse me from my sin" (vv. 1–2). From the depths of his soul David repents and asks pardon from the merciful God he has offended.

Then, in the middle of the psalm, David spells out three absolutely essential things that he desperately needs from God. He has learned something from his terrible fall. What he desires is impossible for him; the Lord must do it. And the work must be done *inside* him.

When you hear David's words, you will be aware of how seldom, if ever, you hear anyone pray like this in today's churches. Unfortunately, we are not asking God for things along these lines. This isn't the way we usually talk. But these three requests of David lie at the foundation of every victorious Christian life.

1. "CREATE IN ME A PURE HEART"

DAVID ASKS GOD to "create in me a pure heart" (v. 10). David is asking for more than having his sin-stained heart washed. He has already asked for cleansing (vv. 2, 7). Now he is going deeper. He wants God to start all over, to *create* a brand-new heart that is pure to the core. He admits that apart from God, he is all twisted inside. He wants to see everything in his world with pure eyes, to hear with holy ears, and to act with godly responses.

His words go far beyond our common language of "vow religion" so prominent today: "O God, I promise to do better in the future. I won't do this ever again." Some of us have turned over more new leaves than Central Park. David has no such hope in his ability to pull this off. He calls on God, instead, to create something entirely new within him. The word *create* here is the same one used in Genesis 1:1, when God created the heavens and the earth. It means a divine act of bringing something wonderful out of nothing. The work is all of God.

> **Some of us have turned over more new leaves than Central Park. David called on God, instead, to create something entirely new within him.** ～

Let me say that receiving a pure heart from God is better than getting healed of cancer. It is better than becoming rich overnight. It is better than preaching marvelous sermons or writing best-selling books. Receiving a pure heart is to be like God at the core of your being.

2. "RENEW A STEADFAST SPIRIT WITHIN ME"

THE SECOND THING David cries out for is God's steadiness in his everyday spiritual living: "Renew a steadfast spirit within me" (v. 10). We all know the feeling of being up one day and down the next ... reading the Scripture every day for a week and then hardly glancing at it the next ... going up and down like an elevator. The Hebrew word for *steadfast* means to be firm, strong, erect, immovable. What David is asking God for is a work of grace within him that will keep him from the kind of rise-and-fall, mountain-and-valley pattern that characterizes far too many of our lives. David wants to resist temptation not just one day, but every day. He knows he cannot do that himself—but with God, all things are possible.

David knows he has been cleansed and forgiven, but he feels he needs something else: a steadfast spirit. He doesn't want to be like Jell-O; he asks to be a *rock*. Isn't that our desire as well? Instead of going up and down in our walk with God, we yearn for God by his grace to do the same work for us that David sought. Do we believe God can do it?

Jesus said to Martha of Bethany, "Did I not tell you that if you believed, you would see the glory of God?" (John 11:40). We must not be content just to hope, or to lament our weak spiritual condition. Instead, we must approach the throne of grace with a bold confidence that what God promised, he will do (Hebrews 4:16). Let us ask him for this steadfast spirit that will hold us through the changing situations of life.

3. "GRANT ME A WILLING SPIRIT, TO SUSTAIN ME"

A THIRD THING that David knows he cannot manufacture on his own is "a willing spirit" (Psalm 51:12). God must grant this spirit, he admits. Beyond being steadfast, he wants to be *willing* to do whatever God asks. When God puts his finger on something in our lives and says, "That's not good for you," or "I want you to do this, or go there," we must be willing to accept his will. We can't go on fighting against God in our spirit.

David realizes that only God's power can make him willing to walk in obedience. In Philippians 2:12–13 Paul urges us to "work out your salvation with fear and trembling, for it is God who works in you *to will and to act* according to his good purpose." God is in the "willing business"—praise his name!

David has recognized that his heart can betray him. His will can consent to the appeals of the world and the flesh, so he cries out for God to give him a willing spirit. This again flies in the face of much of today's Christianity, which bites its lip and tries harder to do what only the Spirit of God can accomplish. In fact, God has to *make* us willing. Salvation is of the Lord—from beginning to end. The sooner we learn that we can stop our futile self-effort and throw ourselves on the strong arms of God, the better off we will be.

We must ask God daily to cleanse us, to hold us, to lift us up and give us a willing spirit so our hearts will "run in the path of your commands" (Psalm 119:32). Then we will actually long to do his will. We will get closer to the attitude of Jesus, who said, "My food . . . is to do the will of him who sent me. . . . I seek not to please myself but him who sent me" (John 4:34; 5:30). It was a *joy* for Jesus to obey his Father, not a burden.

The Holy Spirit wants to impart this same spirit to us, so that Christianity is not drudgery or burdensome, but instead a life of loving the good and hating the evil.

ARE CERTAIN CHANGES IMPOSSIBLE?

HOW OFTEN HAVE you and I prayed as David did that day? Isn't it about time that we say with new faith, "God, *you* give me a pure heart. God, *you* renew a steadfast spirit within me. God, *you* grant me a willing spirit to sustain me. Don't let me fluctuate, Lord. Keep me strong!"

God is able to do this against the most vicious behavior patterns and the most embedded thoughts. Certain sins have been characterized in Christendom as almost too hard for God to change. Even ministers have said to me, "Jim, come on, tell me the truth—have you ever seen a homosexual really change?"

"What do you mean? Of course, I have!" I reply. "They are all over our church, serving in all kinds of ministries today."

> Even ministers have said to me, "Jim, come on, tell me the truth—have you ever seen a homosexual really change?" ～

One pastor was frank enough to tell me, "The truth is, I don't want those gays even coming to my church. Once they've been in that lifestyle, that impurity just gets engrained. I don't care who says they've been saved—I'm keeping one eye on 'em."

With that kind of unbelief and prejudice, there is little chance of witnessing the amazing grace of God in action.

One Sunday night not long ago, a very polished, intelligent man named Steve shared with our congregation what God has done in his life. Born and raised in the 'hood of southeast Washington, D.C., he nevertheless excelled in school and earned a scholarship to a Pennsylvania prep academy. While living there in his mid-teen years, he confessed to a counselor one day that he felt a vague attraction to other boys and didn't know what to think about that. The counselor answered that this was all very natural and was nothing to worry about. Steve wasn't convinced, but he said nothing more.

Steve's good grades next brought him a scholarship to the prestigious Ivy League campus of Dartmouth University in New Hampshire. His first actual homosexual experience came as a freshman at the invitation, not of an overly effeminate guy, but rather a star athlete and a candidate for the U.S. Olympic team.

"The next morning, I felt so hollow, so empty," Steve remembers. "It had been a reaching out for love, but it didn't satisfy."

Walking across campus that day to his part-time job, thinking to himself that he had certainly gotten off track, a voice suddenly said to him, *Get out of it!*

Steve did not heed the warning, however, and without any other spiritual anchor in his life, he yielded to his homosexual impulses again and again. By the time he graduated with honors from Dartmouth, he was experienced in the closet lifestyle—but still not sure if he wanted this for the rest of his life.

The lean young man with the penetrating eyes and electric smile showed talent in the field of dance, and in June 1978 he moved to New York City to accept yet another scholarship, this one at the world-renowned Alvin Ailey American Dance Center. (Eventually he landed a job with the prestigious Martha Graham Dance Company, a position he held for ten years.)

Meanwhile, a cousin challenged him to at least read the Bible, and Steve set about systematically to go through the book, starting with Genesis. It took him a year and a half to reach Revelation. During this time, he was sharing an apartment with four other dance students—all of them gay. A close camaraderie developed in the group.

"They were all very promising dancers, and they warmly took me into their circle," Steve says. "Whenever we would be talking late at night, and I'd say something about a Bible portion I had read that opposed homosexuality, they would reply, 'Oh, don't worry about that—you're reading the wrong parts. Read the Psalms, the Proverbs. God is a God of love, and anything that's loving is fine with him.'

"It made sense to me. I gradually convinced myself that my feelings for other men must be God-ordained."

Love of a Different Kind

Steve went from one liaison to another, until finally a relationship solidified with a very talented artist. The two picked out an apartment to share together—one block from the Brooklyn Tabernacle. On Sundays Steve could not help noticing the crowds on the sidewalk coming in and out of our meetings, and he said to himself that he'd like to visit. In October 1980 he finally did.

"I felt the love of God the minute I came through the door," he says with a touch of amazement. "God's presence was there in a powerful way. Instinctively, I wanted to be there. When I left, I was so full of joy!"

Steve kept coming back. No one sat him down for a lecture on homosexuality. In fact, I don't think any of us knew what he was doing privately. He just kept coming to church, soaking in the Word and the presence of God—and starting to feel more and more convicted about his sin. Although he wanted to be in church, he would run out of the building immediately after the meetings, avoiding contact with other believers.

About that time, a big Gay Pride parade was scheduled in the city, and Steve's friends urged him to go. He knew he didn't want to march in the street, but he did attend the accompanying rally near the waterfront in "the Village," as we call that section of Manhattan.

"I watched the crowds of guys, arm in arm, and listened to the fervent speeches," Steve remembers, "—and I never felt so alone in all my life. Something inside my head asked, *Where will I be ten years from now? Out here 'celebrating' homosexuality in the streets? Surely not!* God was steadily chiseling away at my beliefs."

Not long after that, Steve put himself in a foolish situation one night and exposed himself to a sexually transmitted disease. That meant going to the Gay Men's Health Crisis building for a test. Once again, he felt ill at ease as he looked around the waiting room. *I don't belong here. This isn't my kind of place anymore.*

Soon Steve found himself back at our Tuesday night prayer meeting, crying out to God at a corner of the altar rail. He remembers praying, "O God, I know you love me. And I'm willing to acknowledge that this is a sin in my life. But you have to show me the way out of this. In myself, I just don't have the ability."

The struggle with his emotions continued; there was no quick exit from the gay lifestyle for Steve. He grew depressed at times and lost a lot of weight. But he was determined to believe that God would change him on the inside. In faith he held onto the promise of freedom in Christ. He made the tough decision to stop all gay activity.

Then one cloudy day on his way to work near the end of 1982, he was walking in front of the famous Bloomingdale's department store on East Fifty-Ninth Street, when, for no apparent reason, he felt a release from his bondage. "All of a sudden, I just knew that Jesus had set me free!" he says.

The relationship with his partner dissolved, and the man moved out. Steve joined a men's prayer group, where he found spiritual encouragement, and his life began to overflow with the Holy Spirit. Later he got involved with a Manhattan ministry that worked with gays and lesbians. Such Scriptures as Jeremiah 32:27 came alive to him: "I am the LORD, the God of all mankind. Is anything too hard for me?"

With his articulate speaking ability, Steve soon became a spokesman for the ministry, appearing on college campuses and Christian television shows. He was even invited to the nationally syndicated *Sally Jessie Raphael Show* for the taping of a segment called "Being Gay—Born That Way?" Predictably, he turned out to be the only Christian ex-gay on the show, and the minute he started talking about Jesus' power that had set him free, all chaos broke loose on the set. The audience howled while the other guests vented their anger toward Steve.

"On the way home that day, I was feeling sad about the whole thing. I thought of all the things I should have said that I didn't. I was pretty bummed out.

"But early the next morning, my telephone awakened me. A guy from North Carolina said, 'Were you on TV last night?'

"'Uh, yes, I was.'" (How in the world had he even found my phone number?)

"'Can Jesus really do this for someone?' the young man asked with a voice starting to crack.

"'Yes, he really can!' I replied. I went on to explain the gospel to him. Maybe my words the day before hadn't been for naught after all!"

WHO WOULD HAVE IMAGINED?

IN A FEW YEARS, Steve met a beautiful young Christian woman named Desiree in our church. She also had a desire to minister to people with HIV and AIDS. In time they fell in love and began to talk about marriage.

That presented Steve with an uncomfortable dilemma. "Every partner I had had in years gone by was now dead or at least HIV-positive, I knew. The professional dancing field has been devastated by AIDS. If this thing with Desiree was to go anywhere, I knew I would have to take another test.

"The two-week wait for the results was pure agony for me. Finally the day came. I went to the clinic to hear what had been learned. The verdict was—*negative!* What an act of God's grace that I had not been infected all those years! I left the building weeping for joy."

Steve and Desiree were married June 3, 1989. Desiree knew everything there was to know about Steve—and never flinched. She left a successful sales position and returned to school to earn a master's degree in public health. Soon they started a new ministry in our church, a support group in their home for people with HIV and AIDS. Many were led to the Lord and taught that living for Christ is far more than just gritting your teeth and sitting on your hands. It is walking in faith and joy according to God's plan, which is infinitely better.

Leading the group, of course, also meant coping with loss. In one particular year, fifteen members died with AIDS.

Most recently, Steve and Desiree have moved out of the city a couple of hours away so he could accept an assistant professorship at a well-known East Coast college. Two darling little girls have been born to grace their home as more evidence of God's wonderful love. God's hand is on this couple and their children in a special way.

There is not a doubt in my mind that this wonderful man has been changed by the power of God. He told me once that while attending the National Religious Broadcasters Convention in Washington, D.C., a Christian minister came up to him on the exhibit floor and asked a few things about his work. Then he said to Steve a variation of the same question I mentioned earlier that had been posed to me: "So, you mean to tell me you've been set free from homosexuality?"

"Yes, praise the Lord!" Steve answered with a bright smile. "It's been a tremendous thing that God has done in my life."

The man looked him squarely in the face and dropped his bombshell: *"I don't believe it."* With that, he turned on his heels and walked away, leaving Steve speechless.

I am glad I wasn't there at that moment; some of the "Brooklyn" that's still in me might have come out. But a better reply to that pitiful man would have been what the apostle Paul wrote in Romans 3:3–4. "What if some did not have faith? Will their lack of faith nullify God's faithfulness? Not at all! Let God be true, and every man a liar."

> **No matter how deep and dark the secret, no matter how many times a certain sin has defeated you, God can bring change to your life. ～**

God's grace goes further and deeper than we can ever imagine. Steve's life is a reminder that God alone can give us what we really need: a pure heart, a steadfast and willing spirit. No matter how deep and dark the secret, no matter how many times a certain sin has defeated you, God can bring change to your life. But it must be his Holy Spirit working from within and not your weak attempts to "do better the next time." All God asks of you is to bring the whole, sorry mess to him so he can begin the spiritual transformation you need.

Don't attempt to be strong in yourself, for that is the very opposite of what is needed. God is always drawn to weakness. "The sacrifices of God are a broken spirit; a broken and contrite heart, O God, you will not despise" (Psalm 51:17). That verse is from the same psalm with which this chapter started, and if you will join David in his unusual prayer of faith, you will find that God's deeper work will become real in you.

TWELVE

~

Addition by Subtraction

WHEN ANY OF US goes to buy a piece of fine silver jewelry, we walk into an attractive store with aesthetic lighting and well-dressed personnel waiting to show us the various wares inside their glass cases. Everything about the surroundings is clean and sophisticated.

If we were to track that metal back to its origins, however, the opposite would be true. A silver mine is a dark, dirty, dangerous place. Men dreaming of fortunes have lost their lives in mines like Nevada's Comstock Lode during the 1859 silver rush, the Real de Monte y Pachuca in Hidalgo, Mexico (largest silver mine in the world), or the ancient sources of silver in Greece and Armenia during Bible times.

When the ore is brought to the surface, the work is far from over. The crushing, amalgamating, and smelting is still yet to be done. Silver does not melt until it reaches 960.5 degrees Celsius; only then does it start to yield up its impurities. Both King Solomon and the prophet Isaiah had all that in mind when they wrote about God's purging process, the purifying of our hearts and lives:

> Remove the dross from the silver,
>   and out comes material for the silversmith;
> remove the wicked from the king's presence,
>   and his throne will be established through
>   righteousness (Proverbs 25:4–5).

I [God] will turn my hand against you;
    I will thoroughly purge away your dross
    and remove all your impurities (Isaiah 1:25).

While all of us want our fine jewelry to be of high quality, we do not often think about the need for a similar process
in our hearts. In fact, every year it is getting harder to talk
about topics such as this one, because our churches have
become conditioned by the world. "Feel good" and "Keep it
positive" have become the operative slogans. We tend to bris-
tle at the idea of God wanting to make major changes in our
lives. We like it well enough when God says things such as "I
will never leave you or forsake you . . . I will bless your coming in and your going out" and so forth. Yes, God did say all
those things—but the spiritual realities are a little more complex than that.

> **"Feel good" and "Keep it positive" have
> become the operative slogans. We tend to
> bristle at the idea of God wanting to make
> major changes.** ~

God deals with us as a responsible parent deals with a
child. Sometimes you give a compliment or a pat on the back;
however, at other times you do what the apostle Paul told the
young minister Timothy to do: "Correct, rebuke and
encourage—with great patience and careful instruction"
(2 Timothy 4:2). We like certain parts of that verse but are
not so thrilled about the rest; we appreciate the "encourage"
aspect and the part about "great patience," but we are not so
keen about the correcting and rebuking business.

Pastors today are viewed as doing their jobs properly only
when they are giving "a kind word." How many sermons and

counseling sessions contain inspired correcting or rebuking? In too many places, the clergy have been reduced to hirelings—and they will only stay popular (and employed?) if they keep giving messages the people *want* to hear.

LESS IS MORE

BUT GOD'S WAY IN Scripture is far different from the ways of the American church culture. He knows the absolute necessity of removing the dross from our silver, of heating us up to an uncomfortable point where he can, as the New Living Translation puts it, "skim off your slag" (Isaiah 1:25). He is subtracting in order to add. That is strange mathematics, I admit, but it is reality in the spiritual realm. In God's math, you sometimes get more by having less.

I mentioned in my first book that when my wife and I first came to the Brooklyn Tabernacle in 1972, the church was in disarray. Fewer than twenty people came to the services. Within a month or two, I realized that some of the major problems lay within the tiny group itself! A few did whatever popped into their heads during the services. It was both unbiblical and unedifying. There were other problems with racial tension and with people insisting upon lead positions.

I was young and nervous to face this. I guess my predecessor had felt it was best to do nothing; any correction would probably drive someone away, and then the attendance (as well as the offerings) would be even smaller. But I knew in my heart that wouldn't work. I had played enough basketball to know that sometimes in order to win, you have to kick a guy off the team. The problem player may be spoiling the rhythm of the rest. He may have better-than-average talent, but in the locker room and on the floor he is a bad influence and destroys the cohesion of the team. If he won't change, he has

386 ～ FRESH FAITH

to go. Numerous college and professional teams have experienced this. One *fewer* player sometimes means a better team.

I began to pray, "O God, either change people or have them leave." The Lord helped me to accept subtraction in order to start adding. And that is exactly what took place.

If silver is contaminated with dross, it does no good just to add more ore to the pile. The silversmith will not be able to make something beautiful out of it, no matter how large the pile or how much effort is given. Something has to be removed. As long as the impurities remain, the silver will not be shiny or smooth.

We readily accept this truth in many areas, but spiritually we resist it. Imagine someone who is eighty or a hundred pounds overweight going to the doctor and saying, "Please make me feel better. When I wake up in the morning, I'm just dragging. Give me some pills to pep me up."

The doctor would say, "All the pills in the world aren't going to restore your energy. What you need to concentrate on is losing fifty pounds, just for starters."

"What? Hey, I came here to your office to feel better! I can't change my whole lifestyle. Just give me something to help me."

The person *will* be healthier—by subtracting, not adding.

Imagine another patient, with a cancerous growth, who comes in wanting better aspirin to dull the pain. That won't work; the growth has to be cut out. If the patient protests, "Look, I didn't come in here to lose part of my body!" the doctor would reply, "Well, you *need* to lose this particular part of your body. It's cancer; it's got to go."

"You mean you care about me and say you're my friend, and you're going to cut me with a knife?"

"Exactly! If I don't, you're going to die."

Telling the Tough Truth

MANY OF US ARE quick to shout Hallelujah and celebrate God's blessings. Others of us have a sound intellectual grasp of Bible doctrine. That is all good—but we can easily avoid the fact that all the noise and knowledge in the world will take us nowhere if there is unremoved dross in our lives. All the talking in the world won't produce a godly life without the Lord's intimate, ongoing refining process in our hearts.

Some of us are overextended financially. Others of us have a calendar that is way too busy. The only way to get healthy is to reduce the indebtedness, to cut back the busyness. Whatever clutters our walk with God becomes the target of his purging process.

> **All the noise and knowledge in the world will take us nowhere if there is unremoved dross in our lives.** ∼

So many of us think that the more we do and the more we acquire, the happier we will be. Wrong! This is why so many Christians do not see God's purposes worked out in their lives. They can quote the Bible verse about the peace of God that passes all understanding, but they have little experience of what it means.

Because God loves you, he will always be direct with you. He tells you the truth. He is absolutely ruthless in going after the things that spoil the flow of his grace and blessing into our lives. His process is to subtract in order to add. He will never make a treaty with our secret pockets of sin. "That has to go," he will insist. "You cannot go on with that in your life. I cannot make a beautiful silver vessel with that dross still present."

When Jesus began his public ministry, one of his first stops according to the Gospel of John (see chapter 2) was the cluttered temple. Did Jesus bring new paint colors and expensive furniture to add to the decor? No. He got rid of things that didn't belong there, and he kicked out the profiteering merchants. He showed himself to be a tough refiner that day, because he deeply loved the purpose of the temple as "a house of prayer for all nations," and he wanted it to be restored.

Because God loves you, he will always be direct with you. He tells you the truth. ～

We have to face the fact that in order to be what God wants us to be, he will have to take away things in our life that don't belong. In any life or ministry devoted to him, we must stop and ask, "Are there attitudes here that grieve the Lord? Are there habits that need to be broken? What are the impurities that must go? How about that desire to be seen, that competitiveness, that seeking for glory and acclaim? What about that prejudice or judgmentalism toward others?" We must be absolutely open in inviting God to thoroughly search us and take away anything he sees fit.

One Saturday night I was seeking God in preparation for the next day's meetings, just making a fresh consecration of my life and trying to draw nearer to the Lord, when all of a sudden the names of three people came into my mind. None of them were nearby; they were scattered across the country. In all three cases, my relationship with them was not what it should have been. Nothing on the surface was wrong; I was on speaking terms with all of them. But it wasn't right before the God who is love. I didn't feel I had actually sinned against them, but still. . . .

Jim, the Lord seemed to say, *you know there's a wall between you and each of these people. Something isn't right. Call them up! You need to repair the breach.*

I quickly defended myself: "Look, I'm not the cause of these problems. I honestly feel that they are the ones with wrong attitudes, not me."

But God would not back off: *Call them and repent of any hurt you've caused, whether you meant it or not.*

Within the next week, I made the three phone calls. The humbling was good for me, and I learned new insights into God's ways of dealing in my life. What a blessing it turned out to be as I let God bring that slag to the surface and finally skim it off. Immediately afterward, I studied, prayed, and preached with a new vigor.

UNCOMFORTABLE BUT NECESSARY

LISTEN TO THE PIERCING prophecy by Malachi about Christ: "But who can endure the day of his coming? Who can stand when he appears? For he will be like a refiner's fire or a launderer's soap. He will sit as a refiner and purifier of silver; he will purify the Levites and refine them like gold and silver. Then the LORD will have men who will bring offerings in righteousness, and the offerings of Judah and Jerusalem will be acceptable to the LORD, as in days gone by, as in former years" (3:2–4).

Does your theology include Jesus sitting on a refiner's stool, watching over a cauldron of liquid metal under which the fire is getting hotter and hotter? Can you see him reaching down with a flat ladle from time to time to skim off the impurities that have bubbled to the surface? Is our faith deep enough to yield to the refiner's fire?

Will we always be comfortable in this process? Of course not! Is it pleasant? Not at all! But it is our Savior's method of getting rid of the junk in our lives. And his joy and peace will be felt immediately afterward—far deeper within us than we have ever known.

If you are a parent, you might know what it is to see too much junk food going into your child's mouth and decide to do something about it. Or maybe your child is being affected by some bad influences at school. When you take action, it doesn't exactly make you popular—but you do whatever you can to *subtract* these things from your child's life. You're not trying to rain on your child's parade; you do it because you love him.

The Bible says that "the LORD disciplines those he loves, as a father the son he delights in" (Proverbs 3:12). God's purpose for us is a lot deeper than just how we feel at the moment. He lovingly permits pressures and trials, lets the bottom fall out from time to time, so that our wrong reactions come right to the surface. We see our lack of faith, our lack of love—and that is his aim.

God intentionally places us in situations in which we are beyond our ability to cope. He permits difficulties to come with our children, and we say, "Why, God?" He is refining us. He is teaching us to trust him. He is drawing us away from our strength to his. He knows exactly how much heat to allow in our lives. He will never scorch us, but if we jump out of one cauldron because it's too hot, he has others waiting. The dross *must* be removed.

Do you know how the ancient refiner knew when he was finished, and the heat could finally be turned down? It was when he looked into the cauldron and *saw his own reflection* in the shining silver. As long as the image was muddy and rippled with flecks of slag, he knew he had to keep working. When his face finally showed clearly, the silver had been purified.

This is exactly how it is with our spiritual refining process. God's eternal plan is for us "to be conformed to the likeness of his Son" (Romans 8:29). Jesus Christ continues today as the Refiner and Purifier of his people. As he carefully works on our lives, he keeps looking into us to see his own blessed reflection.

Shall we not trust Christ and surrender to this process, rather than fighting it? Remember that it is a process of love to bring beauty and growth and enlargement in our lives. It is God's way of sanctifying us. And we must never forget that the holier the life, the more true happiness we experience within. It is the spiritual impurities that rob us of God's best.

DON'T FIGHT THE PROCESS

LET US FACE the fact that God will never let us remain the way we are today. That is the reason for this refining process in our lives. We are all "under construction." (Sometimes when I see all the major work still needed in my life, I feel like warning people to put on hard hats around me in case of falling debris.)

> **God will never let us remain the way we are today. That is the reason for this refining process in our lives.** ∼

We only move ahead by losing some things. God still adds by subtraction. Communion with him is our greatest need—but there are an awful lot of hindrances to that, aren't there? Some folks know more about *Home Improvement* than God's process of spiritual improvement for their lives. They're more up to date on sports teams and heroes than on what the apostles and prophets taught in the name of the Lord. These weights slow us down as we try to run the race of faith. We stagger at God's promises because our hearts are clogged with so many unedifying habits and unnecessary things.

When someone stubbornly fights God's purifying process, things can turn ugly. When the dross and impurities are grasped tightly like some kind of treasure, the future turns dark and foreboding. It is a kind of spiritual self-destruction.

We have had our share of spiritual shipwrecks at the Brooklyn Tabernacle. Many years ago, I lost one of my closest associates who, unknown to me, had begun to spend far too much time with a married woman who was a new Christian. His wife slowly began to sense that something was wrong, but he cleverly justified his actions on spiritual grounds and blamed her for being judgmental. She didn't share her suspicions with anyone else.

The church was much smaller then, and this associate was known and loved by all the congregation. One day in a staff meeting, I asked him to lead us in prayer. He stumbled along for a while and then broke down emotionally. Something was going on—some deep conflict of the soul. I regret to this day that I was not more discerning. I didn't confront him as a friend and brother in Christ.

Within a few months, the spiritual infection grew stronger and more ominous. Suddenly I received a phone call—while on vacation, no less—that I should quickly get back to Brooklyn. My associate had disappeared along with his lady friend, leaving behind her two children and her husband. They had taken $10,000 from the church account. They left behind a pitiful note assuring me that "God understands what we are doing."

What a tragedy! And how mightily sin can deceive.

Because this associate had been so visible, I faced the unenviable task of breaking the news as best I could to the congregation on Sunday. I broke down openly as I spoke. I can still remember the audible groans and anguished weeping throughout the church auditorium.

I have often thought how many times God must have dealt with my friend. How many times must he have been warned by the Holy Spirit? How many nights did he lie in bed fighting off the conviction of sin? We all know how persistent the Holy Spirit is when he tries to save us from the disaster of shipwreck.

I don't care how many millions around the world may have become fascinated with the story of the *Titanic* and the fateful night it sank into the cold waters of the North Atlantic. It was child's play compared with the spiritual tragedy of men and women who shun the purging of the Refiner's fire, only to find themselves in cold and dark places they never imagined.

God, I ask you to cleanse and purify our hearts and lives. Melt the dross; remove the impurities—all of it, whether in deed, word, or thought. Save us from ourselves, and establish us in righteousness by your strong right hand. We ask this humbly, depending on you, in Jesus' name. Amen.

THIRTEEN

~

The Atmosphere
of Faith

T HE BATTLE OF THE Christian life has always been not just to believe, but to *keep on* believing. This is how we will grow strong in faith and see the actual fulfillment of God's promises in our lives.

Throughout this book we have seen the biblical primacy of faith and its vital nature if we are to live in the will of God. The writer of Hebrews sums this up in a very famous passage:

> So do not throw away your confidence; it will be richly rewarded. You need to persevere so that when you have done the will of God, you will receive what he has promised. For in just a very little while,
>
> "He who is coming will come and will not delay.
>   But my righteous one will live *by faith*.
> And if he shrinks back,
>   I will not be pleased with him."

But we are not of those who shrink back and are destroyed, but of those who *believe* and are saved (10:35–39).

In other words, the writer is telling us not to be like the Israelites who believed for a while and then fell away. What doomed them from ever entering the Promised Land was not the sin of idolatry per se, or immorality, or greed—it was the horrible offense of unbelief. Though God had promised the land to the men and women delivered out of Egypt, they never put one foot in it due to their chronic lack of faith.

> **Faith is like the hand that reaches up to receive what God has freely promised. If the devil can pull your hand back down to your side, then he has succeeded.** ～

Today we tend to soft-pedal unbelief as little more than a common weakness. We say things such as "You know, Mrs. Smith just has a hard time believing that God will help her." God takes no such easygoing approach. He calls it "shrinking back" and lets us know that he is definitely displeased. In fact, to reject his promises to us is far more destructive than the sensational sins we often talk about. The Bible calls it a "sinful, unbelieving heart that turns away from the living God" (Hebrews 3:12). Those are solemn, awesome words!

We see now why the great target of Satan is *to break down our faith*. He knows all too well that the righteous live by faith, so he aims at cutting our lifeline to God. Faith is like the hand that reaches up to receive what God has freely promised. If the devil can pull your hand back down to your side, then he has succeeded. All of God's intended supply will just stay where it is in heaven.

Remember that this faith is not merely a mental assent to certain truths in the Bible. Many people assume, "God said something, and in my mind I affirm that it is true—that's faith." They are wrong. Even the devil can give mental assent to the truth of many biblical facts, yet he remains Satan—our adversary. Real faith is produced when our hearts draw near to God himself and receive his promises deep within us. There, by its own divine power, his Word will work supernaturally.

The minute this kind of heart-faith starts to grow cold, we lose our capacity to receive from God. The chronic disease that afflicts us is not a lack of works or effort; it's a lack of real faith. Many times we are treating the symptom instead of the cause—the outward behavior and not its source.

We are running the race of faith. Those who drop out along the way are people who have stopped trusting the invisible God. None of us want to pull back or make a shipwreck of our lives as we observed in the previous chapter. We desire to receive not only his ultimate promise of salvation in heaven but also the many other promises he has made to us along the way. We want to live in the will of God.

And we don't have much time to accomplish this. As the Hebrews passage says, Jesus Christ is coming soon.

FAITH FOLLOWS PROMISES

IN RUNNING THIS RACE, we must never forget an important principle: Because of the unique place God has given to faith, *his grace flows along the channels of his promises—not his commands*. God's commands do indeed show his holy character and reveal our sinfulness, but that is all. They have no ability in themselves to empower us to obey—which puts us into a dilemma. How many believers worldwide are struggling this very hour with the realization that "I have the desire to do what is good, but I cannot carry it out" (Romans 7:18). It is not that we don't *know* what is right or that we don't *desire* to live that way. Our problem is the spiritual strength to obey, and the commands of God cannot impart that. In fact, it is not in the nature of the "Thou shalts" and "Thou shalt nots" to draw help from God. It is the ministry of his gracious promises to do that.

Saints down through the ages, while lying on their deathbeds, have not so much clung to the holy commands of God and the accompanying judgment to all offenders as they have rather cherished the promises and revelations concerning his great salvation through Christ:

> Therefore, there is now no condemnation for those who are in Christ Jesus. . . . For what the law was powerless to do in that it was weakened by the sinful nature, God did by sending his own Son in the likeness of sinful man to be a sin offering (Romans 8:1, 3).
>
> If we confess our sins, he is faithful and just and will forgive us our sins and purify us from all unrighteousness (1 John 1:9).
>
> To the man who does not work but trusts God who justifies the wicked, his faith is credited as righteousness (Romans 4:5).

These are the blessed promises of God that, when trusted, release his supernatural grace in and through us.

Listen to a man who often failed while depending upon his own strength, though he knew so well the commands of Christ. The apostle Peter tells us the blessed secret that God "has given us his very great and precious *promises*, so that through *them* [we] may participate in the divine nature and escape the corruption in the world caused by evil desires" (2 Peter 1:4). It is these promises that draw the heart to God in faith. This, in fact, is the great command of the New Covenant—to believe!

Without feeding on the promises of the Word, no faith life will be strong. We will not be able to continue on and persevere without living in the Word. There has never been a great man or woman of faith who was not a man or woman of the Book. My shelves are lined with such biographies as Luther, Wesley, Finney, Spurgeon, Moody—they read the Word, lived in it, meditated on it, and through its divine power working in their hearts, grew strong in faith.

> **There has never been a great man or woman of faith who was not a man or woman of the Book.** ⟿

Of course, you will not succeed with only the words on the page. The Israelites who left Egypt came up short with regard to God's promise of possessing that new land for this reason: "The message they heard was of no value to them, because those who heard did not combine it with faith" (Hebrews 4:2). They heard clearly what God promised, but their hearts did not receive it in faith.

Today it is possible to make a living as an esteemed theologian and yet have no more living faith than a slug. Christians can sit in pews listening to the Word preached every Sunday—and even have a devotional life of sorts throughout the week—without rising above the cynicism, depression, and unbelief that are so prevalent in our culture. We can know the Word in some sense, but the Word must find within our hearts an atmosphere in which its divine power can be released.

That kind of dynamic faith fairly oozes from the words of the great Israelite leader Joshua near the end of his life. He was one of only two men who left Egypt as adults and actually *made* it all the way into the Promised Land. Listen to Joshua's parting instructions, which reveal the atmosphere of faith—the environment in which it blossoms and grows.

LOOK BACK WITH THANKSGIVING

JOSHUA BEGINS HIS FAREWELL address with this ringing state-ment: "You yourselves have seen everything the LORD your God has done to all these nations for your sake; it was the LORD your God who fought for you" (Joshua 23:3). In other words, look back, fellow Israelites, and think about all he has done.

How about *us* recalling right now all that God has done for *us* just in the past twelve months? How many hundreds of mornings did you wake up with strength in your limbs to get up and function? You didn't manufacture the strength your-self; it was a gift from God. When did you last thank God for your mental alertness, for a functional memory, or for the skills to be able to hold a job? "Every good and perfect gift is from above, coming down from the Father" (James 1:17). We forget that truth too often. How can we have faith for the future if we don't often look back and thank God for all he's given us in the past?

We have become numb to his many benefits. More than half the persons on this globe have never had the experience of making a telephone call! What we take for granted as an everyday convenience is unknown to much of the planet. A lack of gratitude is, in fact, one of our besetting sins. In most of our churches, there is no outpouring of vibrant thanksgiv-ing and praise each Sunday because we are too occupied with our problems. We concentrate on what we don't have rather than "enter[ing] his gates with thanksgiving and his courts with praise" (Psalm 100:4).

One day in the lobby of our church, a woman named Donna said to me with great excitement, "Pastor Cymbala, I got my first studio apartment—a place of my own! Praise the Lord!" I began to rejoice with her over the simple blessing that she now actually had a one-room place to live. You might find that a little strange ... but then you don't know where Donna was coming from. Several weeks before, the police had gathered outside our church because a "jumper" seemed determined to end her life from a ledge on the building next to ours.

I moved outside with others of our staff and saw Donna high in the air. She had just left the office of her therapist in that building, who obviously had not provided the answer she needed. She was both anguished and frightened at the same time.

I felt God prompt me to enter the building and run up the stairs to where the officers were trying to talk Donna off the ledge. The panicked therapist stood by helplessly. I asked for permission to speak to her, but the cops warned me not to grab for her if I got close, because she might pull me down with her to the pavement.

In about twenty minutes, God helped me to bring her off the ledge into my arms. A staff member went with her in the ambulance for the required examination at a local hospital. We found out later that she had been staying either on a friend's couch or with a man who was abusive to her. Her life had been very sad, but she soon received Christ as her Savior. We helped her find some temporary lodging. When Donna got to the point of being able to rent her own room, believe me, it was a great day to give God a sacrifice of thanksgiving!

Don't you have at least as much to thank God for as Donna does? Then give him praise! Let him know from the depths of your heart how much you appreciate his goodness. Open up your heart and your mouth. Whether it is part of your religious tradition or not, the Bible tells you to express the gratitude of your heart toward the Lord. Get past your self-consciousness and formality to praise the Lord. Refuse to be embarrassed or hindered by anyone.

How pitiful that millions of churchgoers cheer wildly and unashamedly for their favorite sports teams—but are silent as a corpse when it comes to praising God! Read the Bible about the decibel level in heaven. How comfortable will you feel amid the sounds of saints and angels "numbering thousands upon thousands, and ten thousand times ten thousand . . . in a *loud* voice they sang, 'Worthy is the Lamb . . . !'" (Revelation 5:11–12)? Do you have the kind of worshipful, thankful heart that will want to join what John heard as "a great multitude, like the roar of rushing waters and like loud peals of thunder, shouting: 'Hallelujah! For our Lord God Almighty reigns'" (19:6)? May God help us to praise him more!

> **How pitiful that millions of churchgoers cheer wildly and unashamedly for their favorite sports teams—but are silent as a corpse when it comes to praising God!** ~

Think of the many times we have found ourselves in some kind of a bind and have prayed with desperation, "O God, please—if you'll just help this time, I'll serve you and thank you and honor you forever." If that is your history, then don't forget what God has done. Rather, "through Jesus, therefore, let us continually offer to God a sacrifice of praise—the fruit of lips that confess his name" (Hebrews 13:15).

LOOK AHEAD WITH ANTICIPATION

NEXT JOSHUA TURNS HIS attention to the future. You might think that he would be satisfied, at the end of his years, with his many achievements. The first twenty-two chapters of his book tell how he has led the Israelites in conquering vast sections of Canaan. City after city has already fallen to his troops.

But Joshua is not satisfied. He boldly proclaims, "The LORD your God himself will drive [the remaining Canaanite nations] out of your way. He will push them out before you, and you will take possession of their land, as the LORD your God promised you" (Joshua 23:5). Joshua is still, at this late age, invoking the promises of God and boldly declaring that "the LORD your God *himself*" will do the conquering.

Every one of us, if we are honest, can point to things in our lives today that are not yet the way God wants them to be. There is a good deal of "land" still to be conquered. God wants to make us more like the Savior. He wants to root out things that hinder and mar our Christlikeness. He wants to use us to bless and encourage other people in ways we have never experienced or even dreamed. He wants to destroy the complexes and fears that paralyze us. He wants to revive and bless our local church congregations.

And he *will* do these things himself as we live in this blessed atmosphere of faith!

Among the many definitions of faith, perhaps none is more succinct or important than Hebrews 11:1. "Now faith is being sure of what we hope for and certain of what we do not see."

Notice that faith operates in respect to two special objects:

- Future things ("what we hope for")
- Invisible things ("what we do not see")

Faith is not about the present. It is not about things you could capture right now with a camera. Rather, it is about things in the future promised by God—and faith is certain of them. Faith produces a conviction that those things are going to happen, even though the scientific method and our senses cannot validate that certainty at the moment.

> **Faith is not about the present. It is not about things you could capture right now with a camera. Rather, it is about things in the future promised by God.** ～

Faith is the ability of the human spirit to open up and receive impressions from God that are born from his Word and made alive by the Holy Spirit. This brings about a supernatural conviction of certain facts apart from the senses. Andrew Murray put it this way more than a hundred years ago, "Just as we have our senses, through which we hold communication with the physical universe, so faith is the spiritual sense or organ through which the soul comes into contact with and is affected by the spiritual world."[1] In other words, just as our sense of sight or hearing lies dormant until acted upon by light or sound, so our ability to have faith lies dormant until we open ourselves to receive impressions from the eternal, invisible God.

Then we simply *know* that something is going to happen, for God's Word has been received and has activated this spiritual sense called faith. We now bank our life on it. If somebody says, "Prove it," we cannot—but we still know it is coming.

This is what Moses experienced thousands of years ago. "By faith he left Egypt, not fearing the king's anger; he persevered *because he saw him who is invisible*" (Hebrews 11:27).

How do you see the invisible? Not with the eyes in your head, but with the more powerful eyes of faith.

The senses—touch, taste, smell, sight, hearing—have to do with present and visible things. They can't pick up anything about the future. They have nothing to do with spiritual realities. But faith has to do primarily with these future and invisible things that God has promised us in his Word. Faith makes them more real to us than the headlines of today's newspaper. This other kind of "seeing" is what faith is all about, as the apostle Paul says in 2 Corinthians 4:18: "So we fix our eyes not on what is seen, but on what is unseen. For what is seen is temporary, but what is unseen is eternal."

Faith can be likened to a transistor radio. When you turn the radio on, music pours out. Are there any trumpets or guitars inside that little box? Of course not. Yet the room has sound waves all through it. The human senses can't detect them at all. But the radio can pick them up. The music is not actually in the radio at all. The music is coming *through* the radio from a greater unseen source.

So it is with faith. Faith does not originate within us. It comes from God as we receive his living Word into our hearts. Then a supernatural kind of "music" comes alive in us as the product of this faith. A person filled with faith has an entirely different view of things from the person living merely by the physical senses.

Back in the most difficult days of the Brooklyn Tabernacle, when Carol and I had just come to the little church and were struggling to stay afloat with maybe forty people attending on Sunday mornings, our daughter Chrissy was about two years old. One morning at the breakfast table, we noticed a lump under her eyelid. The next day it seemed bigger. We didn't talk about it, even though the lump grew steadily larger.

406 ～ FRESH FAITH

"What do you think it is?" Carol finally asked one day with worry in her voice.

"I don't know."

"We'd better take her to a doctor," she said. The trouble was, we had no health insurance.

That night I spent time praying about the problem, and the longer I prayed, the more ominous it seemed. Did my little girl have some kind of tumor that would steal her eyesight? I said the right words to God, but I knew there was no faith in my heart. There was only apprehension.

We scraped up the money, and I took her to a doctor. He confirmed, "Yes, this is a growth—[he gave the technical name]—that shouldn't be there. It's not life-threatening, but we will need to cut it out."

The thought of my little firstborn daughter having a knife only millimeters from her eye immediately frightened me. Additionally, I was concerned how we would ever pay for the surgery.

That night, after Chrissy went to sleep, I returned to her room. I picked her up and held her in my arms. I prayed quietly, "O God, heal my daughter."

As I stood there in the semidarkness, holding my child and staring at the lump under her eye, I was filled with doubt and fear. I needed true, living faith. ～

Once again, although I was saying prayer-words, all I could see was a lump that now seemed as large as a boulder. I knew what God had said in the Bible about healing—I had preached from those texts. A dramatic healing had even played a role long ago in my grandmother coming to Christ.

But as I stood there in the semidarkness, holding my child and staring at the lump under her eye, I was filled with doubt and fear. I needed true, living faith, not theoretical faith.

The following Sunday, after the sermon, we were singing and worshiping together at the end of the service. I led the people in praising God for his goodness, while Carol played the organ. Suddenly my heart was flooded with a kind of divine light that brought a new sense of God powerfully to my soul.

I was overcome with God's awesome greatness, which makes everything on earth seem miniscule. Then suddenly— as God is my witness, I am not embellishing the story—I *saw* my daughter being prayed for at the front of the church. *And I saw her being healed!* It was not emotional or spooky; it was a real and definite picture before the eyes of my heart. God had birthed something within me.

My heart was pounding with joy as I reached for the microphone. "Who is holding my daughter?" I asked. (Our church was far too small back then to have an organized nursery.)

A teenage girl's hand went up in the back.

"Bring her up here quickly," I said. We gathered around her and anointed her with oil, praying together for God to heal her.

Within forty-eight hours, the lump was entirely gone, with no surgery, no doctor, no medical intervention of any kind. The God who longs to do great things for his people was encouraging us once again to believe.

Now what would happen in your church or mine if people came to each meeting with greater faith—a spirit of anticipation, a belief that God was about to do something wonderful? This was the very expectancy that greeted Jesus in many places. People fought just to touch him, for they

408 ~ FRESH FAITH

knew something wonderful would happen. What if *we* yielded our hearts to both his Word and his Spirit instead of just mechanically repeating the same old order of service we have been following for the past twenty years? Something tells me things would never be the same.

Unfortunately, I have learned firsthand that many Christians who pound the Bible the hardest and most strongly defend the verbal inspiration of Scripture are the most unbelieving and cynical about God ever doing a new thing in his church. They seem so intent on preserving tradition that any spontaneity is spurned as "emotionalism." My question is: If Jesus is the same today as he was in the Bible we defend, why shouldn't we believe him to do great things among us and through us, so we can touch people's lives in powerful ways as did the first-century apostles? Peter was no perfect saint, as evidenced by his denial of Christ; many churches today would hardly allow such a failure to stand in their pulpits. But God chose him on the Day of Pentecost and used him mightily—and God can do the same with us if we look to him with childlike faith in our hearts.

> **Many Christians who pound the Bible the hardest are the most unbelieving and cynical about God ever doing a new thing in his church.** ~

More than twenty-five years ago, David Wilkerson preached a great sermon called "God Only Uses Failures." Of course, it's true—what else does God have to work with? But if we dare to believe him, we can be valuable instruments in his hand.

LOOK INWARD—BUT CAREFULLY

NEXT, JOSHUA CALLS the people to take stock of their obedience: "Be very strong; be careful to obey all that is written in
the Book of the Law of Moses, without turning aside to the
right or to the left. Do not associate with these nations that
remain among you; do not invoke the names of their gods or
swear by them. You must not serve them or bow down to
them. But you are to hold fast to the LORD your God, as you
have until now" (Joshua 23:6–8).

This separation from ungodly things was for the purpose
of the Hebrews' maintaining their strength for battle. Alliance
with sinful things—even just questionable practices—saps our
strength and leaves us weak before the enemy. If there are
some wrong conversations going on, an inappropriate relationship, or some fascination with a questionable topic or
thing, we slowly but surely undercut our spiritual vitality.
The enemy has subtly stolen our "shield of faith" needed to
protect us in "the day of evil" (Ephesians 6:13, 16).

Joshua knew this all too well from what had happened
back at Ai (see Joshua 7). After the stirring victory at Jericho,
the disobedience of one soldier named Achan clogged up the
carburetor of the whole Israelite war engine. The army suffered an unexpected and humiliating defeat—not because
God had lost his power, but because something had separated
the people from his holy companionship. Joshua had to stop
everything and root out the sin before the military campaign
took another step.

The apostle John wrote, "Do not love the world or anything in the world. If anyone loves the world, the love of the
Father is not in him. For everything in the world—the crav-
ings of sinful man, the lust of his eyes and the boasting of
what he has and does—comes not from the Father but from

the world" (1 John 2:15–16). Love for the world and preoccupation with its sick value system and enticements will wreck anyone's faith life.

Introspection, of course, is a two-edged sword. If we give long periods of time just to looking inward, we can easily get morose and spiritually depressed. There are special times for focusing on these things—for example, at the receiving of Communion (see 1 Corinthians 11:28–32) and other moments of divine searching within us. But if this process consumes us exclusively, Satan can easily gain the upper hand as our accuser, keeping us preoccupied with *our* failures rather than with Christ's pardon and power.

It is interesting to me that "solemn assemblies"—occasions when Old Testament leaders set aside whole days for confession and repentance and weeping—are not found in the New Testament. Yes, the apostles believed in getting right with God, in dealing with sin—but they did not grovel in it for long periods of time. Instead, it seems that they called people to cleanse their hearts before God and then moved on to faith and the fullness of the Holy Spirit. After all, Jesus left a Great Commission of work for the church to do. How would that be accomplished if his followers were continually looking inward at their own faults and shortcomings?

LOOK AWAY TO JESUS

JOSHUA'S FINAL INSTRUCTION is stated very simply: "Be very careful to love the LORD your God" (Joshua 23:11). Our gaze must always be upon him, because he is the one who will perform everything. Only when we are "looking unto Jesus, the author and finisher of our faith" (Hebrews 12:2 KJV) are we truly walking in faith.

Satan wants us to focus on the problem, not the Provider. He constantly points to what *seems* to be rather than to what God has promised to do. If we stop spending time with the Lord in prayer, the concerns of the physical world snatch our attention and dominate us, while the spiritual senses deaden and the promises fade.

> **The number one reason that Christians today don't pray more is because we do not grasp the connection between prayer and the promises of God.** ⟿

I am absolutely convinced that the number one reason that Christians today don't pray more is because we do not grasp the connection between prayer and the promises of God. We are trying as individuals and churches to pray "because we're supposed to" without a living faith in the promises of God concerning prayer. No prayer life of any significance can be maintained by this "ought-to" approach. There must be faith in God at the bottom.

Time and again I get phone calls and letters from hungry believers throughout the nation saying, "Pastor Cymbala, I am so frustrated—I've been to sixteen churches now in my area, and I can't find one that has a prayer meeting!" It is obvious that while pastors and leaders mentally accept the Bible's teaching on prayer, they don't really *see* its potential power through God. Otherwise, they would be leading their congregations to do it rather than just preaching sermons about it.

When real faith in God arises, a certainty comes that when we call, he will answer ... that when we ask, we will receive ... that when we knock, the door will be opened ...

412   FRESH FAITH

and soon we find ourselves spending a lot of time in his presence. We seek him for wayward children to be saved, for a greater sense of the Holy Spirit in our church services, for spiritual gifts and power to be released, for the finances we need to do his work.

But I am speaking about more than just presenting a laundry list of requests to God. Faith is especially nurtured when we just wait in God's presence, taking the time to love him and listen for his voice. Strength to keep believing often flows into us as we simply worship the Lord. The promises of Scripture become wonderfully alive as the Spirit applies them to our hearts.

> **Faith is especially nurtured when we just wait in God's presence, taking the time to love him and listen for his voice.** ∼

When people come to my office overloaded with problems, not knowing where to turn, I sometimes say, "Here is what I want you to do: Go sit with the Prayer Band upstairs in their special room this Friday night from midnight to two in the morning."

They often react with shock on their faces. "Oh, Pastor Cymbala—I'm so discouraged I can't believe that the sun will come up tomorrow. I could never pray for two hours!"

"I didn't ask you to pray," I reply. "I just asked you to go sit there. The Prayer Band will pray for you. And God will operate on your heart as you just wait in his presence."

How many times have I heard back from these people that while they were sitting in that atmosphere, God brought alive his Word and his promises and lifted their spirits to believe. Thanksgiving began to flow. They began to remember the good things God had done in their past. Faith began to spring anew as they waited on the One who can so easily turn everything around in life.

God Is Waiting for You

WHAT DIFFICULTY ARE YOU now facing in your life that you have not been able to overcome? I wonder what God is waiting to accomplish in your life, your home, your work, your service for him. Why don't you and I face our need in Jesus' name and reach out in fresh faith to the Lord?

Let us not be hesitant or unsure about trusting him after reading all these wonderful stories and encouragements. Let us, rather, "draw near to God with a sincere heart *in full assurance of faith*, having our hearts sprinkled to cleanse us from a guilty conscience and having our bodies washed with pure water. Let us hold unswervingly to the hope we profess, for *he who promised is faithful*" (Hebrews 10:22–23). In the end, that is what really matters—not our efforts or pledges, but the wonderful truth that God is a faithful God.

So now, what will it be for all of us? Will we simply be stirred for a moment, or will we lay hold of God and his promises in a new, life-changing way? After all, it is not what happens externally to people that makes for tragedy in their lives; it is the missed opportunities to see God help them, due to their unbelief. That is the real tragedy.

God will be no different tomorrow than he is today. His love for us is the same. His power to meet our needs is unchanged. Right now his hand reaches out as he says, "Why spend money on what is not bread, and your labor on what does not satisfy?" (Isaiah 55:2). Let us stop the futile search for answers outside of God. Instead, let us arise with hope in our hearts, remembering that this powerful "word of faith" is not far away and difficult, but rather "is near you; it is in your mouth and in your heart" (Romans 10:8). This is the faith that not only saves us from sin but can also keep us victorious over every obstacle that life presents to us. "As the Scripture says, 'Anyone who trusts in him will never be put to shame'" (Romans 10:11).

Joshua must have had God's faithfulness in mind when he finished his speech that day with this great crescendo: "Now I am about to go the way of all the earth. You know with all your heart and soul that not one of all the good promises the LORD your God gave you has failed. Every promise has been fulfilled; not one has failed" (Joshua 23:14). We, too, can finish our race in life with the same powerful declaration, if we will only keep believing in the God whose promises are forever true.

EPILOGUE

~

33 Treasures

MORE VALUABLE THAN anything I could write or preach on the subject of faith are the direct declarations and promises of God's Word. Here are gems from the Bible that have inspired me over the years to believe. They have also formed the foundation for many a sermon.

As you read them, let them penetrate your mind and your spirit. Open your Bible and read the full passages in which they occur. Review them often as you seek to strengthen your own walk of faith.

~

SO THEN FAITH COMES by hearing, and hearing by the word of God.

ROMANS 10:17 NKJV

~

THE ONLY THING that counts is faith expressing itself through love.

GALATIANS 5:6

~

EVERYONE BORN OF GOD overcomes the world. This is the victory that has overcome the world, even our faith.

1 JOHN 5:4

~

THEY ASKED HIM, "What must we do to do the works God requires?"

Jesus answered, "The work of God is this: to believe in the one he has sent."

JOHN 6:28–29

~

IT IS BETTER TO take refuge in the LORD than to trust in man.

PSALM 118:8

~

FAITH IS BEING SURE of what we hope for and certain of what we do not see. This is what the ancients were commended for.

HEBREWS 11:1–2

~

WITHOUT FAITH IT IS impossible to please God, because anyone who comes to him must believe that he exists and that he rewards those who earnestly seek him.

HEBREWS 11:6

~

THE APOSTLES SAID to the Lord, "Increase our faith!"

LUKE 17:5

~

WE DO NOT WANT you to become lazy, but to imitate those who through faith and patience inherit what has been promised.

HEBREWS 6:12

~

IF ANY OF YOU lacks wisdom, he should ask God, who gives generously to all without finding fault, and it will be given to him. But when he asks, he must believe and not doubt, because he who doubts is like a wave of the sea, blown and tossed by the wind.

JAMES 1:5–6

~

TRUST IN THE LORD and do good;
 dwell in the land and enjoy safe pasture....
Commit your way to the LORD ;
 trust in him and he will do this....
Be still before the LORD and wait patiently for him;
 do not fret when men succeed in their ways,
 when they carry out their wicked schemes.

PSALM 37:3, 5, 7

~

CAST YOUR CARES on the LORD
 and he will sustain you;
 he will never let the righteous fall.

PSALM 55:22

~

TRUST IN HIM at all times, O people;
 pour out your hearts to him,
 for God is our refuge. *Selah*

PSALM 62:8

~

BUT NOW, THIS IS what the LORD says—
 he who created you, O Jacob,
 he who formed you, O Israel:

"Fear not, for I have redeemed you;
    I have summoned you by name; you are mine.
When you pass through the waters,
    I will be with you;
and when you pass through the rivers,
    they will not sweep over you.
When you walk through the fire,
    you will not be burned;
      the flames will not set you ablaze."

ISAIAH 43:1–2

∼

I AM THE LORD, your God,
    who takes hold of your right hand
and says to you, Do not fear;
    I will help you.

ISAIAH 41:13

∼

TRUST IN THE LORD with all your heart
    and lean not on your own understanding.

PROVERBS 3:5

∼

WHO AMONG YOU fears the LORD
    and obeys the word of his servant?
Let him who walks in the dark,
    who has no light,
trust in the name of the LORD
    and rely on his God.

ISAIAH 50:10

∾

MY EYES ARE EVER on the LORD,
for only he will release my feet from the snare.

PSALM 25:15

∾

TO ALL WHO received him, to those who believed in his
name, he gave the right to become children of God.

JOHN 1:12

∾

"WHOEVER BELIEVES IN ME, as the Scripture has said,
streams of living water will flow from within him."

JOHN 7:38

∾

"HE MADE NO DISTINCTION between us and them, for he
purified their hearts by faith."

ACTS 15:9

∾

WHAT THEN SHALL we say that Abraham, our forefather, discovered in this matter? If, in fact, Abraham was justified by works, he had something to boast about—but not before God. What does the Scripture say? "Abraham believed God, and it was credited to him as righteousness."

Now when a man works, his wages are not credited to him as a gift, but as an obligation. However, to the man who does not work but trusts God who justifies the wicked, his faith is credited as righteousness.

ROMANS 4:1–5

～

AGAINST ALL HOPE, Abraham in hope believed and so became the father of many nations, just as it had been said to him, "So shall your offspring be."

ROMANS 4:18

～

CHRIST IS THE END of the law so that there may be righteousness for everyone who believes.

ROMANS 10:4

～

THEY WERE BROKEN OFF because of unbelief, and you stand by faith. Do not be arrogant, but be afraid.

ROMANS 11:20

～

... SO THAT YOUR faith might not rest on men's wisdom, but on God's power.

1 CORINTHIANS 2:5

～

IN SCRIPTURE IT SAYS:
    "See, I lay a stone in Zion,
        a chosen and precious cornerstone,
    and the one who trusts in him
        will never be put to shame."

1 PETER 2:6

～

NOT THAT WE LORD it over your faith, but we work with you for your joy, because it is by faith you stand firm.

2 CORINTHIANS 1:24

∼

IN ADDITION TO ALL THIS, take up the shield of faith, with which you can extinguish all the flaming arrows of the evil one.

EPHESIANS 6:16

∼

LET US DRAW NEAR to God with a sincere heart in full assurance of faith, having our hearts sprinkled to cleanse us from a guilty conscience and having our bodies washed with pure water.

HEBREWS 10:22

∼

"MY RIGHTEOUS ONE will live by faith.
And if he shrinks back,
   I will not be pleased with him."

But we are not of those who shrink back and are destroyed, but of those who believe and are saved.

HEBREWS 10:38–39

∼

WHEN HE HAD gone indoors, the blind men came to him, and he asked them, "Do you believe that I am able to do this?"

"Yes, Lord," they replied.

MATTHEW 9:28

∼

IMMEDIATELY THE BOY'S FATHER exclaimed, "I do believe; help me overcome my unbelief!"

MARK 9:24

NOTES

Chapter Five—Can I Trust God to Lead Me?

1. *The Works of John Wesley*—CD (Franklin, Tenn.: Providence House, 1995); see also "The Character of a Methodist," *The Works of John Wesley*, 3d ed., vol. 8, p. 339 (London: Wesleyan Methodist Book Room, 1872; reprinted Grand Rapids: Baker, 1996).

2. Sermon entitled "The Eternal Name," preached on the evening of May 27, 1855, at Exeter Hall, London.

Chapter Seven—Faith Runs on a Different Clock

1. "Keep Believing" by Tim Pedigo (Nashville: Meadowgreen Music, copyright © 1985).

Chapter Eight—Overcoming Discouragement

1. Cited in *Words Old and New*, compiled by Horatius Bonar (reprint Edinburgh: Banner of Truth Trust, 1994), pp. 16–17.

Chapter Thirteen—The Atmosphere of Faith

1. Andrew Murray, *The Holiest of All* (1894; reprint Grand Rapids: Revell, 1993), pp. 441–42.

Fresh Faith
Study Guide

Chapter One: Stolen Property

Pastor Cymbala points out that *Satan steals spiritual, eternally significant treasures* that God values. What types of things does Satan do to steal our sense of purpose in life, to cause our zeal and passion for God to wane?

Personal Reflection

Jesus said to the Ephesian church in Revelation 2, "I know your deeds, your hard work and your perseverance.... Yet I hold this against you: You have forsaken your first love." What do you notice when you compare your love for the following today to the love you had when you first became a Christian?

- Your love for Jesus?
- Your love of and desire to know the Scriptures?
- Your energy and passion for the church?

Pastor Cymbala writes about the "unique calling that rests on every Christian's life—the gifting to serve others in the name of the Lord."

- What are some ways in which Satan has sidetracked you from your God-given calling—or hindered you from accomplishing what God wants you to do for him? Did you recognize them as Satan's effort to side-track you? How did you respond? What would you have done differently if you had recognized Satan's efforts to steal, kill, or destroy?

Pastor Cymbala emphasized that Satan intends to destroy our marriages, credibility, and effectiveness. What are some evidences of his "successes" in our society today? Among Christians?

A Time to Share

Break into groups of two or three and discuss the following questions:

- What is faith?
- Which specific events or thoughts cause people to stop trusting God, to stop expecting him to answer their prayers?
- What do you think will happen if we go after specific problems in the name of the Lord?

Pastor Cymbala used the story of the time when David and his men recovered their families and all their possessions from the marauding Amalekites to illustrate that "what the enemy steals, God alone is able to recover."

- Why is it important for us to recognize that we aren't wrestling against flesh and blood but are engaged in spiritual warfare?

- Why is it important for us to use the spiritual weapons of faith and prayer to resist Satan and in the power of God "get up" and recover what Satan has stolen from us?
- Why do some of us refuse to battle Satan and seek the abundant life Jesus promises—in our marriages, in our spiritual calling, in our desire to have a vibrant heart-faith and childlike trust in the risen, supernatural Christ?

Personal Reflection

In what ways do you tend to respond toward God when bad things happen in your life? Do you angrily blame him? Do you, as the psalmist David did, "find strength" in the Lord your God? Do you ask God for guidance and encouragement? What do your responses reveal about your faith?

Romans 1:17 reveals that "the righteous will live by faith," and Hebrews 11:6 reads, "Without faith it is impossible to please God." What must we do to keep our "faith connection" to God fresh and vibrant?

CHAPTER TWO: AMALIA'S STORY

Remember the story Pastor Cymbala told concerning Amalia—her wretched home life, the sexual abuse, drugs, exotic dancing, plans for suicide?

- What things in our lives seem "too impossible" for God to change?

- In light of what God changed in Amalia's life, how might he change the "impossibilities" of our lives if we will in faith ask him to help us reclaim what Satan has stolen from us?

A Time to Share

Pastor Cymbala writes, "You can see Jesus Christ prove himself more powerful than the thief who steals [Satan]. This very moment is critical, even as you read these words. Face the reality of your spiritual situation, and go after anything God has shown you to be stolen property that Satan has cleverly taken from you. The zeal and love for Christ you once had *can* be recovered."

- In what ways would your life change if you were to recover what Satan has stolen from you?
- What might the consequences be if we continue to allow Satan to steal the treasures God has for us—our children, our marriages, our churches?

Personal Reflection

Psalm 50:15 reads, "Call upon me in the day of trouble; I will deliver you, and you will honor me."

- What prevents you from calling on God right now for mercy and grace?
- Think of an area in your life in which you need to ask in faith that Jesus will restore what Satan has stolen. Be honest! Then take some time to ask God for help. Instead of allowing Satan to keep ripping you off, begin to ask Jesus in faith for the abundant life he offers you. Ask him to restore what Satan has tried to steal. (And when God does it, be sure to praise him in a new way!)

CHAPTER THREE:
THE QUESTION NOBODY IS ASKING

Why do you think Christians tend to measure how they are doing spiritually by focusing on what Pastor Cymbala calls "surface things" instead of answering the question: *How active and vibrant is our faith in God?* What is the difference?

Pastor Cymbala writes, "What [the apostle] Paul knew, but what we seem to have forgotten, is that when people break down in their behavior, backslide into sinful living, or grow cold in the Lord, it is because their faith has broken down first."

- Do you agree or disagree with this? Why?
- What specific things cause our personal faith in God to "break down"?

Personal Reflection

We read in the New Testament that Jesus was amazed by some people's faith—for example, the Roman centurion (Luke 7) and the Canaanite woman (Matthew 15). If Jesus were sitting across from you in a restaurant or in your home, what do you think he would say about your faith in him?

The Bible clearly states that our faith is the key to our relationship with God. Pastor Cymbala calls it "the trigger that releases divine power." Jesus said, "According to your faith will it be done to you" (Matthew 9:29).

- How does this truth match what you have learned about God's supreme power and what he will do for you?
- In what way(s) does this truth support or contradict what you have heard about what it means to walk "in faith"?

- If people realize this truth, how might they act and respond differently—toward God? Toward the Bible? Toward prayer?

What happens to our walk with God when we focus on our human efforts and abilities rather than on God's, meaning that we focus on earning God's approval by doing certain things (daily Bible reading, trying to live a good life, etc.) rather than receiving his grace by faith?

Paul writes, "I can do everything through him [Christ] who gives me strength" (Philippians 4:13). What does it mean, in practical terms, to receive "strength" from Christ?

God, on one hand, calls us to live "by faith." Yet Jesus is "the author and finisher of our faith" (Hebrews 12:2 KJV). How would you describe the balance between what we do and what God does in and through us?

In the following verses written by Paul, what might seem contradictory to people who don't yet know Jesus? "The Lord ... said to me, 'My grace is sufficient for you, for my power is made perfect in weakness.' ... That is why, for Christ's sake, I delight in weaknesses, in insults, in hardships, in persecutions, in difficulties. For when I am weak, then I am strong" (2 Corinthians 12:9–10).

Describe a time in your life when, as Pastor Cymbala says, "God used trouble and trials of all kinds" to remind you that you need him to fill you constantly so that you had the faith to use divine resources. What did the troubles and trials teach you about your need for God? Your need for faith?

"Childlike faith in God," writes Pastor Cymbala, "is not only what pleases him but is also the secret of our strength and power."

- What does Pastor Cymbala mean by childlike faith?
- Why is childlike faith so important to our spiritual growth and effectiveness?

A Time to Share

Pastor Cymbala writes, "When we run to him [God] and throw ourselves upon him in believing prayer, he rejoices.... He is not so much interested in our *doing* as in our *receiving* from him."

- What is "believing prayer"?
- Why does God desire us to be in a mode of receiving from him?

As a group, read Psalm 32:6–11 aloud. Then discuss each of these verses, exploring how they relate to faith and trust in God's character. You may use the following questions as a springboard.

- In what way(s) is God our "hiding place"?
- What does God promise to do for us?
- What, according to God, surrounds a person who trusts in him?

CHAPTER FOUR: FREE FROM A HURTFUL PAST

Pastor Cymbala points out that Joseph named his first son Manasseh because God had made him forget all the evil things people had done to him.

- Why is it important for us, when we've been hurt by others, to seek God's help in delivering us from the paralysis of the past?
- What was accomplished when Amalia, who was greatly abused, visited her father and told him that she had forgiven him and loved him?
- What is Satan able to accomplish when he uses the hurts and ugly memories of our past to steal our callings, our peace, and our joy?

Personal Reflection

Think about a time when you or someone you know stopped struggling in his/her own strength and called out to God in simple faith. What happened? Are you fully depending on God today and trusting him to help meet a particular problem or need? Why or why not?

Personal Reflection

Do you believe that, as Pastor Cymbala puts it, "Faith grows best on cloudy days"? Do you believe that God can set you free from painful experiences and hurt? Will you ask him to make you spiritually fruitful even when you face the hardest challenges? Why not approach his throne of grace boldly right now and ask him for the grace to help you right where you need it!

CHAPTER FIVE: CAN I TRUST GOD TO LEAD ME?

Pastor Cymbala writes, "It may not seem obvious at first glance, but the way we make decisions in life tells a lot about the kind of faith we have in Jesus Christ." To what extent do you base your decisions on feelings? On the advice of godly family members and/or friends? On what the living God who reveals himself through the Bible says?

A Time to Share

Pastor Cymbala points out that some Christians follow the spiritual culture into which they were born—such as a particular church, denomination, or religious tradition—rather than using the Bible as their guide and model. Instead of coming to the Scriptures and asking God to teach them, these people hold on to what they have already embraced and are not really open to change and growth.

- How does this "closed" approach to the Christian life influence people's understanding of these words: *prayer, worship, church, evangelism, God's power, faith, Christian?*
- Why is it important, as Pastor Cymbala writes, to "honestly search God's Word and let it shape our spiritual thinking and values"?
- What are some of the dangers of letting our personal background, rather than God's Word, be the main force that shapes our spiritual thinking and values?

What are the consequences of making decisions without seeking God and tapping into his great resources of wisdom? Of doing just about everything *except* praying earnestly until we find God's will for our lives?

A Time to Share

Pastor Cymbala writes, "Wherever God leads us, there is an umbrella of protection and supply that stays over our heads.

Under that umbrella are the divine resources of wisdom, grace, finance, and all the other things we need to do that God has asked. That does not mean there won't be problems and difficulties. But wherever the Lord leads, he must then by necessity help us." Break up into twos and threes and talk about times when you have seen in your lives or in the lives of others how God has provided for people who have obeyed God and gone where he wanted them to go.

When Pastor Cymbala heard about a four-thousand-seat theater in Brooklyn for sale, he asked the associate pastors to look at it and pray about buying it. Unless all of them felt God was leading them, they wouldn't present the option to the congregation.

- In what ways can we seek God's confirmation for decisions we must make?
- Why is it important for us to receive confirmation from God concerning our decisions?
- What role does humility play as we seek God's guidance?

A Time to Share

Pastor Cymbala points out research showing that fewer than 10 percent of churchgoing Christians make important life decisions "based on God's Word and seeking his will." We don't think God really cares about us, are too proud to admit we need God's help, or simply continue the same decision-making habits.

- To what extent does our understanding of God's character influence the degree to which we will seek his leading?

According to Pastor Cymbala, "Too many church leaders, having been turned off by overblown claims and fanaticism in certain quarters, have stopped believing in an active Holy Spirit at all." Discuss your opinions on this and the consequences this may be having in your church today.

Personal Reflection

Do you believe God is interested in every part of your life? That he watches you and wants to lead you? How does your belief affect your life—and people around you?

What situations are you or someone you love facing right now in which you need God's guidance? Have you yielded to his will for your life so you can hear his voice? Why or why not? What will you do in coming days in order to wait and listen in God's presence?

During one Sunday afternoon service, Pastor Cymbala sensed God telling him to preach the gospel right away. So, after giving Calvin Hunt, the soloist, time to speak, Pastor Cymbala interrupted the schedule and preached. As a result, a wayward young man heard and responded to the gospel.

- Why is it important for us to listen to the Holy Spirit's leading—even during our preplanned church services?

CHAPTER SIX: THE HIGH COST OF CLEVERNESS

A Time to Share

Pastor Cymbala writes, "Our culture teaches us to take charge of our lives and call our own shots." In what ways does this view conflict with trusting God completely to lead and guide us?

Selected by God to become king of Israel, Jeroboam received wonderful promises that were conditional on his obedience to God. Instead of having faith in God, obeying God, and trusting in God's promises, he "thought to himself" (1 Kings 12:26) and depended on human cleverness.

- What are some situations in which we do this same thing today?
- How does our unbelief affect our relationship with God?
- What makes it easier to trust in ourselves rather than in God?

King Jeroboam built golden calves in his territory so people would worship in Israel rather than in the southern kingdom. Pastor Cymbala points out, "In the church today, we are still busy inventing new forms of religion as Jeroboam did." In what ways might our new, "user-friendly" kind of Christianity be quite different from a Spirit-filled Christianity?

Why is it important for us to pray honestly to God, tell him our fears, and trust in his faithfulness rather than "talking to ourselves" and trying to figure out all the details?

In what way(s) might each of us benefit from a godly prayer partner who can help us remain focused on God's faithfulness?

CHAPTER SEVEN:
FAITH RUNS ON A DIFFERENT CLOCK

Personal Reflection

When you experience problems, do you believe that God is really "for you" and will supply what you need—or do you believe that you have to face everything on your own? Are you still asking and seeking God—even when you feel pressure to "do something" in your own strength? What are some specific ways in which you can trust God to keep his promises?

A Time to Share

As the story of Zechariah and Elizabeth in Luke 1 illustrates, God accomplishes his will according to his timetable. Let's recall their story and explore a few truths together.

- How do you think Zechariah felt when the angel announced Elizabeth would bear a son?
- The angel said to Mary, who would be the mother of Jesus, "For nothing is impossible with God" (Luke 1:37). How does this relate to us today?
- What does God reveal about himself and our relationship with him when he intervenes in the seemingly hopeless situations in our lives?
- Describe a time when God intervened on your behalf, perhaps when a situation seemed too awful to be fixed.
- What impact did God's action have on you? On others close to you?
- After Elizabeth gave birth, Zechariah praised God. Why is it important for us to praise God after he demonstrates his mighty power and salvation in our lives?

Why, according to Pastor Cymbala, must we "persevere in prayer"—as individuals and as a body of believers? Relate your answer to James 4:2: "You do not have, because you do not ask God."

Personal Reflection

When do you, as Zechariah did, find it hard to believe God's promises? Are you persevering in prayer, or are you trying to get by on your own? What may be keeping you from completely trusting God, who can accomplish so much when you have faith in him? " Do you believe what your feelings and circumstances tell you or what God has promised to do?

When you read the following lyrics, what do you *feel?*

> Keep believing what you know is true;
> Keep believing—you know the Lord will see you
> through.
> When troubles arise in your life, and you don't know
> what to do,
> You'll be fine if you just keep believing.[1]

In *Fresh Faith*, Pastor Cymbala describes Wendy Alvear's search for a husband and good marriage and how she learned to keep her eyes on God rather than on her situation. "Wait for God," she later shared with the Brooklyn Tabernacle congregation, "he knows how to give you the best."

- What does it mean, in practical terms, to "keep on believing and waiting for God"?

---

[1]"Keep Believing" by Tim Pedigo (Nashville: Meadowgreen Music, copyright © 1985).

CHAPTER EIGHT: OVERCOMING DISCOURAGEMENT

"The promises of God," Pastor Cymbala writes, "are appropriated only by faith. God is looking for a people who will believe him and take him at his word no matter what the circumstances say or what other people are telling us."

- Why is it more difficult for us to place our faith in God and what he has promised to do than to believe what our feelings and circumstances tell us?
- Why do you think God values our faith in him so highly?

A Time to Share

Pastor Cymbala writes, "The battle is always not about giving in to what we see around us, but about holding on to God's promises." Do you agree or disagree? Why? Share some experiences you have had relating to trusting God with important issues. Describe how you fought the battle.

Colossians 1:10–12 reads, "And we pray this in order that you may live a life worthy of the Lord ..., being strengthened with all power according to his glorious might so that you may have great endurance and patience, and joyfully giving thanks to the Father, who has qualified you to share in the inheritance of the saints in the kingdom of light." Which parts of these verses are especially meaningful and encourage you to live a life that is worthy? Why?

Satan, according to Pastor Cymbala, uses loose talk and loose emotions to discourage us.

- What are some signals that reveal we should try to limit our time with a particular person because of his or her negative effect on our spirit?

440 ～ Fresh Faith

- What are some ways to deal with a person who discourages us?
- Describe what Pastor Cymbala calls "loose emotions" and identify their causes.
- What is the biblical antidote to loose talk and loose emotions?

What are some differences between Christians who are able to endure life's challenges and other Christians who become discouraged in the face of attacks on their faith?

"The longer I live, the more I treasure people who just keep walking with God," Pastor Cymbala writes. "They aren't up or down, left or right; they're always steady on the course, praising God and believing his Word." Why is praise important in our walk with God?

Chapter Nine: Grace That Is Greater

Judah, the Old Testament patriarch, wasn't exactly a model of godly obedience. He married a pagan, lost two evil sons to God's judgment, and had sex with a woman he believed to be a prostitute. He was a moral failure, hypocrite, and a disgrace to God and his family.

- Why do you think God included Judah's ugly story in the Bible and included Perez—Tamar's son from her union with Judah—in the genealogy of Jesus? What does his story reveal about God's view of sin and forgiveness in light of our own sins and feelings of unworthiness?

- What is the difference between proclaiming God's grace in changing and redeeming sinful people on one hand and emphasizing God's commandments and expressing self-righteous disdain over other people's sinful lives?

"God's specialty," Pastor Cymbala writes, "is forgiving and putting away people's sins from his sight." In what ways could we better emphasize the mercy God has for every person who messes up?

Personal Reflection

When you read the story of Calvin Hunt's addiction to crack cocaine, how does what God did in his life and in the life of his family relate to your life? To the life of someone you know? To what our powerful God can do?

In what way(s) does what the apostle Paul says in the following verse, 1 Timothy 1:16, relate to each of us today? "But for that very reason I was shown mercy so that in me, the worst of sinners, Christ Jesus might display his unlimited patience as an example for those who would believe on him and receive eternal life."

CHAPTER TEN: FATHER OF THE FAITHFUL

Pastor Cymbala writes, "When you walk by faith, God never lets you settle into some plateau." In what ways have you found this to be true in your life?

A Time to Share

Break into small groups and discuss these questions:

- What happens when we try to live off God's commands rather than God's promises?
- If we woke up every morning thinking about God's wonderful promises—what he has said he will do for us today—how might our lives be different?
- What price do we pay when we don't step out in faith and believe God's promises?

What are the dangers of concentrating on external evidences of God's work, such as "the secret of church growth," rather than receiving the power God has promised to give his people as they walk in faith?

Just as Abraham headed to Egypt without consulting God because of a famine, trouble ensues when we stop living by faith and do what we think is smart or what circumstances dictate. How will God respond to anyone who turns back to him, to what Pastor Cymbala calls "an altar of consecration and faith"?

Personal Reflection

"Jesus Christ," writes Pastor Cymbala, "can do anything but fail his own people who trust in him." Why is it so important to trust in God—in his care for you and those you love—rather than worrying? Do you find it hard to trust God sometimes, even though you know God's promises? Set aside time this week to carefully and prayerfully search the Scriptures, asking God to make his promises come alive to you and also reviewing his promises included at the back of *Fresh Faith*.

Regardless of whether you have strayed from God, he is waiting to receive you.

CHAPTER ELEVEN: GOD'S DEEPER WORK

Over and over, Pastor Cymbala emphasizes that walking by faith brings us into the realm of God's supernatural power. Often we expect God to work in external areas, such as healing our bodies and supplying jobs. But where, according to Ephesians 3:20, does God often exhibit his great power? What does he want to accomplish?

"God," Pastor Cymbala writes, "knows that our problems are not merely due to our environment; they are deeply personal." What does he mean by this statement? In what way(s) does this statement go against current perspectives concerning our problems?

A Time to Share

Nearly a year after David's affair with Bathsheba, he admitted his guilt and came clean. In the middle of Psalm 51, he spelled out three essential things he needed from God. Break into groups of two or three and discuss these three things.

1. "Create in me a pure heart" (Psalm 51:10)
   - What did David admit here about himself?
   - Why did David want a brand-new heart?
   - If this prayer were the cry of our hearts, how might our lives be different?

2. "Renew a steadfast spirit within me" (Psalm 51:10).

- Why is "steadfastness" in everyday spiritual living important?

- What causes many Christians to have a "rise-and-fall, mountain-and-valley" relationship with God?

- What keeps us from boldly asking God to make our faith firm and do what he has promised?

3. "Grant me a willing spirit, to sustain me" (Psalm 51:12).

- According to this verse, how do we obtain "a willing spirit" that will do whatever God asks us to do?

- What happens when we try to do God's will on our own rather than depending on his Holy Spirit to work from within us?

- What has happened to Christians who view Christianity as drudgery and burdensome rather than a joyous life of loving the good and pleasing God?

God, according to Pastor Cymbala, will give *anyone* a pure heart, renew a steadfast spirit, and grant a willing spirit. It doesn't matter how deeply evil thoughts are embedded or how vicious a person's behavioral patterns have become. Jeremiah 32:27 reads, "I am the LORD, the God of all mankind. Is anything too hard for me?"

- What, then, do Christians who are unwilling to realize that God can fully redeem anyone and change even the "worst" behaviors believe?

- What conclusions do we come to when we believe that God's power isn't effective for all sins, that he can't completely change anyone from the inside out? What are the consequences of such beliefs?

Personal Reflection

Is your Christian walk all you want it to be? What might be keeping you from walking in faith and joy according to God's plan? What, in practical terms, happens when you believe your faithful God has the power to completely change your life—and the life of anyone else no matter how deeply rooted sin may be in his or her life?

Psalm 51:17 says, "The sacrifices of God are a broken spirit; a broken and contrite heart, O God, you will not despise." Why is God always drawn to weakness?

CHAPTER TWELVE: ADDITION BY SUBTRACTION

In which area(s) of your life are there "secret pockets of sin"? Is your faith deep enough to yield to God's refining fire and allow him to purify your life and take away anything he sees fit that hinders your communion with him?

A Time to Share

God clearly expressed his desire to remove our impurities through a purging process, yet many of us don't like to think that God wants to make major changes in our lives—including correcting and rebuking us.

- What is the intent of pastors who focus only on kind, "feel good" topics that people want to hear?
- What consequences does this focus create for individual Christians listening to their sermons? For the church as a whole?

- What might God want to accomplish when we become uncomfortable as we recognize our impurities and how they are affecting our relationship with him?
- Pastor Cymbala writes, "He [God] will never make a treaty with our secret pockets of sin." What is God seeking to accomplish as he ruthlessly goes after things—attitudes, habits, actions—that spoil the flow of his grace and blessing into our lives? What does this process of spiritual refinement reveal about who God is and why he will never allow us to remain the way we are today?

Why do some Christians hold on to their impurities and fight God's purifying process despite the Holy Spirit's persistent warnings and conviction of sin? If you feel comfortable sharing, describe times when you resisted God's purifying process and share what happened as a result.

CHAPTER THIRTEEN: THE ATMOSPHERE OF FAITH

Do you agree or disagree with this quotation from Pastor Cymbala: "The battle of the Christian life has always been not just to believe, but to *keep on* believing"? Why? What kinds of things can cause us to believe for a while and then fall away?

What is the difference between giving mental assent to a biblical truth on one hand and drawing near to God?

Why does God consider our chronic lack of faith to be such a serious sin rather than just a weakness?

Why does Satan work so hard, in Pastor Cymbala's words, to "break down our faith"?

A Time to Share

Pastor Cymbala points out that many believers struggle with this realization: "I have the desire to do what is good, but I cannot carry it out" (Romans 7:18).

- Why don't the commands of God make us strong enough to obey him?
- What tends to happen to believers who know what is right and desire to live that way yet can't seem to do it?
- Why must we understand that God "has given us his very great and precious promises, so that through them . . . [we] may participate in the divine nature and escape the corruption in the world caused by evil desires" (2 Peter 1:4)?
- If we don't feed on God's promises of the Word, what will happen to us? Why?

Personal Reflection

The Israelite leader Joshua encouraged people to look back and see what the Lord had done for them. What has God done for you within the past year? Which "good and perfect gift" has he given you? (See James 1:17.) Do you "enter his gates with thanksgiving and his courts with praise" (Psalm 100:4)? Are you opening up your heart *and* your mouth to express the gratitude of your heart toward the Lord?

Think of several things in your life that are not yet the way God wants them to be. What is keeping you from invoking his promises and letting him do his work in these areas of your life?

Pastor Cymbala writes, "How pitiful that millions of church-goers cheer wildly and unashamedly for their favorite sports teams—but are silent as a corpse when it comes to praising God." Why do you think this occurs? What compels us to praise God?

We read in Hebrews 11:27, "By faith he [Moses] left Egypt, not fearing the king's anger; he persevered because he saw him who is invisible." Note how it was possible for Moses to persevere. What does it mean to see "him who is invisible"?

Faith "comes from God as we receive his living Word into our hearts," writes Pastor Cymbala. What is involved in receiving God's Word into our hearts?

Personal Reflection

Pastor Cymbala shares a story of how God miraculously removed a growth from under his daughter's eyelid. What great thing(s) has God done for you or someone you know that he may be using to encourage you to once again believe in him? What may be keeping you from believing that God is about to do something new and wonderful in your life? In your church? In your community? What will happen, if you haven't already done so, if you yield your heart to God's Word and his Spirit?

When we ally ourselves with sinful things or questionable practices, our spiritual strength and vitality are weakened. Thus the "shield of faith" that we need to protect us has been stolen by the enemy. Without dwelling on your failures so much that you lose focus on Christ's pardon and power, think about your life. What sin in your life is separating you from God's holy companionship? Which steps will you take to cleanse your heart before God and then, as Pastor Cymbala expresses, move on "to faith and the fullness of the Holy

Spirit"? What seemingly insurmountable difficulty are you facing that you need to bring before God in fresh faith?

"I am absolutely convinced that the number one reason that Christians today don't pray more," writes Pastor Cymbala, "is because we do not grasp the connection between prayer and the promises of God." What is this connection, and how is it established?

What is the difference between waiting in God's presence, taking time to love him and listen to his voice, and simply presenting him with a list of requests?

Hebrews 10:23 tells us to "hold unswervingly to the hope we profess, for he who promised is faithful." In what ways do our lives change when we embrace this truth?

Fresh Power

What Happens When God Leads and You Follow

Jim Cymbala
with Dean Merrill

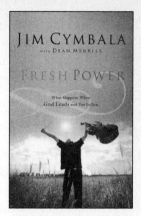

Pastor Jim Cymbala of the Brooklyn Tabernacle has taught his congregation how God's mighty power can infuse their present-day lives and the mission of their church. He continued that teaching nationally in his bestselling books *Fresh Wind, Fresh Fire* and *Fresh Faith*, which tell about the transforming power of God's love to convert prostitutes, addicts, the homeless, and people of all races and stations in life.

Now in *Fresh Power* Cymbala continues to spread the word about the power of God's Holy Spirit in the lives of those who seek him. Fresh power, Cymbala says, is available to us as we desire the Holy Spirit's constant infilling and learn what it means to be Spirit filled, both as individuals and as the church. With the book of Acts as the basis for his study, Cymbala shows how the daily lives of first-century Christians were defined by their belief in God's Word, in the constant infilling of his Spirit, and in the clear and direct responses of obedience to Scripture. He shows that that same life in Christ through the power of the Holy Spirit is available today for pastors, leaders, and laypeople who are longing for revival.

Softcover 0-310-25154-0
Audio Download, Unabridged 0-310-26150-3
Audio Download, Abridged 0-310-26044-2

Pick up a copy today at your favorite bookstore!

ZONDERVAN®
.com

Breakthrough Prayer

The Secret of Receiving What You Need from God

Jim Cymbala

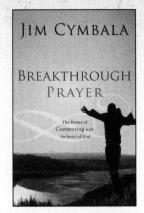

A practical and visionary approach to the principles of prayer that will revolutionize our lives—and enable us to receive all God has for us

Many people are missing the great things God wants to do in their lives because they don't know how to receive answers to their prayers. This revolutionary book is not a step-by-step guide on how to pray but an inspiring vision that moves people to greater hope as they see the tremendous potential of prayer.

Breakthrough Prayer is peppered with amazing stories of answered prayer from the Brooklyn Tabernacle, including the story of the final survivor of the World Trade Center collapse and the prayers she prayed before becoming the last person pulled from the wreckage alive.

Unique features include:

- **Breakthrough to Holiness:** What is the connection between how we live and how we pray?
- **Breakthrough to Power:** What are the prayers that really have power with God?
- **Breakthrough to Listening:** How can we learn to recognize God's answers to our prayers?

Jesus said and did only the things he received from the Father. When we do the same, the real potential of our lives will unfold, and prayer will enable us to become people with instructed tongues who are able to sustain others in fearful times—times much like those we face today.

Softcover 0-310-25518-X

The Life God Blesses

The Secret of Enjoying God's Favor

Jim Cymbala
with Stephen Sorenson

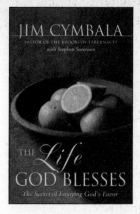

Think of what it means to have God bless your family, your relationships, your ministry, your finances . . . every aspect of your life. Think how wonderful it would be to have the Creator of the universe "show himself strong" on your behalf.

Good news! That's exactly what he wants to do. God is so eager to bless people that he is constantly searching for that special kind of heart on which he can pour out his goodness. Yours can be that kind of heart.

Pastor Jim Cymbala shares stories from the Bible and from the lives of men and women he has known to reveal inner qualities that delight our heavenly Father. Cultivate them in your heart and stand amazed as God answers your most heartfelt prayers and makes the impossible come true in your life.

Hardcover 0-310-24202-9
Audio Download, Unabridged 0-310-26159-7

Pick up a copy today at your favorite bookstore!

The Church God Blesses

Jim Cymbala
with Stephen Sorenson

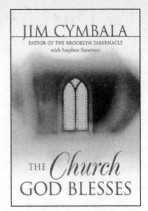

God wants to transform his church into a people of power, joy, and peace. Jim Cymbala reminds us that Christianity is only as strong as the local church and that God wants to bless our churches in ways we can't possibly imagine. It doesn't matter whether a church is alive and growing or barely surviving on life support. God has a plan for it. It doesn't matter whether a church is facing financial challenges, internal divisions, or strife among its leaders. God has a plan for it. God is able to deal with any problem a church will ever face—as long as his people earnestly seek him.

As the pastor of the Brooklyn Tabernacle, Cymbala knows that God's blessing and grace is available to us today just as much as it was in the early church. Then, as now, God chose the church to manifest his presence to the world.

Hardcover 0-310-24203-7

He's Been Faithful

Trusting God to Do What Only He Can Do

Carol Cymbala
with Ann Spangler

Carol Cymbala's ministry in a tough inner-city neighborhood in New York can be summed up in one word: unlikely. She is the director and songwriter for a Grammy Award-winning choir—yet she doesn't read music. She is the pastor's wife in a six-thousand-member congregation filled with people of color—and she is white. A shy girl who struggled to get through school, she is the last person you'd expect to stand before a packed house at Radio City Music Hall, confidently directing the Brooklyn Tabernacle Choir.

But Carol's God is the God of the unlikely. *He's Been Faithful* is an honest story about the struggles we all face and the power of God to help us. It is told through Carol's eyes as well as through the eyes of various members of the Brooklyn Tabernacle Choir, who have experienced the grace of Christ in remarkable ways. *He's Been Faithful* tells the story of the way God works despite—or maybe because of—our many inadequacies.

But Carol's faith hasn't always come easily. There have been times of wavering and challenge, like the time a man walked down the aisle of the church pointing a gun at her husband, Jim. Or like the time she was assaulted outside the church. Or like the time she wanted to pack up her children and run away from the city for good because of what was happening to her family.

Whether you are a pastor, a choir director, or someone who is seeking a deeper experience of God, *He's Been Faithful* will renew your faith and increase your understanding that only Jesus can fill that deep, deep longing we all have for something more in life.

Hardcover 0-310-23652-5
Audio Download, Abridged 0-310-26055-8